Mike Chick

DIMENSIONS OF VOCABULARY KNOWLEDGE

Dimensions of Vocabulary Knowledge

Edited by

James Milton

and

Tess Fitzpatrick

First published 2014 by
PALGRAVE MACMILLAN

Palgrave Macmillan in the UK is an imprint of Macmillan Publishers Limited,
registered in England, company number 785998, of Houndmills, Basingstoke,
Hampshire RG21 6XS.

Palgrave Macmillan in the US is a division of St Martin's Press LLC,
175 Fifth Avenue, New York, NY 10010.

Palgrave Macmillan is the global academic imprint of the above companies
and has companies and representatives throughout the world.

Palgrave® and Macmillan® are registered trademarks in the United States,
the United Kingdom, Europe and other countries.

ISBN 978–0–230–27572–0   hardback
ISBN 978–0–230–27573–7   paperback

This book is printed on paper suitable for recycling and made from fully
managed and sustained forest sources. Logging, pulping and manufacturing
processes are expected to conform to the environmental regulations of the
country of origin.

A catalogue record for this book is available from the British Library.

A catalog record for this book is available from the Library of Congress.

Printed and bound by CPI Group (UK) Ltd, Croydon, CR0 4YY

Typeset by MPS Limited, Chennai, India.

Contents

List of Tables and Figures   viii

Notes on the Contributors   x

Preface   xiii

Acknowledgements   xiv

1   **Introduction: Deconstructing Vocabulary Knowledge**   1

    James Milton and Tess Fitzpatrick

    Introduction   1
    Component approaches to word knowledge   1
    Developmental approaches to word knowledge   8
    Metaphorical approaches to word knowledge   9
    Reassessing the elements of word knowledge   11

2   **Knowledge of Spoken Form**   13

    James Milton, Thomaï Alexiou and Marina Mattheoudakis

    Introduction   13
    Spoken word recognition   16
    Current research work   22
    Practical implications and suggestions for further research   28
    Questions for discussion   29

3   **Knowledge of the Written Word**   30

    Imma Miralpeix and Paul Meara

    Introduction   30
    Written word recognition   32
    Current research work   37
    Practical implications and suggestions for further research   42
    Questions for discussion   44

4   **Knowledge of Word Parts**   45

    Katja Mäntylä and Ari Huhta

    Introduction   45
    Recognition of word parts   46
    Current research work   49
    Practical implications and suggestions for further research   57
    Questions for discussion   59

5 **Knowledge of Form and Meaning** 60

María Pilar Agustín Llach and Soraya Moreno Espinosa

Introduction 60
Associating word form and meaning 61
Current research work 64
Practical implications and suggestions for further research 71
Questions for discussion 72

6 **Knowledge of Word Concepts and Referents** 73

Parto Pajoohesh

Introduction 73
Words, concepts and referents 75
Current research work 82
Practical implications and suggestions for further research 90
Questions for discussion 91

7 **Knowledge of Word Associations** 92

Tess Fitzpatrick and Ian Munby

Introduction 92
Developing word association networks 93
Current research work 100
Practical implications and suggestions for further research 104
Questions for discussion 104

8 **Knowledge of Grammatical Use** 106

Jeanine Treffers-Daller and Vivienne Rogers

Introduction 106
Word patterns and use 108
Current research work 118
Practical implications and suggestions for further research 121
Questions for discussion 121

9 **Knowledge of Collocations** 123

Dale Brown

Introduction 123
Knowledge of collocations 124
Current research work 131
Pedagogical implications and suggestions for further research 138
Questions for discussion 139

10 **Knowledge of Constraints on Use** 140

Clarissa Wilks

Introduction 140
Constraints on use 141

Current research work   147
Practical implications and suggestions for further research   152
Questions for discussion   153

11   Confidence in Word Knowledge   **154**

Jim Ronald and Tadamitsu Kamimoto

Introduction   154
Confidence in word knowledge   155
Current research   157
Pedagogical implications and suggestions for further research   171
Questions for discussion   172

12   Conclusion: Reconstructing Vocabulary Knowledge   **173**

Tess Fitzpatrick and James Milton

Appendix 1: The Non-Word-Based Test of Derivation (Chapter 4)   178
Appendix 2   180
Glossary of Terms   183
References   185
Index   205

List of Tables and Figures

Tables

1.1	What is involved in knowing a word?	5
2.1	X-Lex and A-Lex vocabulary scores	25
2.2	Mean scores in A-Lex and X-Lex	26
3.1	Descriptive statistics for each measure including all the participants	40
3.2	Groups according to receptive vocabulary sizes	40
4.1	Scores on the three derivation tests	51
4.2	Item characteristics of the non-word-based test	53
4.3	Correlations between the three derivation tests	53
4.4	Relationship between derivation skill and more general language proficiency	56
4.5	Derivation test performance at different CEFR levels	57
5.1	Test results	66
5.2	Between-groups comparison of differences across grades	68
5.3	Target word rendering across grades	70
7.1	Correlations between the word association test scores and the proficiency measures	103
8.1	Frequency of the verbs *courir* and *run* in Sketchengine/BNC	111
8.2	Word order differences between French and English	119
8.3	Summary of participants	120
8.4	Calculations of overall measure of verb movement	120
9.1	Frequency in English of the recurrent responses	133
9.2	Correlations between the recurrence of the participants' responses and the frequency and MI scores for those collocations in COCA	137
9.3	Correlations between the recurrence of the participants' responses (acceptable responses only) and the frequency and MI scores for those collocations in COCA	137
11.1	Descriptive statistics	158
11.2	Mean item facility indices	158
11.3	Frequency of IF differences by word level	159
11.4	Mean score	160
11.5	Mean frequency count	161
11.6	Accuracy rates of translation equivalents as compared with V_States ratings (Hiromi)	166

11.7	Accuracy rates of translation equivalents as compared with V_States ratings (Yoko)	166
11.8	Results for all looked-up and not looked-up target words (Hiromi)	167
11.9	Results for all looked-up and not looked-up target words (Yoko)	167
11.10	Initially unknown (0/1-rated at T0, T1) looked-up target words (Hiromi)	168
11.11	Initially unknown (0/1-rated at T0, T1) not looked-up target words (Hiromi)	168
11.12	Initially unknown (0/1-rated at T0, T1) looked-up target words (Yoko)	169
11.13	Initially unknown (0/1-rated at T0, T1) not looked-up target words (Yoko)	169

Figures

1.1	The lexical space	9
1.2	Strong links in the word web	10
2.1	Coverage provided by sub-corpora of the British National Corpus (BNC)	15
2.2	Example of the Vocabulary Levels Dictation Test	16
2.3	Aural word recognition and frequency	19
2.4	Aural vocabulary recognition and level	19
2.5	Comparison of class scores on A-Lex and X-Lex in Greek and Arabic native-speaking learners of EFL	20
2.6	Mean A-Lex scores in X-Lex score bands	21
2.7	Comparing written and oral/aural strategy choice	26
6.1	Mean average for English syntax measure of definitional quality scale	84
6.2	Mean average for English superordinate measure of definitional quality scale	84
6.3	Mean average for English complement measure of definitional quality scale	85
6.4	Mean average for English definitional feature measure of definitional quality scale	85
6.5	Mean average for measures of definitional quality scale in Farsi	86
8.1	Patterns found with the verbs *courir* and *run*	111
9.1	The number of responses given by various proportions of participants	133
9.2	The part of speech of the recurrent responses	133
9.3	The number of acceptable recurrent responses produced by various proportions of participants	134
11.1	Sample question	161

Notes on the Contributors

María Pilar Agustín Llach received her PhD in Applied Linguistics from the Universidad de La Rioja, and is a lecturer at the Universidad de La Rioja, in Spain. Her main research interests are second and foreign language acquisition, particularly vocabulary acquisition in a foreign language and the factors that influence this process. The variables she has attended to are: L1 influence, age, L2 proficiency, gender, or L2 learning context (CLIL vs non-CLIL). She is a member of the research group on Applied Linguistics GLAUR.

Thomaï Alexiou is a lecturer in the Department of Theoretical and Applied Linguistics, School of English, Aristotle University of Thessaloniki, Greece. She holds an MA in TEFL from Canterbury Christ Church University and a PhD in Applied Linguistics from the University of Wales Swansea, UK. She teaches methodology of language teaching, pedagogical foundations in learning a foreign language and research methods in applied linguistics. Her research interests concern early foreign language learning and material development for young learners.

Dale Brown teaches undergraduate and postgraduate courses at Osaka University, Japan, and is pursuing a PhD in Applied Linguistics with Cardiff University, Wales, UK. His primary research interests are in extensive reading, the analysis of language teaching materials and vocabulary acquisition. In his PhD research, he is looking into the development of EFL learners' collocational knowledge.

Tess Fitzpatrick is Professor of Applied Linguistics at Cardiff University, Wales, UK. Her research interests, originating from the years she spent working at Swansea University, are in the areas of vocabulary acquisition, storage and retrieval, with a specific focus on word association studies and vocabulary measurement tools. An experienced EFL teacher and teacher trainer, she has also worked on projects exploring extreme language learning methodologies and the role of formulaic sequences in second language use.

Ari Huhta is a researcher at the Centre for Applied Language Studies at the University of Jyväskylä, Finland. He specializes in language assessment, with particular interest in performance ratings, diagnostic assessment and the development of assessment procedures for SLA research.

Tadamitsu Kamimoto obtained his PhD in Applied Linguistics from Swansea University, Wales, UK. His professional and research interests include language testing and L2 acquisition. He is a professor in the Department of Foreign Languages, Kumamoto Gakuen University, Japan, and teaches a variety of undergraduate and postgraduate courses related to theory and practice of foreign language acquisition.

Katja Mäntylä is Associate Professor of English at the Department of Languages at the University of Jyväskylä, Finland. She has focused on L2 vocabulary development in research projects on metalinguistic awareness, writing skills and assessment.

Marina Mattheoudakis is an Assistant Professor at the Department of Theoretical and Applied Linguistics, School of English, Aristotle University of Thessaloniki, Greece. She holds an MA in TEFL from the University of Birmingham, UK and a PhD in Applied Linguistics from the Aristotle University of Thessaloniki. She teaches courses in second language acquisition and language teaching methodology at both the undergraduate and graduate levels. Her main research interests lie in the areas of second language acquisition, language teaching methodology and corpus linguistics.

Paul Meara recently retired from Swansea University, and is currently Honorary Professor in the Centre for Language and Communication Research at Cardiff University, Wales, UK. He began his career studying the psycholinguistics of syntax, but soon realized that vocabulary acquisition was a lot more interesting. His Vocabulary Acquisition Research Group at Swansea University for many years both guided the research careers of the students and colleagues associated with the programme, and contributed hugely to the renaissance of interest and publications in the field of lexical studies.

James Milton is Professor of Applied Linguistics at Swansea University, Wales, UK. A long-term interest in measuring lexical breadth and establishing normative data for learning and progress has led to extensive publications including *Modelling and Assessing Vocabulary Knowledge* (CUP, 2007, with Michael Daller and Jeanine Treffers-Daller) and *Measuring Second Language Vocabulary Acquisition* (Multilingual Matters, 2009).

Imma Miralpeix is currently a lecturer and researcher in the Department of English Studies, University of Barcelona, Spain. Her main research interests are in second language vocabulary acquisition, especially lexical development and assessment, and in multilingualism. She has taken part in several research projects funded by the Spanish Ministry of Education, on topics such as the age factor or the role of input, age and aptitude in the long-term attainment of English proficiency in foreign settings.

Soraya Moreno Espinosa teaches English as a foreign language at the Official Language School El Fuero de Logroño, Spain. She obtained her PhD in Applied

Linguistics at the University of La Rioja. Her fields of study are L2 vocabulary assessment and second language learning and teaching. She forms part of the GLAUR Research Group (http://glaur.unirioja.es), which investigates issues concerning second language acquisition, learning and teaching.

Ian Munby taught English in France, Spain and his native UK before moving to Japan. He currently teaches at Hokkai Gakuen University, Sapporo, Japan. He completed his PhD on word associations in an L2 at Swansea University in 2011. His research interests include vocabulary and testing.

Parto Pajoohesh is a part-time faculty member at the Department of Applied Linguistics of Brock University, Ontario, Canada. Her research and academic interests include academic/language development of bilingual and minority language students, L2 vocabulary development and assessment, and settlement issues of immigrant professionals.

Jim Ronald teaches at Hiroshima Shudo University, Japan. He gained a PhD in Applied Linguistics from Swansea University in 2007. As a teacher and researcher, his interests include vocabulary acquisition, dictionary use, learner development and pragmatics.

Vivienne Rogers received her PhD from Newcastle University in the UK in 2009, which examined syntactic development in instructed English speaking learners of French. Her research interests include the second language acquisition of syntax and vocabulary and she is currently developing a project examining the possible link between the two. In 2011 she joined Swansea University as a lecturer in Applied Linguistics.

Jeanine Treffers-Daller is Professor of Second Language Education at the University of Reading, UK. Most of her research focuses on bilingualism and language contact, in particular on code-switching, borrowing and contact-induced language change. She also works in the field of vocabulary richness and explores ways of measuring lexical diversity in oral or written productions of bilinguals and L2 learners and has recently obtained funding from the European Science Foundation for an exploratory workshop on thinking, speaking and gesturing in two languages.

Clarissa Wilks is Associate Dean of the Faculty of Arts and Social Sciences at Kingston University, London, UK. She teaches and supervises in the area of second language acquisition, sociolinguistics and French language. Her research into second language vocabulary acquisition explores the power and appropriacy of metaphors used to describe lexical storage and uses word association data to examine the comparative density and structure of lexical networks. She has also published on attitudes to lexical change and discriminatory language in France.

Preface

The origin of this book lies in the annual conference of the British Association for Applied Linguistics (BAAL) held at Swansea in September 2008. The BAAL conference hosts papers on a wide range of linguistic-related subjects, but in this conference, perhaps because it was held at Swansea where we have an interest in the subject, there was a strong Vocabulary Studies strand running through it. These papers showed that in the wider international Vocabulary Studies community the research that is being carried out is very diverse; so diverse, in fact, that much of the work presented contained aspects and approaches which were novel even to experts in the field. It is easy even in a field as specialized as Vocabulary Studies to specialize further in a specific area of research, such as measuring lexical breadth or investigating the development of word association patterns, and in doing so to overlook other aspects of vocabulary knowledge and the way all these aspects and dimensions inter-relate. It was clear that in some areas, such as the assessment of vocabulary breadth, research has homed in on a number of definitions of the subject and as a result standardized testing approaches have emerged which allow this aspect of the lexicon, and the way it is acquired, to be usefully modelled. Other areas, such as the range of aspects of knowledge which might fall under the umbrella of vocabulary depth, are still searching for the commonly accepted constructs which will allow standardized tests and normalized scores to emerge. But there is much interesting work which is attempting to achieve such a goal. It was very refreshing to be given the opportunity at the Swansea conference to be able to view our understanding of the mental lexicon in so many different ways. The chapters in this volume, therefore, are an attempt to bring together our knowledge and research across the entire the range of our attempts to investigate the mental lexicon as it relates to language learning. It presents as many challenges as it does answers to questions of how words are organized in the mind and how they are learned.

JAMES MILTON
TESS FITZPATRICK

Acknowledgements

The authors and publishers wish to thank Cambridge University Press, Multilingual Matters and Wiley/Blackwell for permission to reproduce copyright material:

Figure 1.2 The lexical space, H. Daller, J. Milton and J. Treffers-Daller, *Modelling and Assessing Vocabulary Knowledge* (Cambridge: Cambridge University Press, 2007).

Figure 1.3 Strong links in the word web, J. Aitchison, *Words in the Mind* (Oxford: Blackwell, 2003).

Figure 2.1 Coverage provided by sub-corpora of the BNC, J. Milton, *Measuring Second Language Vocabulary Acquisition* (Bristol: Multilingual Matters, 2009).

Figure 2.2 Example of the Vocabulary Levels Dictation Test, P. Nation, *Learning Vocabulary in Another Language* (Cambridge: Cambridge University Press, 2001).

Table 8.4 Proposed stages in the L2 development of English questions, R. Hawkins, *Second Language Syntax: A Generative Introduction* (Oxford: Blackwell, 2001).

Introduction: Deconstructing Vocabulary Knowledge

James Milton and Tess Fitzpatrick

1

Introduction

The study of words and word knowledge has a very long history. For hundreds of years the ancient Greeks and Romans struggled to understand the functions of words and their relationship with meaning. It proved difficult for ancient scholars even to divide words meaningfully into different functional classes. Two thousand years later we are still wrestling with words and most recently we have been puzzling over the nature of word knowledge, and how and where this knowledge is stored. Knowing a word is an elusive concept and we are still unable to capture, in a simple description, everything that knowing a word might involve. Word knowledge, it seems, is complicated and it is hard to capture all of its many facets in a simple yet comprehensive definition.

Because word knowledge is complex and difficult, the descriptions we use often take different approaches in attempts to characterize the idea. One approach, a *component approach*, attempts to list the different aspects of knowing a word or, often, describes contrasts between different aspects of knowing a word. A second approach, a *developmental approach*, tries to characterize the parts of word knowledge that learners acquire at different stages of learning. A third approach might be described as a *metaphorical approach*. Word knowledge cannot be seen or touched or even measured very readily and sometimes it can be more usefully characterized by metaphors, such as describing word knowledge as a 'web' of words (Aitchison, 1987, p. 84). Just like the ancient Greeks' classifications of word types, these attempts at description have grown over time to reflect the multi-faceted nature of word knowledge and in many ways these descriptions are still far from perfect.

Component approaches to word knowledge

Spoken form, written form and meaning

One of the earliest attempts to characterize word knowledge is the distinction made by Aristotle in the fourth century BC. Like other Greek philosophers he was concerned with clarifying the relationship between thought, usually articulated in words, and the reality the thought and words represent. In his *De Interpretatione*, Aristotle described four fundamental components:

- real world things,
- impressions (perhaps the idea or concept of those things),
- spoken signs, and
- written signs.

Knowing a word, then, can involve knowing both its spoken form and its written form. While the teaching of modern languages routinely distinguishes between the skills of reading and writing, and those of listening and speaking, in the study of vocabulary knowledge this distinction is often overlooked. Studies presume that if learners know one form of a word they will also know the other form. But even in modern and more literate times than those of ancient Greece, it can be hard to know both word forms equally. When a foreign language involves a different orthography, it can be very hard to learn to recognize words in writing. Western European travellers to China, for example, may be unnerved by the experience when the signs they are surrounded by in airports or elsewhere are completely incomprehensible. Across Europe, on the other hand, where the Roman alphabet is mostly used, such signs continue to convey some sort of information, and can be sounded out for example, even if the meaning is not always completely clear.

Aristotle's four fundamental components also introduce a distinction that has a very modern sound. He recognizes that there is a distinction to be made between the form of a word and the meaning or concept it represents. It is the kind of distinction made by Saussure (1916) who draws a distinction between *signifiant* and *signifié*, where *signifiant* is the thing that signifies or the sound image, and *signifié* is the thing being signified. The idea that language is a representation of reality, and not part of that reality, is an idea that has been at the root of linguistic debate for centuries.

Receptive and productive word knowledge

While there is a wealth of linguistic thought and description in Western Europe between the ancient times and the twentieth century, Aristotle's idea of a written form, a spoken form and a meaning underlying them, was not systematically advanced on. For much of this period Aristotle's opinions were taken, like the Bible, as reflecting an absolute truth. However, with the growth of modern linguistics fresh ideas emerged. In 1921 Palmer makes the distinction between being able to recognize a word when it is encountered with the support of other words for context, and being able to use it in speech or writing, which involves being able to call the word to mind spontaneously for production. This distinguishes, therefore, between *receptive* and *productive* knowledge, also sometimes called *passive* and ***active* vocabulary** knowledge. The significance of this for Palmer was that it pointed to the need to administer different vocabulary tests to learners to try to characterize their vocabulary knowledge fully and accurately. This has proved to be a useful and enduring distinction which we still commonly make today, and the call for multiple tests to adequately understand a learner's vocabulary competence is still being repeated (for example, Nation, 2007; Richards and Malvern, 2007). It will be appreciated that this idea overlays Aristotle's distinctions and that both the spoken and written forms of a word may be known receptively or productively.

This is not the only new set of qualities which emerged at this time. In 1917 Palmer commented that the term 'word' is vague and might include very frequent **collocations** and phrases like *in spite of* and *as a matter of fact* (Palmer, 1917, p. 40). He also comments that a word might include functional units like **affixes** such as *-ly* and *-ment* at the end of words and *multi-* and *poly-* at the beginning. His terminology, *polylogs* for collocations for example, and *miologs* for morphological affixes, failed to catch on, however.

A simple three-part model of word knowledge has now expanded to include a variety of other potential factors. From this point onwards it becomes logical to attempt to systematically list all of these possible qualities which might be included in a definition of word knowledge.

Lists of word knowledge

The earliest modern list of word knowledge components is probably by Cronbach (1942). In this paper he distinguishes between:

- generalization
- application
- breadth of meaning
- precision of meaning
- availability.

Knowledge of the form of the word has disappeared in this analysis, and Palmer's ideas of an appreciation of how words can combine is implied rather than clearly stated. Nonetheless, a consideration of **polysemy** has emerged, that a word form may carry several different meanings or uses. At the general level, therefore, *generalization* refers to the word's definition, and *application* to using it appropriately. *Breadth of meaning* refers to an appreciation that the word may have several different meanings, and *precision of meaning* being able to use them correctly in different situations. The receptive and productive distinction is preserved, however, since *availability* refers to productive use.

Richards (1976) expanded this list further and suggested eight assumptions which could be made about vocabulary knowledge:

1. The native speaker of a language continues to expand his vocabulary in adulthood, whereas there is comparatively little development of syntax in adult life.
2. Knowing a word means knowing the degree of probability of encountering that word in speech or print. For many words, we also know the sort of words most likely to be found associated with the word.
3. Knowing a word implies knowing the limitations imposed on the use of the word according to variations of function and situation.
4. Knowing a word means knowing the syntactic behaviour associated with the word.
5. Knowing a word entails knowledge of the underlying form of a word and the derivatives that can be made from it.
6. Knowing a word entails knowledge of the network of associations between that word and the other words in the language [sic].
7. Knowing a word means knowing the semantic value of a word.
8. Knowing a word means knowing many of the different meanings associated with a word. (Richards, 1976, p. 83)

Many of these assumptions are repetitions of earlier ideas. Knowing a word involves knowing the meaning of a word (number 7 in the list), or several meanings (number 8), and its restrictions on use (numbers 2 and 3). Number 2 on the list implies recognition of both spoken and written forms. Other assumptions expand still further the idea of word knowledge to include knowledge of a word's associations (number 6), its derived forms (number 5), its **collocations** (number 4) and the subtleties of **connotation** and meaning the word might carry (number 8). It also includes assumptions which might seem out of place in a component analysis, such as the idea that native speakers can continually expand their vocabulary while other aspects of language are relatively fixed and unchanging in adult life. As a list it continues the process of refining and adding detail to the idea of word knowledge, but it is a relatively unorganized list.

Nation (2001) produces the latest and, to date, most comprehensive version of this type of analysis. He adds further to the list of word knowledge components and codifies this knowledge under three broad headings: knowledge of form, knowledge of meaning and knowledge of use. This is tabulated and shown in Table 1.1.

This table includes knowledge of spoken and written forms and also, within the form category, knowledge of the inflected and derived forms of words which allow speakers to add to the meaning or function of a word. The meaning category now includes not merely the simple idea that a word has a meaning, but includes the connotations and associations which words can carry with them and which a learner will need to know if the word is to be used

Table 1.1 What is involved in knowing a word? (from Nation, 2001, p. 27)

Form	Spoken	R	What does the word sound like?
		P	How is the word pronounced?
	Written	R	What does the word look like?
		P	How is the word written and spelled?
	Word parts	R	What parts are recognizable in this word?
		P	What words parts are needed to express the meaning?
Meaning	Form and meaning	R	What meaning does this word form signal?
		P	What word form can be used to express this meaning?
	Concepts and **Referents**	R	What is included in the concept?
		P	What items can the concept refer to?
	Associations	R	What other words does this word make us think of?
		P	What other words could we use instead of this one?
Use	Grammatical functions	R	In what patterns does the word occur?
		P	In what patterns must we use this word?
	Collocations	R	What words or types of words occur with this one?
		P	What words or types of words must we use with this one?
	Constraints on use	R	Where, when and how often would we expect to meet this word?
		P	Where, when and how often can we use this word?

Note: R = receptive, P = productive.

appropriately. Finally, the use category defines the places in which words can be used and the company they are likely to keep. If a word is a noun, for example, then it will commonly be preceded by an article, if it is a pronoun then it is likely to be followed by a verb. Some words like to associate closely

together while others do not; *Red Sea* and *Yellow Sea* are geographical entities and commonly co-occur, we often speak of a *blue sea* or a *turquoise sea*
(in places sunnier than Swansea), but *purple sea* or *pink sea* occur much less
frequently together. Still other words are restricted in the places and occasions
they are likely to be used. Swear words and taboo words are good examples of
this. Swear words are much more likely to be heard on the football terraces than
found in the pages of a textbook like this one. At each division, knowledge
continues to be sub-divided into productive and receptive knowledge producing a list of 18 different aspects of word knowledge.

It will be appreciated that this has now become quite a considerable taxonomy. It becomes difficult at this level of complexity to operationalize the list
and to devise ways to adequately capture a learner's knowledge across the
whole range of qualities. The prospect of a learner taking 18 separate tests to
try to achieve this is quite unthinkable. It is not clear from this list either to what
degree these separate elements interlink with each other. Do they function entirely separately or does a growth in one element, say an increasing number of spoken word forms, give rise to similar growth in other elements – for example,
how often these words can be used? Alongside this growing list of the many
and varied qualities that make up word knowledge, therefore, is a process to
simplify the model and to reduce it to a smaller number of dimensions which
can usefully characterize a learner's word knowledge.

Dimensions of knowledge

Anderson and Freebody (1981) appear to have initiated the idea that there
may be a smaller number of broad categories of word knowledge when they
introduced a further dimension by contrasting *breadth* of word knowledge
and *depth* of word knowledge. The distinction appears simple. Breadth of
knowledge is the number of words a learner knows and depth of knowledge is what the learner knows about these words. This is potentially useful
in that it allows a distinction to be made between learners who may have
learned lots of words, perhaps through the rote learning of translation lists,
but cannot use them idiomatically or appropriately, and learners who have
also learned how the words they know associate with other words or the
nuances of meaning they carry. It is not entirely clear how these terms map
onto Nation's (or anyone else's) list of the many aspects of word knowledge.
It appears that word breadth includes a knowledge of word form, whether
spoken or written. But does it also include a knowledge of word parts, the
inflections and derivations which allow new words to be created and words
to change to reflect their grammatical function? Nation categorizes these
as part of knowledge of form, but this aspect of knowledge could equally
well be placed in the depth dimension. Questions might also be raised about
the link between form and meaning in Nation's table. Does breadth require
the purely receptive ability to recognize that a word exists in a foreign language or does it also require some knowledge of the meaning that is attached

to the form once it is known? Or, yet again, does depth of knowledge include having a translation or appreciation of the semantic qualities of the word as part of this overall idea of things a learner knows about a word? This quality of word knowledge might equally well be included in either the breadth or depth dimensions and there is no hard and fast rule to say which of these alternatives is best.

In practice, it seems that researchers choose the definition which suits them best and this is often dictated by the availability of the testing instruments they have to hand. Checklist tests such as X-Lex (Meara and Milton, 2003) attempt to test passive word recognition, while Nation's Vocabulary Levels Test (VLT) (to be found in Nation, 2001) requires the learner to link a word with a possible meaning. Both tests are considered tests of lexical breadth but it seems likely that they will produce quantitatively different estimates of vocabulary size given the different constructs which underlie the tests.

The idea of dimensions of lexical competence, such as depth, also implies that there is some link between the elements that make up this competence, although it is often not clear how this should happen. How should a learner's knowledge of fixed idioms, for example, develop in relation to their knowledge of, say, **collocations**? Are they separate entities which can develop in isolation from each other or are they connected in some way so that a change in the knowledge state of one will influence the knowledge state of the other? Most researchers treat each element of the aspects that make up depth separately and test only one or two of the qualities. Meara (1997) has argued, however, that all of these elements in the depth dimension are meaningfully connected by the notion that they relate to the links between words. The links may be descriptively separable, there are collocational links, grammatical links and associational links, for example, but they are all still links. The development of a learner's lexical depth involves increasing the number of links between the words in the lexicon. There is an implied connection with lexical breadth here, since any increase in the number of words a learner knows will also increase the possible number of links between words. A few words can generate only a handful of connections, but thousands of lexical items can, potentially, be linked in millions of different combinations.

Meara (1996a) also extends the number of dimensions suggested by Anderson and Freebody and contrasts *breadth* and *depth* dimensions with the ease with which a word can be accessed. Daller *et al.* (2007) call this third dimension a *fluency* of knowledge dimension. This three-dimensional framework makes it possible to distinguish between learners who know lots of words and lots about them but struggle to use them (**declarative knowledge**), and learners who can quickly and naturally activate this knowledge for communication (**procedural knowledge**). Essentially, this is to reintroduce the receptive and productive distinction back into word knowledge analyses, but the idea of a theoretical three-dimensional **lexical space**, within which a learner's knowledge can be categorized, appears an attractive one, though it has yet to be successfully operationalized.

Developmental approaches to word knowledge

It might be expected that developmental approaches to word knowledge would draw heavily on component or dimensions approaches. Some of the components of word knowledge appear, very obviously, to precede others. Knowledge of form ought to precede knowledge of **collocation** or association, for example. It is almost inconceivable that a learner could systematically link together words which are not even recognized as words. The relationship between **vocabulary breadth** and **depth** also appears to be one where breadth must develop before the dimension of depth can emerge, since, as has already been pointed out, the possibility of a dense matrix of links between words can only exist once many words have been acquired. It has also been suggested that receptive and productive knowledge are stages of development, or points at either end of a continuum of development, as well as qualitatively different aspects of word knowledge (Melka, 1997).

Although component and developmental approaches are clearly related, they are often described in very different terms. However, it is possible to infer how developmental stages relate to the componential aspects of knowledge in frameworks such as Nation's. Dale (1965), for example, suggests a four-stage developmental model where learners place test words into one of four categories.

Stage 1: I never saw the word before
Stage 2: I've heard the word but I don't know what it means
Stage 3: I recognize the word in context, it has something to do with _____
Stage 4: I know the word

This model implies recognition of form as a requirement of the development of other aspects of word knowledge, including the link to meaning. If it could be demonstrated empirically that learners really do move through these stages sequentially then this might help make sense of the breadth and depth dimensions and where to draw the line between them. Breadth might be viewed as the number of words that can be recognized, and depth as the degree to which the form can be linked to meaning in all its many aspects.

Paribakht and Wesche (1993) propose something similar in the Vocabulary Knowledge Scale (VKS). This hierarchical model of learning has five stages.

Stage 1: The word is not familiar at all
Stage 2: The word is familiar but the meaning is not known
Stage 3: A correct synonym or translation is given
Stage 4: The word is used with semantic appropriateness in a sentence
Stage 5: The word is used with semantic appropriateness and grammatical
        accuracy

Paribakht and Wesche (1993, p. 180)

This model appears to add stages beyond the recognition of form and the link to meaning, and suggests that knowledge of word use, and appreciation of the semantic appropriateness of words and their grammatical functions, emerge late. It implies that Nation's 2001 table is almost a developmental sequence as well as a component list: knowledge of form precedes knowledge of meaning, which precedes knowledge of use. The VKS has been quite widely used, for example in Horst and Meara (1999) and Milton (2008), but practical difficulties emerge. As Wolter points out (2005), its mechanism for testing knowledge beyond recognition of meaning is scarcely robust. The VKS is a self-reporting scale and is not intended to be too rigorous a testing instrument, but the effect is that reaching the highest points on the scale is undemanding. Producing a convincing sentence demonstrating the correct use of a word can often be done even in the absence of an understanding of its meaning. The five-point scale, in practice, often collapses down to two points; learners either feel they do not recognize the word, or they recognize it, think they know the meaning, and think they can use it.

In comparison to the detail included in the component approach to word knowledge, these developmental approaches appear unsophisticated and, as yet, are unable to specify with any level of certainty how or when the various elements of word knowledge are acquired. The testing mechanisms – self-reporting scales, for example – are also not as robust as many of the tests we have for assessing awareness of different aspects of vocabulary knowledge.

Metaphorical approaches to word knowledge

Several metaphors for word knowledge have already been used in this chapter; indeed, it is often difficult to describe the abstract nature of some aspects of word knowledge without the use of metaphor. One of these metaphors is that of the **lexical space** (Daller *et al.*, 2007) comprising dimensions of breadth, depth and fluency. Daller *et al.* even draw this up (Figure 1.1) as a cubic space,

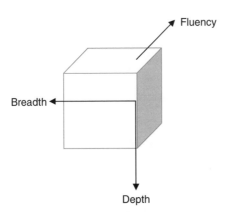

Figure 1.1   The lexical space (Daller *et al.*, 2007, p. 8)

which implies that each dimension can function and develop independently of the others.

The attraction of such a space metaphor is that it allows learners with different kinds of vocabulary knowledge to be systematically distinguished and positioned separately within the space. Learners who have learned lots of words through word lists but have little ability to call them to mind and use them correctly can be clearly distinguished from learners who may know fewer words but who can use these quickly and appropriately. These are not abstract differences; English as a foreign language (EFL) practitioners will be very familiar with non-native English-speaking students who exhibit these kinds of difference. Japanese students, for example, often appear to have large recognition vocabularies and typically communicate well in writing, but function poorly in oral communication where this vocabulary has to be processed and activated quickly. By contrast, Arabic-speaking students often possess much less English vocabulary but nonetheless present themselves fluently in speech. Of course, there is no real lexical space, but even at a metaphorical level it seems that the idea needs to be amended since the dimensions cannot operate entirely independently. It seems impossible to have great depth of vocabulary knowledge when only a few words are available to communicate with, but the relationship between breadth and depth, which will govern the shape of the lexical space, has yet to be convincingly characterized.

A further metaphor, that of a web of words, is often used to describe the depth axis and the way the words interact with each other. The idea of a web has emerged because when connections are plotted with lines between words, the result is meant to look a little like a spider's web. This is not the only way to turn these relationships between words into a useful image and Aitchison (1987, p. 84), who introduces the web idea, also uses overlapping balloons and lines, as in Figure 1.2, to show especially strong links.

There are attempts to turn this metaphor into a model of lexical depth which can be empirically tested with real language users (for example, Wilks and Meara, 2007, and Schur, 2007). Meara and Wolter (2004) have developed

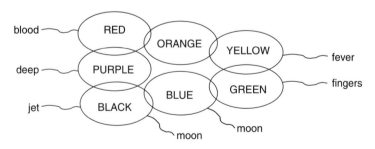

Figure 1.2 Strong links in the word web (Aitchison, 2003, p. 94)

a test which allows learners to draw up these webs so that a score can be assigned to them. At first sight this looks like a promising innovation, but there are problems which emerge in deciding exactly what to include in the definition of a link. At what point, for example, do **collocations**, which clearly should be included in this kind of test, become sufficiently infrequent to be excluded? And should **word associations** be included in the test or not? Many word associations, like green and grass, are conceptual rather than linguistic links and it might be thought that such links exist in all languages. A test of associational knowledge potentially tells us very little of the nature of the developing foreign language lexicon except, perhaps, its breadth and whether the words forming the link are known or not. There are clearly many details to be worked out before this kind of metaphor becomes a really useful tool for linguistic description.

Reassessing the elements of word knowledge (and the structure of the book)

The development of our understanding over the last 100 years or so has entailed breaking down the idea of word knowledge into progressively smaller and smaller areas. This has made the analysis of the subject progressively more complex but not necessarily more clear. Some of the distinctions we like to work with may be artificial in the sense that they may lack psychological reality in the minds of learners who may work with a different set of divisions. The separation of associations and **collocations** may be one such distinction and it is noticeable that Meara treats them as equivalents in his tests of association networks. Simultaneously, and perhaps in response to this increasing complexification, there has been an attempt to try to capture the nature of word knowledge in a much smaller number of meaningfully distinct dimensions. However, it is not precisely clear how these dimensions should work or what should be included in them.

All of these things might become clearer if we understood better the processes of the acquisition of words and the ability to use them easily, accurately and appropriately. But the developmental approaches to word knowledge description are not well advanced. The place of vocabulary in the curriculum has been downplayed for many years and even now, with a resurgence of interest in vocabulary studies, we have only a hazy idea of how words are learned within the greater process of the mastery of a foreign language.

One of the effects of progressively dividing word knowledge into smaller and smaller units is that research becomes increasingly focused in smaller and more precisely defined areas and it becomes difficult to join the areas together to gain a good impression of the bigger picture of word knowledge and its development. Thus, we have research literature on the acquisition of collocation knowledge and associational knowledge separately, but little idea of how these two areas might interact if, indeed, they do. Inevitably too, some areas come in for far greater attention than others. We have for example, quite a large volume of research into the growth of word recognition when the word is in written form, but almost no work which parallels this investigating the acquisition of words in their spoken form.

The subsequent chapters are an attempt to pull together and summarize work which has focused on the various different aspects of word knowledge, and to give a more detailed account of some of the most recent research in these areas. For practical purposes we have used Nation's 2001 taxonomy as the basis of this. This allows us to highlight the way learners' knowledge in one area might link to knowledge and development in other areas. Each chapter is dedicated to one aspect of word knowledge from Nation's framework and, in the light of research carried out by colleagues in the Swansea Vocabulary Acquisition Research Group, we have also added a chapter on confidence in word knowledge. This is not in Nation's list but nonetheless seems to add a further dimension to our understanding of the way words are known and used. The final chapter will draw these strands together to see if a clearer picture of word knowledge and the way it is acquired can emerge.

Knowledge of Spoken Form

James Milton, Thomaï Alexiou and
Marina Mattheoudakis

2

Introduction

Form	Spoken	R	**What does the word sound like?**
		P	**How is the word pronounced?**
	Written	R	What does the word look like?
		P	How is the word written and spelled?
	Word parts	R	What parts are recognizable in this word?
		P	What words parts are needed to express meaning?

Knowing the spoken form of a word involves both recognizing it receptively and being able to produce it in speech to express meaning. Although the recognition of a word's spoken form appears first in Nation's list of knowing a word, it seems that it is an area much less intensively researched among foreign language learners than some other areas of word knowledge and, in particular, knowledge of written word form.

At first sight, learning the spoken form of a word appears to pose rather more potential problems to the learner than learning the written form. Recognizing a word, as a word and separate from other words, may not always be easy in speech, since in this form words are run together and are not conveniently separated by gaps as are written words on a page. For the listener too, there is pressure of time. Speech is usually heard once only and, unlike in writing, there is little opportunity to go back and review speech again. Listeners may rely heavily on context and on the correct anticipation of meaning in streams of sounds that may have several possible interpretations. For example, phrases such as *ice cream* and *I scream* are pretty much identical phonemically, /aɪs kriːm/ and /aɪ skriːm/. The gap between the words is a convention in transcription and does not exist in normal speech. Such phrases can often only be distinguished by context: the words which surround such phrases and the likely meanings that will associate with them.

There also appears to be more variation in the pronunciation of words than there is equivalent variation in written form. This can be the product of **assimilation** and **elision** as words which come together in normal speech influence each other, or it can be the product of the kind of variation that goes with dialect, regional accent or differences in group identity. Assimilation can significantly alter the way a word is spoken. For example, a word such as *and* is rarely fully pronounced in normal speech unless it is emphasized for some reason, and in a phrase like *fish and chips* is reduced to an –*n*– linking the two nouns /fɪʃ n tʃɪps/. Again, the pronunciation of a word such as *car* can vary. In spoken British English, when a pause follows, it has no /r/, /ə kɑː/. But if *car* is followed immediately by a vowel sound, as in *the car is red*, then the /r/ sound is added, /ðə kɑːr ɪz red/. By contrast, in rhotic varieties of English, such as American English, the /r/ in car is pronounced in all circumstances. A listener will need to be able to recognize this kind of systematic variation. There is much less of this kind of variation in the written form of English.

As Nation (2001, pp. 41–4) points out, for very young learners acquiring a first language phonological short-term memory capacity appears a significant element in the progress of learning. Very young first language learners acquire language from normal speech and interaction, and the advantages of a larger short-term memory are not hard to guess. Learners with large short-term memories are able to search greater strings of sounds for something that might be recognized and to search too for other words and meanings that might provide a key to the comprehension of unrecognized strings of sound. This link diminishes with age, so for most second language (L2) learners, who are likely to be of school age and will quite likely be adolescents, memory ability of this kind appears unimportant. This may be connected with the way new words are presented in foreign language learning, normally separated from strings of other sounds.

Knowing the sound of a word productively likewise appears to offer more potential complications to the learners than learning the equivalent written form. Producing words in spoken form will involve being able to produce all the sounds of a language, and in some languages like English there are more of these sounds than there are letters in the alphabet; but it will also require the learner to be able to put stress and emphasis in the right place and combine these sounds correctly. Languages can vary considerably in the range of sounds they produce and how these sounds can combine. Foreign language learners often struggle to master all the sounds of their new language and substitute sounds from their first language in pronouncing. They can also struggle to combine them. For example, English likes to join its consonants together to form clusters, as in the three-consonant sounds at the beginning of the word *string*. Learners with native language backgrounds where this does not happen – for example, Japanese – often put extra vowels between these consonants to help them make the pronunciation easier and pronounce a one-syllable word such as *string* with three syllables, something like *sitiring*, /sɪtɪrɪŋ/. A further example of the difficulty in mastering the phonological form of a word would be in stress placement. Since a language like English does not mark where the stress falls in written words, it is not surprising if stress and emphasis are often misplaced by learners. Where, in a word like *tentative*, for example, should the stress fall? Non-native speakers in our experience often favour placing it on the middle syllable and introducing a diphthong into the pronunciation, /ten'teItIv/. British pronunciation of this word, which learners may rarely encounter in speech, would place stress on the initial syllable, /ten'teItIv/. Writing words has its own problems, of course (these are considered in Chapter 3), and for learners of English the absence of a strong one-to-one relationship between sound and symbol can cause great difficulties. Nonetheless, there does not appear to be as much variation in spelling words as there is in speaking words.

Spoken word form and word frequency

One of the things that should influence knowledge of the spoken form of a word is the frequency of occurrence of that word. It has been assumed for many years that the more frequent a word is, then the earlier it is likely to be learned (Wesche and Paribakht, 1996, p. 14) and a number of recent experiments have demonstrated that this does occur in reality (for example, Milton, 2007; Richards and Malvern, 2007). These rely on tests of written vocabulary knowledge and word frequencies drawn from written **corpora**. However, the frequencies of words in spoken corpora are slightly different. Some words, such as the personal pronoun *I*, are rather more frequent in speech than in writing, for example. More generally, there is a tendency for the most frequent words in language to be even more frequent in speech than in writing. In Figure 2.1 the coverage provided by words from the written sub-corpus of the British National Corpus has been plotted alongside those provided in the two spoken sub-corpora. One spoken sub-corpus is called *demographic*, which contains transcripts of conversations, while the second is called *context-governed* and

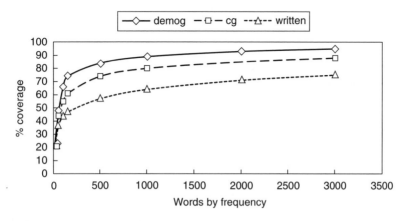

Figure 2.1 Coverage provided by sub-corpora of the British National Corpus (BNC) (Milton, 2009, p. 58)

contains rather more formal speech transcribed from lectures, meetings, sermons and the like. Because the most frequent words in the spoken sub-corpora are more frequent, they provide greater coverage than the same number of the most frequent words in the written sub-corpus.

If the relationship between frequency and learning, observed in written language, holds good in spoken language, then there should be an enhanced tendency for the learning of the most frequent words early in the learning process. The converse will be also true. Because infrequent words will be comparatively even less frequent than in writing, it will be more difficult to encounter and learn these words, making it more difficult to build a large lexicon in spoken form.

Spoken word recognition

Measuring knowledge of spoken words

Given the complexity of the spoken form of a word, perhaps it is not surprising that we know comparatively little of learners' knowledge in this area and the way this knowledge develops with progress in language learning. There is no standard or even a most frequently used test to draw on for information, as is beginning to emerge in other areas of vocabulary knowledge. This is possibly because, as Milton (2006, p. 130) notes, 'until very recently the technology for the reliable, fair and consistent delivery of vocabulary tests including sound did not exist'. A review of the literature suggests that only a handful of tests address this area of knowledge: three receptive tests and only one productive test.

Fountain and Nation (2000) report a dictation-based version of Nation's levels test where test words from the various **frequency bands** of the levels test are read to testees in a dictation passage. The words occur in context, therefore, and the testee has to be able to write them down. An example is provided in Figure 2.2. The passage is read once only and testees are instructed to write down what they hear. There are pauses where the slashes are marked and only the italicized words are scored.

Introduction

The *demand* for *food* / *becomes* more *important* / as the *number* of *people* in the *world* / *continues* to *increase*. /

Paragraph 1

The *duty* to *care* / for the *members* of a *society* / *lies* with those who *control* it, / but *sometimes governments* / *refuse* to *deal* with this *problem* / in a *wise way,* / and *fail* to *provide enough* to *eat*. / When this *occurs* many *ordinary* people *suffer*. /

Figure 2.2   Example of the Vocabulary Levels Dictation Test (from Nation, 2001, p. 429)

This test has certain attractive characteristics which include high reliability, and the possibility of generating parallel forms of the test with very similar performance characteristics. The test is reliant on oral delivery by a teacher, however, and this must introduce some variety in the presentation of the test material which will have an unknown impact on the scores learners can obtain.

Read (2007a) is interested, likewise, in testing the spoken form of a word in some kind of context. In his test,

> spoken words are associated with two kinds of sentence context: one providing a lexically bare syntactic context and the other a semantically richer one (Read 2007[b]). The contexts may add to the basic format not only a more accurate identification of the target word but also a link to a specific use of the word, which could result in more valid judgements by the test takers as to whether they know the word or not. (Read, 2007a, pp. 111–12)

In neither case, however, do we have data from learners at different levels of knowledge and from different backgrounds, which would allow us to model how learners' knowledge is likely to grow during learning.

Milton and Hopkins (2005) take a different approach and have designed a test of decontextualized aural word recognition, Aural-Lex (A-Lex), which deliberately parallels an established test of written word recognition, X-Lex (Meara and Milton, 2003). Tests of this kind for recognition of written form are described in greater detail in the next chapter. Both tests attempt to estimate knowledge of the most frequently occurring 5000 words in English. The wordlists they use are drawn from Hindmarsh (1980) and Nation (1984) and are lemmatized. The tests are computer-delivered **yes/no** tests which present learners with 120 words, one by one. Learners have to indicate whether they know each word. There are 20 randomly selected words from each 1000-word frequency band and a further 20 **pseudowords** which are designed in the case of X-Lex to look, and in Aural-Lex to sound, like words in English but are not real English words. The number of Yes responses to these pseudowords allows the score on the real words to be adjusted for guessing and overestimation of knowledge. There is no time limit to the test, which generally takes five or ten minutes to complete. A learner's vocabulary knowledge is calculated by counting the number of Yes responses to real words and multiplying this by 50 to give a raw score out of 5000. The number of Yes responses to pseudowords is then calculated and can be used to exclude data which is thought to be unreliable (for example, David, 2008), or it can be used to adjust the raw score for guessing. There are a variety of ways of achieving this, but, generally, the number of Yes responses to pseudowords is multiplied by 250. This figure is deducted from the raw score to give an adjusted score, which thus includes a compensation for guesswork. It is the adjusted scores which are thought to provide the better estimate of learners' **passive receptive vocabulary** size.

The Aural-Lex test format has the advantage that it allows scores for knowledge of the sound form of a word to be compared directly with knowledge of its written form. This should provide us with an insight into the structure of the mental lexicon and the way words are stored in memory. It can provide us, for example, with an insight into whether words are stored primarily in written or in spoken form or in both forms. Because estimates of written vocabulary size correlate well with overall foreign language competence, this test format also allows knowledge of the sound of a word to be placed in this broader, language-general context. A test in this format is not without its drawbacks, however, and users comment on the accent used in this test, native-speaker English received pronunciation (RP), when the testees are more familiar with non-native varieties. Words are also presented in citation form. The accent, it appears, can be a distraction and this, combined with the potential difficulty of recognizing many of the more frequent words removed from context, may explain the higher rates of false alarms in this form of the test than are usually found with the written equivalent. For many learners it appears to be more difficult to tell whether they know a word when only the sound is heard in isolation. Nonetheless, we do have studies (Milton and Hopkins, 2006; Milton and Riordan, 2006) where Aural-Lex data have been collected and appear to be reliable.

Aural-Lex is a receptive test of aural vocabulary knowledge and there appear to be almost no tests which systematically investigate productive knowledge of word form in a way that is designed to make sense of the learning process. However, Fitzpatrick and Clenton (2010) report a spoken/oral version of Lex30, a test based on a **word association** task, which they run in parallel with a written version of the Lex30 test. Their results indicate a modest positive correlation between written and oral **productive vocabulary** form knowledge, and no statistically significant difference in the scores obtained. Their conclusion is that productive knowledge in written mode cannot be assumed to mirror exactly knowledge in spoken mode, although clearly they are often related.

What research tells us about knowledge of the spoken word

Frequency and spoken word recognition

One thing that emerges from the data we have concerning knowledge of spoken word form is that word recognition is quite closely associated with word frequency. Figure 2.3 demonstrates this relationship and summarizes the data from Milton and Riordan's (2006) study of Arabic learners of English who were tested using Aural-Lex and whose sub-scores for each 1000-word **frequency band** can be calculated. The figure shows that the mean scores at each frequency level diminish with the frequency of the level, giving a downward-sloping profile.

Phonological vocabulary growth over time

Existing data also suggest, not surprisingly, that as learners progress, and spend progressively more time learning in class, then they have greater vocabulary knowledge in spoken form. Figure 2.4 summarizes data from 88 Greek learners (Milton and Hopkins, 2006), 11 drawn from each of eight levels ranging

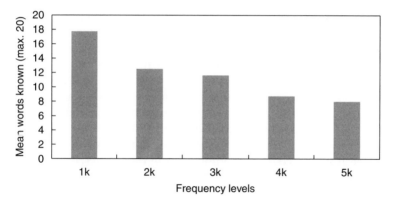

Figure 2.3   Aural word recognition and frequency

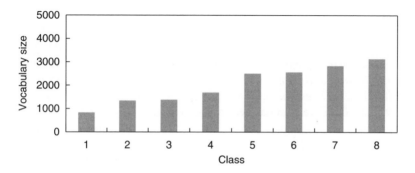

Figure 2.4   Aural vocabulary recognition and level

from elementary (class 1) through to highly advanced Cambridge Proficiency level (class 8).

In each succeeding class the mean estimated size of vocabulary in spoken form increases. A feature of elementary learners is that they have small vocabularies, less than 1000 words in this form, and a feature of advanced learners is that they have much larger vocabularies, they know about 3000 out of the most frequent 5000 words in English.

The inter-relationship between vocabulary in spoken and written form

The figures at each level for vocabulary size often appear to be lower than those recorded by the same students taking an equivalent written form of the test. It may be surmised that this is the frequency effect of spoken English coming into play. It was noted above that the most frequent words in spoken English are more frequent than the equivalent words in written English and that thresholds for comprehension can be met with smaller vocabulary resources in speaking than would be possible in writing. One interpretation of this observation is that learners' knowledge of the aural form of words will plateau earlier than their knowledge of written form because they will encounter the comparatively infrequent words less often and will have less need to learn them for communicability. However, it is suspected that not all learners behave in this way and demonstrate higher written word recognition than aural word recognition scores. Both Milton and Hopkins (2006) and Milton and Riordan's (2006) studies were designed to investigate whether native Arabic-speaking learners, in particular, behaved differently and learned words predominantly in aural form.

One of the principal motivations behind the creation of Aural-Lex, and for these two studies, was to have equivalent tests of words in both spoken and written forms so vocabulary knowledge in these different forms could be meaningfully compared. The evidence we have suggests that there need not be a direct one-to-one relationship between the words known by sound and by writing, and if a word is known in one form, it is by no means certain that it will be known equivalently in the other. The 88 Greek learners of EFL in Milton and Hopkins (2006) took both written and aural versions of the vocabulary size test and a comparison of the mean vocabulary size shows that, among these learners, written vocabulary tests scores typically exceed the aural test scores. The difference is statistically significant (t (87) = 10.02, p < .01). The Arabic-speaking learners in this study produced a different response pattern from Milton and Riordan (2006), where the reverse is true, although here the difference between the scores is not statistically significant (t (37) = 1.73, p = .09). The data are summarized in Figure 2.5.

Tentatively, it is suggested that the Arabic speakers in this investigation are particularly tied to phonological decoding of writing in English, producing scores on the two tests which are much more similar than for other learners of English who do not phonologically decode. However, Milton and Hopkins argue that this observation disguises the subtlety of this relationship. By dividing the data into bands according to X-Lex scores a rather more interesting picture of the inter-relationship emerges and this is illustrated in Figure 2.6.

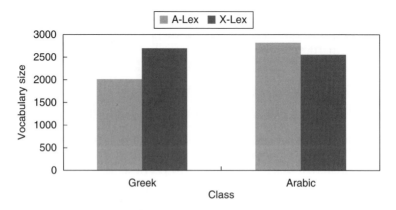

Figure 2.5 Comparison of class scores on A-Lex and X-Lex in Greek and Arabic native-speaking learners of EFL

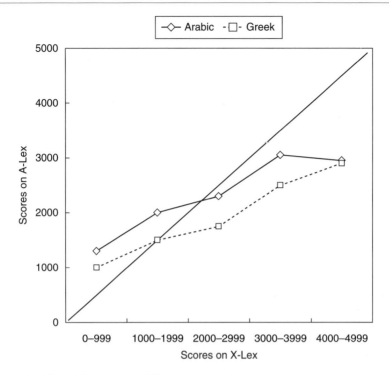

Figure 2.6   Mean A-Lex scores in X-Lex score bands

It appears that learners with very low vocabulary knowledge, from both language backgrounds, tend to have aural vocabulary scores larger than their written vocabulary scores. As learning progresses and vocabulary knowledge increases, however, this reverses and written vocabulary knowledge begins to exceed spoken knowledge. This is seen in Figure 2.6, where the trend lines cross the diagonal which represents a point at which written and aural vocabulary knowledge are equal. Learners who have very large vocabularies are characterized by having written vocabulary recognition that very considerably exceeds spoken recognition, possibly because access to the infrequent words lies principally through the written media where they will be comparatively more frequent. The difference between the Greek- and the Arabic-speaking learners lies in the timing at which this change from aural preference to written preference in vocabulary knowledge occurs. The Arabic learners, for reasons possibly connected with the educational system, are slower to make this change than the other learners.

This raises a question about how words are stored in the mental lexicon. It is entirely conceivable for learners to know a word by sound only, without any written representation. Non-literate people can and do learn foreign languages. However, it is less obvious that a word can exist in written form only, without a sound representation. One of the routes that readers use to access a foreign language word and its meaning is to sound it out. It has been argued that sub-vocalizing while reading is a natural and inevitable process (Carver, 1990). If a word can be read, and it has to be read to be known in written form, then somewhere there has to be a sound equivalent in the mind of the learner. Some languages lend themselves to this process better than others. Alphabetic languages, with a strong sound/ symbol correspondence, can provide an apparently straightforward phonological route to meaning when the word is encountered in written form. Nonetheless, it appears that advanced learners recognize many words by sight only and would fail to recognize the sound equivalent. Possibly, learners who encounter infrequent words by reading have sound versions which are somewhat different from the RP citation form they will be presented with in a test. This would be good enough to function when reading, and might explain aberrant pronunciations like the / tent'teɪtɪv/ for *tentative*, described earlier in the chapter, which emerge when a learner is forced to speak a word they have never encountered in sound. But, equally, it may be that, as Suárez and Meara (1989) and Segalowitz and Hulstijn (2005) have suggested, advanced learners develop a direct route to meaning from the written form, cutting out any intermediate phonological form.

It is not completely clear, therefore, why learners should favour the sound representation at the earliest stages of learning but increasingly favour the written representation thereafter. Two possible explanations have emerged. Possibly this reflects the nature of word frequencies in these two forms. The most frequent words are more frequent in spoken form while the less frequent words are more frequent in written form, and since vocabulary learning is particularly tied to frequency, these trends may be a manifestation of these differences. Possibly too, there may be features in the learning experience which help promote one form of vocabulary knowledge over another.

Current research work

The research presented here attempts to explore more in depth the strategies used by learners and the potential for learning experience to influence the learning of words in spoken or written form.

Research questions

The research hypothesis investigated is that there is a relationship between strategy use and vocabulary size/knowledge. The intention is to test the hypothesis that there is a relationship between learners' selection of written or aural strategies in learning, and the size of the written and aural lexicon that emerges.

Participants

In Greece, 81 learners of Greek as a second/foreign language participated in the study. The virtue of this, we believe, is that since they are learning the language in the country where it is spoken, then they have the advantage of immersing themselves in aural input in a way that learners in the traditional foreign language environment probably never can. The participants were of diverse origin and their age ranged between 18 and 52. Some of them had been living and working in Greece for quite some time, whereas others needed to certify their knowledge so as to be admitted to a Greek university. Thus, their level of Greek varied and ranged between A1 and B2 according to the Common European Framework of Reference (**CEFR**) for languages.

Instruments

The participants agreed to be tested so that their written and aural vocabulary sizes could be estimated. To this aim, two different tests were administered: Greek versions of the English X-Lex and A-Lex (described above) – the former testing their written vocabulary size, the latter estimating their aural vocabulary size.

The Greek X-Lex is a checklist test and presents the written form of 120 words. Of these, 20 words are selected from each of the first five 1000 lemmatized word **frequency bands**. The frequency information is taken from the Hellenic National Corpus (HNC) (Hatzigeorgiu *et al.*, 2001). There are also 20 false words that resemble the Greek morpho-phonology and the responses to these are used to adjust the scores for guesswork and overestimation. This provides an estimate of the learner's written vocabulary size out of the most frequent 5000 words, which gives a good, useful and efficient estimate of knowledge. Learners are presented with a written list of words and are required to indicate whether they recognize each word or not. The Greek X-Lex is currently available only in a pen and paper format.

The Aural-Lex (Milton and Hopkins, 2005) is developed to be directly comparable with X-Lex in construction and the criteria for word selection and, thus, its structure is identical with that of X-Lex, the only difference being that the words are presented in the oral mode in order to test aural vocabulary size. Learners are presented with words one at a time in sound only. The test word can be heard as often as wanted and then learners are required to indicate whether or not they know the word by clicking on the relevant button.

In addition, participants were required to fill in the SILL strategy questionnaire (Oxford, 1990) which had been previously modified and simplified to suit the purposes of our study. There were two versions of the questionnaire, one in English and another one in Greek (Psaltou-Joycey, 2010) to allow the participants to choose the language they felt most confident with. The questionnaire included 50 question items in a rating scale format; they were broadly classified into six sections investigating (a) mnemonic strategies, (b) practising strategies, (c) guessing strategies, (d) reflective strategies, (e) affective strategies and (f) interactional strategies. The following examples are taken from the questionnaire to indicate use of each type of strategy:

I think of relationships between what I already know and new things I learn in Greek (mnemonic strategy)
I say or write new Greek words many times to learn them (practising strategy)
To understand unfamiliar Greek words, I make guesses from context (guessing strategy)

I try to find as many ways as I can to use my Greek (reflective strategy)
I try to relax whenever I feel afraid of using Greek (affective strategy)
If I do not understand something in Greek, I ask the other person to slow
  down or say it again (interactional strategy).

For the analysis of individual strategies and their relationship with vocabulary size scores, the rating scales were used. However, to investigate overall strategy use and vocabulary size scores, the questions were divided into two groups: those that involved the aural/oral use of the language and those that promoted the written form of the language. The rating scale was not used but the numbers of strategies that were reported to have been used allowed four different types of strategy user to be distinguished:

1. Learners who reported high use of both oral/aural and written strategies (38 students, Group 1).
2. Learners who reported high use of oral/aural strategies and low use of written strategies (ten students, Group 2).
3. Learners who reported low use of oral/aural strategies and high use of written strategies (11 students, Group 3).
4. Learners who reported low use of both oral/aural and written strategies (seven students, Group 4).

Students using three or fewer strategies from either the written or oral/aural group of questions are classified as low users. Students using more than three strategies from either group are classified as high users. Among the students 15 generated incomplete responses which were unusable.

Procedure and data analysis

Participants took the X-Lex and A-Lex tests followed by the strategy questionnaire in the presence of the researcher. Regarding the vocabulary size tests, students were clearly instructed to be honest in their answers and advised against cheating as this would be penalized.

The relationship between vocabulary size (as measured by X-Lex and A-Lex) and strategy use (as measured by SILL) was investigated by means of two statistical tests. Paired t-tests were conducted to investigate the relationship between learners' written and aural vocabulary scores. Correlations were calculated between strategy use and written vocabulary scores as well as between strategy use and aural vocabulary scores.

Results and discussion

Relationship between written and aural vocabulary scores

Results shown in Table 2.1 indicates that X-Lex scores are higher on average than Aural-Lex while there is a good correlation between the two scores.

Table 2.1 X-Lex and A-Lex vocabulary scores (n = 81)

	Mean	s. d.	Comparison of means
X-Lex	2754.94	939.668	t = 9.908 (p < .001)
A-Lex	2090.12	996.695	

The mean X-Lex score is 2755 while the mean A-Lex score is 2090 – about 25 per cent smaller; this difference is statistically significant (t = 9.908, sig < 0.001). This means that learners in this sample tend overall to have written vocabulary sizes which are larger than the aural vocabulary sizes. Closer analysis of these results suggests that learners with less than 22,000 words have aural scores higher than written scores. However, the trend is that, as vocabulary sizes get larger, the written vocabulary size scores increase disproportionately and become increasingly larger than the aural vocabulary size.

Rather disappointingly for this investigation, there is a good correlation (r = .807, p < .001) between the two sets of scores and there are no learners with very high aural and very low written vocabulary size. This actually validates the two instruments and indicates that both tests measure different aspects – written and aural – of the same feature (lexical knowledge). But it makes the investigation of factors that might promote one type of learning rather than another difficult to investigate.

Relationship between strategies and vocabulary scores

If the total number of strategies used by students is compared with vocabulary size scores, no obvious relationship is apparent. The correlations which emerge are both very small and are not statistically significant. The correlation between strategy use and written vocabulary size is close to zero (r = 0.009, p = 0.942), while the correlation with aural vocabulary size is negative and very small (r = –0.135, p = 0.271). Figure 2.7, however, shows that the students in this study are not uniform in the choice of strategies and can be distinguished both in the numbers of strategies they report using and whether they choose aural or written strategies.

When divided into groups by strategy use, however, it appears that strategy use can exhibit a relationship with vocabulary size. The mean scores in X-Lex and A-Lex for all four groups are displayed in Table 2.2.

In each test Group 2, the learners who reported high use of aural/oral strategies and low use of written strategies, produces the smallest mean vocabulary size score. Group 3, students who report high use of written strategies and low use of oral strategies, produce higher mean scores. The highest mean scores on both tests are produced by students who report low use of both types of strategy. In order to determine whether these differences are significant, an analysis of variance (ANOVA) was performed. This analysis indicates that the differences between the A-Lex mean scores are not statistically significant (f (3, 65) = 2.188, sig. = 0.098). The differences between the mean X-Lex scores are statistically

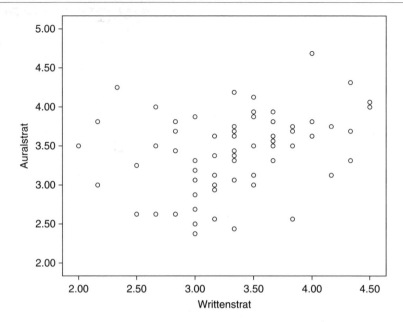

Figure 2.7   Comparing written and oral/aural strategy choice

Table 2.2   Mean scores in A-Lex and X-Lex

Group	Mean A-Lex score	Mean X-Lex score
Group 1 – high aural, high written	2216	2970
Group 2 – high aural, low written	1595	1875
Group 3 – low aural, high written	2477	3041
Group 4 – low aural, low written	2593	3286

significant ($f (3, 65) = 5.499$, sig. $= 0.002$), and a Post-hoc Tukey analysis iden-tifies this difference is because the Group 2 scores are statistically distinct from the other three test scores in this analysis.

It was expected that some sort of relationship would emerge between strat-egy use and the vocabulary development in both aural and written form. What seems to be suggested in these results is that the use of aural/oral strategy associates with lower written vocabulary scores, and use of written strategies associates with higher written vocabulary scores. This makes sense in that it is thought that reading in particular increases exposure to infrequent words, allowing a bigger vocabulary size to emerge. However, these data also appear to suggest that the same trend is emerging with the aural vocabulary scores, although the differences in means are not significant. It appears that use of oral/aural strategies associates with low aural scores rather than high scores, and it is the use of written strategies which associates with higher aural scores. Of course, in a language such as Greek the development of a large written vocabulary implies that there must be some kind of aural representation of the new words also present, since the Greek alphabet is strongly phonological and it may be that this trend confuses the issue.

There may, however, be other features in the strategies investigated which help to explain the association of oral/aural strategies with low vocabulary scores. Only a very small number of the strategies investigated produce statistically significant correlations with vocabulary size and this aggregation of the strategies with other, non-significant, strategies may be misleading.

Relationship between specific strategies and vocabulary scores

Three strategies positively associate with both A-Lex and X-Lex scores:

I try to think of relationships between new Greek words and old ones
I read books or magazines in Greek
I write notes, messages, letters, or reports in Greek (in class or on my own).

One strategy produced a positive correlation with X-Lex only:

I read Greek texts without looking up every new word.

Our tentative interpretation of this is that the strategies associated with meaningful reading and writing, or with language analysis, appear to associate with larger vocabulary size. These are all activities where, it can be argued, there is not just access to and use of the written form of the word but also a high involvement load.

There are eight strategies which negatively associated with both X-Lex and A-Lex scores:

I connect the sound of a new Greek word and a picture of the word
I use rhymes to remember new Greek words
I mime new Greek words to remember them
I review Greek lessons often
I say or write new Greek words many times to learn them
I practice the sounds of Greek
I notice my Greek mistakes and use that information to help me do better
I write down my feelings in a language learning diary.

Two strategies correlate negatively with A-Lex only:

I try to relax whenever I feel afraid of using Greek
I encourage myself to speak Greek even when I am afraid of making a mistake.

Again, our tentative analysis of this is that strategies associated with low vocabulary size tend to be strategies also associated with low involvement load. These activities, repeating a word in isolation or copying the sounds of Greek, are not just oral/aural activities but are activities disassociated from meaningful language exchange. These activities might be useful in the context of learning other aspects of language but their use does not appear to associate with the development of the kind of large vocabularies which are associated with great fluency.

The hypothesis that there is a relationship between learners' selection of written or aural strategies in learning, and the size of the written and aural lexicon, has been partially borne out in this study. It can be argued that oral/aural strategies do associate more with smaller vocabulary sizes, whether aural or written, than strategies involving the use of the written form of the word. Associations of this kind do not, of course, demonstrate a causal link, although this may be possible. Learners who interact with the aural form of the language predominantly will probably be exposed to fewer infrequent words and, therefore, have less opportunity to grow a large lexicon. However, the nature of the individual strategies which provide correlations suggests that it may be equally possible that it is the vocabulary size which governs the choice of strategy use. Extensive reading of books and magazines in a foreign language may not be possible and certainly will not be easy if the learner has only a small vocabulary to work with. It may be that these strategies only become realistically available for use to learners once a threshold of vocabulary size has been passed.

Practical implications and suggestions for further research

One of the implications of research into the recognition of the sound form of words in a language is that it allows us to create a better representation of the way words are stored in the mental lexicon. It appears as though words will not inevitably have both sound and written representations even when the language being learned has a strongly phonetic written form. This leads to the conclusion that the form of a test of vocabulary knowledge, especially size, may be crucial if the desire is to capture the full extent of the learners' foreign language lexicon. A written-only test may well underestimate at very low levels of knowledge, and an oral test looks likely to underestimate knowledge at higher levels of knowledge and performance. Estimation of vocabulary size is not an arcane matter, but, because of the links which have emerged with language level and performance, is a matter of importance to language learners and their teachers. Knowing the number of words recognized by sound may be particularly relevant where oral performance needs to be assessed, and knowledge of the number of words recognized in their written form is particularly relevant if the ability to perform in reading and writing are assessed. Unlike other areas of language, it appears this aspect of language knowledge can be assessed comparatively objectively.

The area is comparatively lightly researched, however, and there are many ways in which research might usefully develop. Almost everything discussed in this chapter has considered receptive knowledge of word form and there are no comparable studies of productive knowledge in this area. There is no standard test to use although an oral/aural version of Fitzpatrick's Lex30 test might prove illuminating since we now have data produced by written versions of the test against which the sound version could be compared. Nation's table specifically characterizes the productive form as knowledge of pronunciation, and work on the development of the phonological systems in the L2 has yet to be built into a model of the development of the lexicon as a whole.

We also have much less idea of how knowledge of the sound form of words ties in with other dimensions of vocabulary knowledge and with language performance more generally. The limited information we have has already proved illuminating, however, in helping to explain the relationship between lexical size and productive performance. Tests of the written form of words had left an unexplained gap in this relationship where the volume of words recognized appeared to contribute to skills such as reading and writing but where no comparable connection could be found with speaking skills. As Milton *et al.* (2010) demonstrate, knowledge of the written form of words correlates well with performance in skills involving the written form of words, knowledge of the sound form of words correlates well with skill involving the use of the sound form, and skills which involve both forms of the words can be explained by a combination of both written and sound word knowledge. Tests such as A-Lex and X-Lex, because they are very directly comparable in their structure and the range of scores they are designed to produce, appear to be useful tools in the language testers' armoury.

Research might also usefully develop into the factors which govern the growth of the sound knowledge of words. We have some idea, for example, of how knowledge of sound and written word form interrelate in the growth of a foreign lexicon, but only assumptions as to why they develop as they do. It appears unsafe to assume that the form of the word, spoken or written, is unimportant in the presentation of vocabulary for learning. Further experimentation, building on the type of study described in this chapter, might usefully help explain how lexicons develop as they do, and how to expedite learning in this area so that learners can move as quickly and painlessly as possible to the levels of communicability they aspire to. Reworking this study with a revised strategy questionnaire to make written and aural strategies assessment more directly comparable would appear a useful start.

Questions for discussion

- Why might knowledge of spoken word form develop faster than knowledge of written word form in beginner learners of Greek? Why might knowledge of written form develop faster once the 2000-word threshold is passed?
- What sort of teaching interventions might help learners develop written and spoken word knowledge simultaneously?
- Why do you think the group who reported lowest use of aural or written strategies produced the highest vocabulary size scores?
- How might productive knowledge of spoken word forms be tested in an objective way?
- How might you gather information on strategy use to better illuminate the way knowledge of spoken and written word form are developed by learners?

Knowledge of the Written Word

Imma Miralpeix and Paul Meara

3

Introduction

Form	Spoken	R	What does the word sound like?
		P	How is the word pronounced?
	Written	**R**	**What does the word look like?**
		P	**How is the word written and spelled?**
	Word parts	R	What parts are recognizable in this word?
		P	What words parts are needed to express meaning?

According to Nation (2001), one of the aspects involved in knowing a word receptively is being familiar with its written form so that it is recognized when it is met in reading. Regarding productive knowledge and use, knowing a word also entails being able to write it correctly, as the table above shows.

This chapter will focus on written word recognition, which is the ability of a reader to recognize words correctly and effortlessly. In his discussion about knowledge of the written forms of words, Nation focuses mainly on spelling, as translating sounds into appropriate graphemes (or vice versa) is not always an easy task but a quite demanding one, especially when more than one language is involved and when these languages do not share the same alphabet.

However, there are other factors that can affect the recognition of visually presented words. These factors have been traditionally classified depending on whether they were more related to the form or to the semantic properties of words. Among those referring to the form, we find word length and word shape, as words are usually seen as patterns more than the sum of their letter parts, but also word structure, especially in words with recurrent clusters of letters such as common **affixes** or inflectional endings. It has also been shown that the morphological structure of a language exerts great influence on lexical representation and processing in different languages and that morphological awareness does definitely play a role in written word recognition (see, for instance, the special issue of the journal *Reading and Writing* on morphology in word identification and word spelling edited by Verhoeven and Carlisle, 2006). The stimulus quality is another formal aspect to be taken into account (an ink blot or different letter sizes can be disturbing), as well as analogy, because readers sometimes use known words to help them recognize new ones.

Other aspects that may help in visual word recognition are more closely related to semantic information provided by words. As Hauk *et al.* (2006) acknowledge, they are actually 'lexico-semantic' properties, as opposed to those described above that would be 'surface' properties. In this second group we would find aspects such as imageability (more imageable or concrete words tend to be processed faster) and word frequency, as words that are frequently found in a language are more easily recognized by the reader than those that are only met occasionally (De Groot *et al.*, 2002): there is a steady relationship between the written forms that learners identify and those that are more frequent in a language, which has also been observed in studies using vocabulary profiles. When words are not presented in isolation, **priming** can also be determinant in efficient word identification, as it can accelerate response.

The distinction between these two types of properties (formal and semantic) already appears in early word-processing models. Some of these models claim that surface properties are processed earlier (e.g., 'form-first theories') or focus on possible ways of letter processing (e.g., 'serial' vs 'parallel' models of letter recognition etc.); while others put the emphasis on the interaction of both types of properties (e.g., 'cascaded models'). Several studies have recently enquired into the effects of these and other similar properties on written word identification (e.g., Yap and Balota, 2007; Zoccolotti *et al.*, 2009) and coincide in revealing that, more than one factor alone, it is their interaction which leads to successful word recognition.

It is also worth mentioning that in a second language (L2) word recognition will also be affected by the way/s in which L1 words are usually identified. A good example is provided by Chikamatsu (1996), who shows that native speakers of Chinese tend to rely on visual information to recognize Japanese words, while native English speakers learning Japanese use phonological procedures. These results are better explained as an influence of the L1 orthographic system. It has been demonstrated as well that **cognates** are easier to learn and more accurately processed than non-cognates (e.g., De Groot and Keijer, 2000; Tonzar *et al.*, 2009).

In sum, research has shown so far that lexical decision is a complex process and as such it is also difficult to model. In addition to spelling, all these other factors can give account of how accurately and quickly a written word is recognized. As Hauk *et al.* (2006, p. 819) indicate, both 'accuracy and reaction time measures conflate these influences'.

In L2 research, written word recognition tasks have been extensively used for two main purposes. The first is assessing the knowledge learners have of a word – that is, whether the word is known or not. Very often, the claims learners make about their knowledge of individual written words are used to estimate their **receptive vocabulary** sizes – that is, the number of words they know. The second purpose is testing accessibility to familiar items (i.e., speed of response, how quickly words are accessed). The basic procedure involves measuring the time needed to classify a set of words as belonging to a particular category (e.g., word/non-word, animate/inanimate etc.). Results from these tests are thought to be a good measure of lexical access and of fluency.

The next section reviews research that has been conducted to assess accuracy in **lexical decision tasks** (i.e., the extent of written word recognition). More precisely, it focuses on tests that estimate learners' receptive vocabulary sizes from their answers to a word recognition task. Typically, these tests are known as **yes/no** tests and there are many instances in the literature. Then (in the following section), we will concentrate on speed of written word recognition (i.e., timed recognition research) and will revise some of the more prominent studies and tests used in the field so far. Apart from enquiring into the nature of the experiments that have been carried out in these two areas of investigation, the chapter also explores in more detail in the successive sections whether there is a relationship between how accurate and how quick a learner is at recognizing written words. Accuracy and speed of word recognition have usually been seen as two dimensions of vocabulary knowledge (breadth and fluency) and have sometimes been associated in the literature, although the nature of this relationship, if there is one, is an issue that deserves careful attention.

Written word recognition

Measuring the extent of written word recognition: yes/no tests

In order to assess the number of written words that learners are able to recognize effortlessly using a **yes/no** test, L2 students can be presented with a list of written words in a context-free environment and asked to decide whether they know the meaning of each of them. The words are selected from different **frequency bands**, which allows the tester to make an estimation of the number of words known by the testee. **Pseudowords** (words that do not exist in the target language) are also included in the test in order to control for guessing and the scoring is adjusted downwards when the testee claims to know many pseudowords. Meara and Buxton (1987) and Meara and Jones (1988, 1990) were the first to develop the technique for L2 speakers.

A considerable amount of research has been published since then, most of which suggests that the yes/no methodology works quite well, with a few exceptions (e.g., Cameron, 2002). The tests have been considered a useful indication of the number of words recognized by L2 learners and a helpful and simple measure of vocabulary size (Meara, 1994). Furthermore, yes/no tests assess more words than a multiple-choice test in the same amount of time and they are quick to mark.

However, interpreting yes/no scores is not always straightforward, especially where false alarms are concerned – that is, the cases in which the learner says 'yes' to a pseudoword. Imaginary words that look like L1 **cognates** (thus apparently sharing 'surface' and 'lexicosemantic' properties with the L1 word) are a particular problem in this respect. Work by Beeckmans *et al.* (2001), Huibregtse *et al.* (2002) and Eyckmans (2004) addresses the problem of adjusting raw scores by taking into account the false-alarm rates, although none of them presents a completely satisfactory solution (see also Mochida and Harrington, 2006; Shillaw, 2009).

One of the latest versions of a yes/no test to assess **receptive vocabulary** size is X-Lex, which is a computer test proposed by Meara and Milton (2003) and which forms the basis of the A-Lex test of aural word recognition (Milton and Hopkins, 2005) described in the previous chapter. X-Lex can estimate how many words learners accurately recognize by presenting words in five different frequency bands, which correspond to the most frequent words in English up to the 5,000 most common words. This allows the program to generate a profile showing the proportion of words known in each frequency band. Several years of research with this test (Meara, 2005a) have been useful to, among other things, identify different aspects that should be taken into account when interpreting the data the test produces. First, vocabulary size results in English correlate well with general proficiency level in this language, although it might not happen in other languages. Second, high false-alarm rates or large numbers of errors compromise the validity of the results. Third, the tool is sensitive to the L1 of the learners, as those speakers of Romance languages may score higher than expected due to the large number of borrowings between English and French.

In short, yes/no tests assess receptive knowledge of L2 written words. Learners' answers for the words presented at each frequency level are used to calculate their vocabulary sizes. Although there is no perfect scoring method, close approximations can be obtained and these are useful for a variety of purposes, such as having an indication of the learner's lexical proficiency in a quick and easy way. Additionally, the extent to which learners recognize written words might also be related to how quickly this recognition takes place.

Measuring accessibility to written words: timed recognition

Although **yes/no** tests share some methodological similarities with the **lexical decision tasks** used in psycholinguistics (e.g. De Groot *et al.*, 2002), there are some significant methodological differences between the two approaches. Research using lexical decision tasks typically focuses on the time it takes learners to decide that they recognize a word or not. Yes/no tests do not usually take response time into account, only the total number of words known, together with the errors and false alarms, is considered for the final estimation. Thus, we say that this sort of test assesses response accuracy. However, recognizing written words implies much more: the speed at which these words are recognized is also believed to be crucial for the development of abilities such as reading fluency. For instance, Van Gelderen *et al.* (2004) report remarkable correlations between speed of processing and reading comprehension. It has also been observed that lexical retrieval speed can be enhanced and that learners are more prone to use in writing those words they have been trained in (Snellings *et al.*, 2002).

Nevertheless, research has concentrated more on how many words learners know than on how quick the lexical knowledge is accessed, as noted by Schmitt (2010). Most of the studies on speed of recognition have been conducted in the area of psycholinguistics and neurolinguistics by using different tasks. For instance, one of the most typical measures how long it takes people to decide that a particular set of letters is a word they know or not. Although it is difficult to calculate reaction times very accurately, we know today that usually L1 words that are context-free are recognized by normal adult native speakers in exposures of about 600–700 milliseconds. The average reading time for a word when it is read in a natural reading environment would be lower than words that are presented in a context-free environment (about 250 milliseconds), as context clues help to identify the word. For a non-native speaker of a language, the recognition normally takes longer and it is assumed that the time L2 learners require to recognize a word depends on how well they know the language. Therefore, we can tell how accessible a vocabulary is by comparing the lexical recognition times of a particular population with that of native speakers of the language. More recently, innovative techniques such as measurement of eye movements and event-related potentials have also proved useful to determine very precisely word recognition when reading (e.g., Sereno and Rayner, 2003).

However, as Meara (1994) has already suggested, an important drawback of laboratory studies is that they rely on sophisticated measuring equipment to detect differences in the response times and also very careful controls. In addition, the differences between groups of subjects in reaction times are really small (some of the order of 20 milliseconds). All this makes the methodology not suitable for everyday testing purposes and it was also one of the main reasons why he included in the Dígame Project a **lexical decision task** that was different from the ones used until that moment: in this case, testees had to recognize a hidden word, which was six letters long, embedded in a string of 20 letters. Although it was seen that L2 recognition took longer than L1 recognition, it was also shown to be quicker as L2 learners progressed.

This method of looking for hidden words, which was new at the time, sought to obtain reaction times in the region of one to two seconds, which could be measured by using any computer and without any need of specialist equipment. The same method is being used nowadays by Coulson (2010) to test speed of word recognition: using the same format of hidden words in long strings of letters, he measures lexical access in learners and native speakers.

The program he uses to present the letter strings and compute reaction times is called Q-Lex and it requires the participants to press a key whenever they are able to identify the hidden words. The program also records the time each participant uses to complete the identification of each word and compares it against the time native speakers use for the identification of these words.

Development of written word recognition techniques has often gone hand-in-hand with research on bilingualism. According to Lambert (1955) and Lambert *et al.*, (1959), speed of word recognition could help identify the dominant language in the case of bilinguals, as they will be able to recognize written words faster in their stronger language; the so-called 'bilingual deficit'. The more these speakers approach the notional state of balanced bilingualism, the more similar their thresholds will be. For instance, depending on the reaction times needed to recognize 20 English and 20 French words, Lambert could identify the dominant language of an English/French bilingual. However, reaction times might have also been influenced by other aspects: for instance, frequent words in the L2 can be accessed as easily as frequent words in the L1.

More recently, in an attempt to explore the bilingual deficit in lexical retrieval in more detail, Bialystok *et al.* (2008) analysed the performance of a group of monolinguals and two groups of bilinguals (a high proficiency and a low proficiency one) on several tests of vocabulary size (using the Peabody Picture Vocabulary Test and an expressive vocabulary task) and on efficiency of word retrieval (with the Modified Boston Naming Test and letter and category fluency tasks). They saw that bilinguals with matched vocabulary scores outperformed monolinguals on letter fluency, while bilinguals with lower vocabulary scores performed at the same level as monolinguals. A possible explanation they offer for these results is that 'bilinguals balance their deficits in vocabulary against their advantages in executive functioning when performing lexical retrieval tasks' (ibid., p. 536). Thus, lexical retrieval under certain conditions can be better for bilinguals than for monolinguals. A final peripheral implication of their study is the real need to assess the vocabulary size of the participants in order to carefully interpret bilingual effects on lexical retrieval.

There are other authors that have gone a step further and have enquired about the mechanisms that underlie increased recognition speed. According to Segalowitz and Segalowitz (1993), increased speed can be reached through two different routes. The first is a simple speeding up of a process that learners already possess – that is, performance becomes faster because underlying component processes are executed more quickly. Nevertheless, there could also be changes that involve much more than just a simple speed-up. New processes could also be developed due to practice and experience and this would mean that some mental reorganization makes language processing more efficient and allows quicker operations. Among the reasons that may bring about a restructuring of the underlying processes, Segalowitz and Hulstijn (2005, p. 375) give examples such as, 'when the L2 visual word recognition proceeds directly from the printed stimulus to meaning activation without first passing through a stage of phonological recoding or translation into L1' or 'more parallel processing'.

This second route to increase speed is what Segalowitz and Hulstijn call 'automaticity' and they devise a specific coefficient to measure it, when most studies use simple reaction time (RT) measures to evaluate word recognition skills. The new measure, the 'coefficient of variation' (CV) is computed by dividing the mean standard deviation by the mean RT. It is considered to be a measure of response stability on the following premise: in a case where there is just speed-up involved, the standard deviation will drop proportionally to the mean RT. On the contrary, when the standard deviation changes by a greater proportion, it will probably mean that the change involved is not just related to the speeding up and the differences must be attributed to other qualitative changes in the underlying processes. It is assumed that differences in CV will show differences not only and simply related to RT. This coefficient has lately been used to assess L2 gains, as, for instance, those obtained by learners in classroom settings at home and in abroad contexts (Segalowitz and Freed, 2004) and has also been studied in relation to proficiency levels (Harrington, 2006).

However, the distinction between what RT and CV measure has also been questioned by Hulstijn *et al.* (2009). At a theoretical level, they point out that it is problematic to say whether CV is actually a good indicator of automaticity, as it is very difficult to capture the distinction between gains in knowledge itself ('accumulation' of knowledge) and gains in skill of processing that knowledge ('acquisition' of knowledge). According to them, in language acquisition, knowledge accumulation is actually part of skill acquisition.

Accuracy and speed of written word recognition

Research on the written word has reported interesting findings about L2 learning. It has shown, for example, that the number of written words that L2 learners efficiently recognize can be a good predictor of classroom performance (Read, 2000) and a good indication of language proficiency level (Harrington and Carey, 2009; Miralpeix, 2009). In fact, **yes/no** tests have been used as placement tools (Meara and Jones, 1988). Similarly, some studies have evidenced that tests of **receptive vocabulary** size correlate with the performance exhibited in tests of reading and writing, and to a lesser extent to listening abilities (see, for instance, Beglar and Hunt, 1999; Qian, 1999; Staehr, 2008). The difference between these correlations might be due to the fact that the words tested come from frequency lists extracted from written **corpora** and that learners are also provided with written forms – not oral stimuli – to identify in the tests (for a more detailed discussion see Milton, 2009, chapter 8).

There are very few studies in the literature, though, that put in relation the number of words a learner recognizes effortlessly (receptive vocabulary size) and recognition speed in an L2. However, the joint behaviour of these two variables can be determinant for successful L2 vocabulary acquisition and development. A good example can be reading comprehension: a large vocabulary size is important for word recognition in reading because learners usually build a sight vocabulary to perform this task. Consequently, Schmitt (2000, p. 50) emphasizes that 'it is an advantage to have as large a vocabulary as possible to recognise any word that happens to come up'. However, speed of written word recognition is a determinant factor for this reading to be fluent.

Two of the most recent studies to address this issue are Laufer and Nation (2001) and Harrington (2006). In the first study, the authors explore a number of different issues that relate lexical size and speed of access using a tool called Vocabulary Recognition Speed Test (VORST). The study suggests that there might be a modest correlation between vocabulary size and the speed with which a target word can be matched to its meaning. The data also suggest that increases in automaticity do not immediately reflect increases in vocabulary size. Harrington (2006) also measures both performance accuracy and speed of response to familiar items. His results suggest that reaction times systematically decrease as a function of increasing proficiency (CVs were lower when performance improved).

Current research work

In the light of what has been presented on accuracy and speed of written word recognition, we would like to explore in more depth the relationship between them in L2 learning. In the following sections, we present a study devised for this purpose.

Research question

This study aims at providing answers to the following research question: is there a relationship between the number of written words recognized (**receptive vocabulary** size) and recognition speed (lexical access) in L2 learning? If there is, how can this relationship be described?

Participants

Our participants were 145 university students of English Philology at the University of Barcelona. They were all Spanish/Catalan bilinguals and were studying English as a foreign language in this instructional setting. Their levels ranged from intermediate to advanced proficiency. We will refer to Spanish/Catalan as 'L1' and English as 'L2' in spite of the fact that English was actually a FL.

Instruments

Two tests were used for this particular study. One was a **yes/no** vocabulary size test and the other a lexical access test. X-Lex and Y-Lex were the yes/no tests taken as measures of **receptive vocabulary** size (accuracy in written word recognition). The X-Lex version used for this study was an adaptation of Meara and Milton's (2003) X-Lex, whose scores ranged between 0 and 5000 words known receptively. For the present study, the sample of words tested was selected from the JACET list (Ishikawa *et al.*, 2003). Ways in which participants' L1 might confound their performance were accounted for (by controlling for the number of **cognates**, for example). As our participants were estimated to have vocabularies of more than 5000 words, a new test was devised (Y-Lex), which enabled us to estimate students' receptive vocabulary size up to 10,000 words. Y-Lex (Meara and Miralpeix, 2006) is an advanced version of X-Lex and it is aimed at more advanced speakers. It tests vocabulary in the 6000–10,000 word range by presenting the student with a set of words, one at a time, in a context-free environment in the same way X-Lex does. Levels 6, 7 and 8 of the new lists are based on the appropriate levels of the JACET 8000 list (Ishikawa *et al.*, 2003). Levels 9 and 10 are based on Kilgarriff's listing of the BNC (Kilgarriff, 1998).

The background research on Y-Lex is much less extensive than the equivalent work on the lower-level X-Lex tests. Nation's Levels Test (Nation, 1990) and Schmitt's reworking of the original tests (Schmitt, 2000) both contain a 10K section, but in practice this level is often omitted by researchers working with less advanced learners. Meara's original yes/no tests (Meara and Jones, 1990) included items from the 6–10K range, but the higher levels were omitted from the later development of these tests. This means that the Y-Lex tests are one of the few instruments available for testing proficiency at this level (Miralpeix, 2009).

A test devised by Segalowitz was used to assess lexical access in the L1 and the L2. It consisted of a semantic classification task presented to the students on a screen using DMDX software (Foster and Foster, 2003). Students were shown a frequent word on the screen and they had to decide as quickly as possible on whether the word was animate or inanimate. The words were shown in a randomized order but they always consisted of nouns with the corresponding article to avoid confusion (e.g., *a bird, a lady, a pencil, a lamp*…). The actual test was preceded by some trials (practice items for the learners to become accustomed to the task) followed by 100 experimental words, for which students had to indicate their animacy condition by pressing the appropriate key on the computer keyboard. More detailed explanations of the test can be found in Segalowitz and Freed (2004, pp. 180–1). Both reaction times and accuracy were recorded and two measures were obtained from the results:

1. RT (reaction time) is the index used to quantify speed of L2 processing or speed of lexical access. It was computed by partialling out L1 from L2 reaction times, so as to control for individual differences in general speed of processing.
2. CV (coefficient of variation of the RT) is the measure of efficiency of lexical access (automaticity) and was the result of dividing the standard deviation of an individual's RT by the person's mean RT.

Procedure and data analysis

Participants took the X-Lex and Y-Lex tests followed by the lexical access test in a computer room where the researcher was present. These were part of a larger battery of tests the students took for research purposes, which aimed at assessing their English proficiency. Regarding the vocabulary size test, students were clearly instructed to be honest about the answers, and they were advised that cheating was penalized. As far as the lexical access test was concerned, they did it both in Spanish or Catalan (they were told to choose the language they found themselves more comfortable in) and in English. Word responses were made using the forefingers of each hand on particular keys of the computer keyboard for the animate/inanimate distinction. Five students with an unusually high false-alarm rate in the yes/no tests were not included in the final sample, as it has been shown that this could affect the reliability of this measure (Miralpeix, 2009).

The relationship between vocabulary size (as measured by X-Lex and Y-Lex) and lexical access (as measured by RT and CV) was investigated by means of two statistical tests. Preliminary analyses were also performed to ensure no violation of the assumptions of normality, both in the whole data set and in each of the groups that were compared. Pearson product-moment correlation coefficients were obtained between the variables of size and speed and a one-way ANOVA for independent measures was conducted to see if there was any statistical difference in speed of lexical access between groups with different vocabulary sizes.

Results

Table 3.1 presents the descriptive results for the three measures (**receptive vocabulary** size, RT and CV).

There was no correlation between the two variables (size and access), whether lexical access was measured by means of RT [$r = .037$, $n = 145$, $p = .653$] or by means of CV [$r = .002$, $n = 145$, $p = .983$].

Learners were also divided into three groups which were shown to be significantly different according to the size of their receptive vocabularies (Miralpeix, 2009). The vocabulary size scores ranged between 3400 and 8500 words – a difference of just over 5000 words. We divided this range into three sub-ranges (3400–5100 words, 5100–6800 words and 6800–8500 words, as presented in Table 3.2) and computed the mean scores of learners in each sub-range. This table also shows the RT and the CV for each group. As can be observed, RT is similar in groups G1 and G2 and just decreases in G3. The CV only decreases in G3, which is the group with the largest vocabularies.

A one way ANOVA between groups was conducted to explore the impact of vocabulary size on lexical access, as measured by RT and CV, with the groups shown in Table 3.2. Levene's test for homogeneity of variances was non-significant (.626 for RT and .803 for CV), thus confirming the normality

Table 3.1 Descriptive statistics for each measure including all the participants

		Mean	S. d.	Min.	Max.
English learners	Vocabulary size	6020	1054	3400	8500
(N = 145)	RT L1	784	131	525	1167
	RT L2	815	121	570	1119
	CV L1	.3052	.0901	.12	.56
	CV L2	.3078	.0834	.16	.54

Table 3.2 Groups according to receptive vocabulary sizes, given by X-Lex and Y-Lex and their corresponding means of RT and CV

Group	N	Vocabulary sizes	RT L2	CV L2
G1	29	3400–5,100 words	825	.3083
G2	81	5100–6,800 words	821	.3088
G3	35	6800–8,500 words	794	.3053

of the variables under study. There was no statistically significant difference between any of the groups at the p < .05 level in RT [F(2,147) = .970; p = .381] or CV[F(2,147) = .069; p = .934].

Discussion

Taken together, these results indicate that there is no consistent relationship between **receptive vocabulary** size and speed of word recognition. No correlations are found between these variables in the present study, regardless of the measure used to assess lexical access: RT (quickness) or CV (automaticity).

This lack of systematic correspondence leaves the door open to different interpretations. It may be possible to have a large vocabulary size from which it may take time to retrieve words. It would also be possible to have a small vocabulary size from which words are quickly and easily retrieved. Actually, it is not difficult to find people with knowledge of just a few basic English words which can be rapidly accessed – for instance, people that need just a few words in the L2 to communicate effectively in their jobs and who use these words very often. Another possibility that the results do not exclude is that learners with similar vocabulary sizes may actually show different rates of accessibility to words. In this case, those with a higher recognition speed would probably be better than their peers with similar vocabulary sizes at input comprehension or more successful when reading.

The results do not show that the relationship between size and speed is a totally random one either, as both RT and CV are lower for the group with the biggest vocabularies. One of the viable explanations could be that accessibility may not play a determinant role until lexicons reach big enough sizes, or that a close relationship between the two can just be observed at specific stages of the learners' interlanguage development (Serrano and Miralpeix, 2010), and it might not be a linear relationship. However, none of the differences between groups is significant, so this explanation is not proved by our data.

Therefore, the results from our study do not parallel those obtained in studies by Laufer and Nation (2001), who find a moderate correlation between size and speed, and Harrington (2006), who observes a consistent decrease in recognition time as vocabulary size increases. We believe that our results show that the relationship between vocabulary size and access is not a straightforward one, and that statements such as 'an increase in automaticity lags behind increase in size' (Laufer and Nation, 2001, p. 23) could actually be, in Coulson's words, 'a simplification of a potentially richer mechanism' (Coulson, 2010, p. 21). As can be observed in Table 3.2, the group of learners with vocabularies between 5100 and 6800 words have actually a similar mean RT to that of learners with vocabularies smaller than 5100 words. Further research can investigate in more detail if increases in vocabulary size could result in, at least temporary, stable or slower recognition speed.

A point that should also be taken into consideration is that many different variables may account for word recognition speed in the process of learning an L2. **Receptive vocabulary** size can certainly be one of these variables, although the extent of this probable effect will need to be carefully determined. For instance, Jean and Geva (2009) investigated the role of vocabulary knowledge in predicting English as a Second Language (ESL) word recognition ability in primary school children. A hierarchical multiple regression showed that it explained a small proportion of variance, but that phonological awareness or working memory influenced word recognition to a greater extent. Therefore, a relationship between size and access can also be mediated by factors that have not been assessed in the present study.

One of the possible factors that may account for our findings is that the tests we use are different from others previously used for this purpose. Laufer and Nation used VORST, which is a computer version of the Vocabulary Levels Test that counts and averages response times on independent items and on different frequency levels. Harrington's test contains words from different frequency levels to which the learners have to answer if they know the word or not: the vocabulary it presents – 150 stimuli – was chosen from the 2k, 3k, 5k and 10k of the VLT and the Academic Word List (AWL). Our study makes use of different stimuli to compute the scores for vocabulary size and for lexical access.

There also exists the possibility that the lexical access test used in this case does not actually gauge the difference in reaction times that may exist between the participants, due mainly to their L1 and to the selection of words that appear in the test. According to Wang and Koda (2005), there are both common and unique processes in learning to read English for students from different L1 backgrounds. In our case, participants were speakers of Spanish/Catalan learning English, which is a combination that does not appear in studies by Segalowitz or Harrington. In addition, words to be classified as animate or inanimate were common words (and sometimes **cognate**) and research suggests that non-native speakers respond more slowly to infrequent words (Laufer and Nation, 2001). It may be possible, then, that this word selection can have influenced the results obtained, as explained below.

First, Spanish orthography is almost entirely regular, there is nearly always a one-to-one correspondence between letter and sound. In English, on the contrary, phonological rules do not usually predict the pronunciation of a word, as there is a lack of one-to-one correspondence between sound and letter, and written forms are not a consistent reflection of pronunciation in English. The fact that English spelling is highly irregular is one of the reasons that explains why English speakers most probably develop a set of phonological procedures and a set of orthographical procedures in order to access their mental lexicons (e.g., 'dual-route' theory by Coltheart, 1978). According to this, there must be some sort of grapheme-phoneme correspondence rules. However, Spanish speakers may not actually need to develop a set of rules of this sort or any additional orthographic procedures, as their orthographic system is more regular and they could rely on the phonological route to access their lexicon (studies such as Meara *et al.*, 1985, would support this hypothesis). The development of another route would just imply redundancy, and we know that language functioning usually prioritizes economy. Spanish speakers can usually turn any written form into a phonological one and the other way round.

Suárez and Meara (1989) pointed out that Spanish learners of English probably develop new ways of recognizing words if they want to be competent in English, such as a direct visual route. They tested three hypotheses in relation to Spanish speakers' behaviour when recognizing English words. The first was that they would behave like English speakers and use both routes. The second was that they would rely on the direct visual route and the third that they would rely entirely on the phonological one. None of these hypotheses was clearly supported by the results obtained. However, the authors suggest that these learners may continue to rely on the phonological access route and that the direct visual access route can operate for very highly frequent words.

The lexical access test in our study does not tap into this aspect of word recognition. We cannot see whether participants might have developed an orthographic route or continue using the phonological route for some words and the direct route for highly frequent items, as most of the words used in the test are very frequent (*boy, cat, dog*) and some are cognates in the two languages (*television, secretary, dictionary*). Therefore, this would call for an exploration of test formats and how these formats work in relation to different languages.

Practical implications and suggestions for further research

The fact that no clear relationship is found between vocabulary size and lexical access suggests that research should be conducted on several issues.

Recommendations for further work include exhaustive longitudinal studies that look at how much variation there is in the way that vocabulary is recognized and how this can be related to vocabulary gains in size. Having more detailed information about this possible relationship will be useful mainly for two reasons.

The first one is a theoretical one. It is quite likely that the lexicon can be better described and studied in terms of the three-dimensional model that Meara (1996b, 2009, p. 29) proposes, which is composed of size (how many words the learner knows), organization (how the words s/he knows are structured) and accessibility (how easily s/he has access to the words known). Moreover, according to Meara (1996b) speed of lexical access may probably be a matter of amount and kind of interconnections in the mental lexicon instead of a specific feature of a particular lexical item. This leads to the second reason why information on accuracy and speed of word recognition would be of interest and it is a practical one: as type of instruction can have an influence on fluency (Nation, 2001), specific training could also help learners establish new links between words and thus promote efficient vocabulary learning (for a detailed description of motives and implications, see Segalowitz, 2010). Certainly, knowing when and how to enhance fluency at different stages of vocabulary growth can help learners to develop more effective vocabularies.

In relation to the measurement of the three dimensions that are part of the model, some tools to measure vocabulary size and organization have already been developed and validated and information on the behaviour of these two dimensions starts being available. However, very little is known about the role that accessibility performs in the model, and this would probably remain the case until more measures that capture speed of word recognition are validated and put in relation to the behaviour of size and organization. Regarding the vocabulary size tests used in this study, the latest versions are downloadable from http://www.lognostics.co.uk/tools/index.htm. The Spanish–English versions of the lexical access tests were very slightly adapted from Segalowitz and Freed (2004) and just the Catalan translation was added.

Some more research is already being conducted on these grounds: Coulson (2011) works with Q-Lex, an alternative to **lexical decision tasks** to gauge speed of written word recognition. Additional lines of research may stem from the use of auditory lexical decision tasks (Goldinger, 1996) or from the analysis of productive oral performance. Further issues about the implementation of these tasks or the study of learner's speech would go beyond the scope of this chapter, as it has focused on the written word. Nevertheless, the triangulation of results from these measures would shed light on important issues of L2 vocabulary development and, as the present book shows, studies on the different dimensions of word knowledge should always tend to complement one another.

Questions for discussion

- Why might you expect recognition time to a) decrease, b) increase, c) stabilize as vocabulary size increases?
- What sort of teaching interventions might help learners to improve the speed with which they recognize written words?
- What variables other than vocabulary size might account for differences in word recognition speed?
- Are word recognition speed and fluency in a foreign language the same thing, and if they do differ, how do they differ and why?

Acknowledgements

We acknowledge the help of the GRAL Group from the English Studies Department (Universitat de Barcelona), coordinated by Dr Carmen Muñoz. We especially thank Dr Joan Carles Mora and Dr Raquel Serrano for this version of the lexical access test and for the computation of its results from raw data. Thanks also to the editors of this volume for their suggestions, patience and commitment.

Knowledge of Word Parts

Katja Mäntylä and Ari Huhta

4

Introduction

Form	Spoken	R	What does the word sound like?
		P	How is the word pronounced?
	Written	R	What does the word look like?
		P	How is the word written and spelled?
	Word parts	**R**	**What parts are recognizable in this word?**
		P	**What words parts are needed to express meaning?**

When encountering a new word, we have two important tools to help us to decipher its meaning: context and morphology. The sum of **morpheme** meanings more often than not gives us an idea what the word is about. In his reference to knowledge of word parts, therefore, Nation is drawing attention to the way words can be comprised of several morphemes with **affixes** attaching to a base form; all of which contribute to the overall meaning of the word. Knowledge of word parts, and in particular the system of affixes, is an essential part of over-all word knowledge. This kind of knowledge of word parts is usually implicit to language users but is seldom explicitly taught. For an L2 learner, however, morphological information is a valuable asset in expanding both **receptive** and **productive vocabulary**. Word parts have been shown to play a role in vocabulary acquisition, and knowing what parts are recognizable in a word and what parts are needed to express a given meaning, contribute to the essence of knowing a word (Nation, 2001, p. 27; Thornbury, 2002, pp. 106–11).

In this chapter we will discuss word part knowledge, derivational knowl-edge in particular, from the viewpoint of L2 learners. We introduce a study of Finnish learners of English and their ability to recognize and apply dif-ferent affixes. Since there are no established tools to investigate derivational knowledge (Schmitt and Zimmerman's 2002 test is a rare exception), the study also examined how knowledge of affixes could be studied by trying out three different measures that test the use of affixes in context.

Recognition of word parts

Word parts in English

English has over 60 **affixes** (Jackson and Zé Amvela, 2000, p. 74) and, thus, the English language is also rich with derived forms: **corpora** reveal that about 12.8 per cent of words we use have been formed through derivation, and over a fifth (21.9 per cent) are inflected forms (Nation, 2001, pp. 265–6). Of all word formation methods in English, derivation is reported to be the most fruitful and frequent (Yule, 2006, p. 57). For each base form, there are 1.5 to four derivations (Nation, 2001), in addition to the small number of inflections which English uses (Carstairs-McCarthy, 2002, p. 56). Thus, mastering affixation is clearly an asset for a language user. Although what we know about vocabulary and lexical chunks seems to suggest that language users process bigger entities, such as **formulaic sequences,** as wholes rather than building them up every time they encounter them (Schmitt and Carter, 2004), research is still searching for agreement as to how words comprising a stem and affixes are processed.

Among English speakers, there is evidence that at least the more infrequent derived forms are not stored as entities but rather are reformed **morpheme** by morpheme every time they are used, especially if the stem–affix combination is transparent – that is, the meaning of the whole is the same as the sum of stem and affix meanings – for example, *happiness* (Nation, 2001, pp. 46–7, 269). Milton (2010, p. 220), however, suggests that only the most frequent and regular inflections are likely to be handled this way and that infrequent derived forms are likely to be stored whole as separate lexical forms. An important factor that may affect the language users' perception and processing of derived forms, therefore, may be the frequency of the affix itself, together with its productivity; *-ly* for instance, is a common suffix to form adverbs from adjectives, it behaves in a similar manner from one stem to another, and is being actively used to form new words. On the other hand, the frequency of an affix does not always indicate its productivity: *-ment* appears fairly frequently, but is nowadays seldom used to form new words (Ballard, 2002, pp. 51–5).

Affixes vary also according to their predictability. The meaning added by *–ly* does not change from one derived form to another, but, for example, another very productive suffix, *-ee*, although fairly predictable, has exceptions: *testee* and *employee* reveal their meaning if we add up stem + suffix meanings, but *goatee* does not follow the pattern and is thus less transparent. Affixes that behave more irregularly, due to factors such as phonology (*in-, im-, ill-, ir-*), may be more challenging for a language user to perceive as affixes although there is no conclusive evidence of this. (Ballard, 2002, pp. 51–5; Leech *et al.*, 2006, pp. 24–9; Nation, 2001, p. 271).

Word parts and learning in English

Among English native speakers it appears that knowledge of word derivations is a process that continues through school years and into adolescence – that is, after a substantial lexicon has been built and the speakers are highly fluent (McBride-Chang *et al.*, 2005; Mochizuki and Aizawa, 2000, pp. 291–2; Nation, 2001, pp. 263, 270; Schmitt, 2010). When it comes to L2 learners, the strategy of developing derivational competence would be useful, too, but it is seldom taken advantage of (Virkkunen, 1992, p. 58; Pavičić Takač, 2008, pp. 58–90; Schmitt, 2008). The reasons for this may be many. For an L2 learner, the large number of **affixes** and the fact that they do not always behave in a regular manner may pose a problem (Laufer, 1997b, p. 146). For instance, there are eight different prefixes in English that add a negative or reverse meaning to the stem (Ballard, 2002, p. 52), and trying to memorize whether to use, for example, *mis-*, *dis-*, or *un-* increases the learning burden. Furthermore, affixes vary as to their productivity and frequency: for instance, in English, most suffixes are used to form nouns and adjectives (Ballard, 2002, p. 51). Laufer (1997b, p. 146; see also Cvikić, 2007, p. 159) also warns about deceptive transparency – that is, we might misinterpret the morphology of a word and think there are two **morphemes** when in fact this is not the case – for example, *discourse*. Nevertheless, raising awareness of derivational patterns could be used to help language learners actively notice affixes, and thus increase the tools they have to understand and also to an extent to produce new vocabulary (Thornbury, 2002, p. 109).

Studies of L2 learners and word formation are scarce. An early study by Takala (1984) on Finnish learners of English concluded that at the end of compulsory schooling, the students' word formation skills were very poor.

Schmitt and Meara (1997), in their study of Japanese students of English, observed a link between the breadth and depth of students' vocabulary – that is, the relationship between learners' vocabulary size and **word associations** and recognition of suffixes, in particular the compatibility of verb stems and suffixes. As could perhaps be expected, there was a correlation between vocabulary size and suffix knowledge, as well as general L2 proficiency. They concluded that L2 students' suffix knowledge was rather poor, with the exception of knowledge of rule-based and regular inflectional suffixes (*-ing*, *-ed*, -s). Mochizuki and Aizawa (2000) investigated the acquisition of both prefixes and suffixes and reached the same conclusion that a relationship exists between knowing affixes and the size of vocabulary. Mochizuki and Aizawa (*ibid.*) also wanted to see whether the participants were able to categorize non-word + suffix combinations (e.g., *dutical*) according to their word class. The results of this also correlated with the general vocabulary size of the participants. Mochizuki and Aizawa mention that the participants' L1, Japanese, and its affix system may have had an effect on the results, in particular in understanding prefixes.

Part of the problem with learning the less frequent derivational forms may be the inconsistency with which they are used in English. Schmitt and Meara

(1997) also gathered data from native speakers of English and found that there was variation in native speaker judgements as to which derivational suffixes were applicable to which stems, sometimes contradicting dictionaries and grammar books in their judgements. This is also noted by Schmitt and Zimmermann (2002). Thus, it seems only natural that L2 learners vary when they are asked to judge the acceptability of affixes connected to certain word stems. Schmitt and Zimmermann (*ibid.*) also suggest that knowing one word in a family does not necessarily mean that the learner will be able to produce other forms in that family. Nouns and verbs appeared to be the parts of speech best known to their testees, but other derived forms could not reliably be recognized or produced. Their conclusion was that derivative forms are not taught and, thus, are not well enough known, which may lead to avoidance in learners who are afraid of making mistakes.

In a more recent study on derivation and L2 learners, Nyyssönen (2008) investigated derivational skills of sixth-graders in Finland. Her participants were thus 12 years old, having studied English for three and a half years. Nyyssönen adapted a set of tests of affix knowledge (described in detail in the next section) for young participants using a **think-aloud** procedure. Nyyssönen concludes that the participants' receptive knowledge of derivational affixes was fair, but only the most advanced pupils could use this knowledge productively. She also attributes this at least in part to the absence of explicit teaching of word formation. This is despite extensive knowledge of word derivation and the possibilities of affixation from their native language.

The sum of research in this field is not extensive, therefore, but, to sum up, vocabulary size correlates with some aspects of knowledge of word parts. Recognition of affixes and recognition of suitable affix + stem combinations does not appear to tell us about the ability to produce, or even understand the affixes. It also seems that inflectional suffixes are acquired before derivational ones (Ward and Chuenjundaeng, 2009). This would make sense as inflectional affixes are often specifically taught, and since they are frequent and there is usually quite a lot of input, as Ward and Chuenjundaeng (2009) emphasize. They also stress the structural equivalence between a learner's mother tongue and the L2. Indeed, before mastering the morphology of the L2, the learner must be familiar with the morphological system in their mother tongue and be able to process the similarities and differences in the systems of the two languages (Singleton, 1999, p. 142). The relationship between L1 and L2 morphological systems could indeed serve as one starting point for raising awareness of word parts.

Knowledge of word parts and derivation would appear to be useful to a language learner, although it is not much emphasized in teaching. Further research in this area of language knowledge would appear to be beneficial. Although we know of some factors, such as frequency and transparency, that may affect the perception of affixes, we do not know to what extent L2 learners notice affixes or are able to use this information in their language learning. In the study described below, focusing on the affix knowledge of Finnish learners of English, we attempt to move this area of investigation forward.

Current research work

Data and methods

To investigate L2 learners' derivation skills further, data were collected from seventh- to ninth-grade (12–16 years) Finnish students (n = 327), who had studied English for four to six years. Data collection took place as part of the CEFLING project that examines how L2 proficiency develops across Common European Framework of Reference (**CEFR**) levels. The participants completed a three-part test on derivation. In addition, as part of the CEFLING project, the students completed four structured writing tasks ranging from an informal email to a narrative. The writing tasks were assessed against the CEFR levels by four raters.

To our knowledge there are no established tools to measure word part knowledge in context other than Schmitt and Zimmerman's 2002 test, which uses a very minimal context. The relationship between overall language proficiency and the ability to produce and understand **affixes** is unclear. Based on the fact that some affixes are more frequent and productive than others, Nation (2001, p. 268; modified in 2005, p. 592) gives a sequential list of the stages in which affixes might be taught, drawn largely from Bauer and Nation (1993). However, there is little evidence of a fixed order of acquisition among affixes relating to frequency or otherwise. In Schmitt and Meara's (1997) study, the Bauer and Nation levels were not reflected in the ability of learners to recognize derivational suffixes. Also, the frequency of an affix does not necessarily correspond to the frequencies of single derived forms (Mochizuki and Aizawa, 2000). It was decided not to base a test purely on frequency of affix occurrence, therefore, and various test methods, using different criteria, were used to choose the words for the testing in this research. A general recommendation in language testing is to use multiple measures of the skills of interest, whenever possible, and this also applies to vocabulary studies (see, e.g., Schmitt, 2010).

The first part of the test was a productive gap-fill task of 18 sentences. The students were presented with sentences with gaps, with clues to the answers in Finnish. The sentences were mostly presented in pairs so that, in addition to the Finnish clue, either the base or derived form appeared in the task. The words were taken from the Waystage (equivalent to A2 level in CEFR) word list (Van Ek and Trim, 1990), so the students could be assumed to be familiar with them:

(1) I am _____ (varma) that he will get the job in London.
     He will _____ (varmasti) get the job in London.
     → sure – surely

Since it was possible to do well in the first part of the test by good general vocabulary knowledge, the other two parts concentrated more heavily on affixation.

The second part strongly called for affix knowledge, since it consisted of non-words and, thus, general vocabulary knowledge was of no assistance:

(2)   She could bourble animals very well because she was a good _____
      bourble_____.
         (= henkilö, joka tekee lihavoidun sanan kuvaamaa toimintaa/työtä
         [*a person who does the action described by the word in bold*])
         → bourbler

To explain the task, the non-word test (Appendix 1) provided the students with an example with real Finnish words; Finnish non-words in the example proved to be too challenging for the students in a pilot test since the whole concept of non-words was unfamiliar to many. The non-words were taken from a list of **pseudowords** developed by Paul Meara for the Dialang test (Alderson, 2005). Thus, their morphology, written form and the possible spoken form followed the English system.

The third part of the test was a list-based gap-fill test. The students were presented with 12 sentences with gaps, and a list of prefixes to choose from.

(3)   He did not follow the instructions. He had ___ understood them.

The target words for this part were chosen from Ballard (2002). The aim was to include words and contexts that would be manageable to teenagers. The task was made more challenging by including 22 prefixes for 12 gaps, and by allowing one prefix to appear more than once. Thus, the students could not rely on a ruling-out strategy.

The students first completed the productive gap-fill test and the non-word test. These were collected, and only then were the students presented with the list-based gap-fill test. This was done in order not to let the students copy prefixes from the third part into the first and second part of the test. The tests were assessed by two raters independently. In the productive gap-fill test, the scale for each item was 0–4, whereas for the other two parts it was 0–2. Spelling errors were penalized if they changed the meaning of the word (*shore→sure*), or if the result deviated greatly from the target word (*deffreno→different*). If the target word could be detected despite erroneous spelling, it was accepted as correct (*unbelievubl, unbelievevabl, unbelievobl→unbelievable*). The students were very creative in their answers, and this is why, with some items, there were several possible correct replies. For instance, when the students were asked to produce a small *gabl (gablet)*, also *minigabl* was marked as correct.

Results

The results of these tests have been analysed using classical item analyses carried out with the TiaPlus program (Heuvelmans, 2009). As Table 4.1 shows, the tests clearly differed in terms of difficulty. The easiest test for the population

Table 4.1 Scores on the three derivation tests

	Items	Mean score (per cent)	Standard deviation (per cent)	Standard error of mean	Cron-bach's alpha	Average item/ total correlation
A Productive gap-fill test (n = 310)	**18**	**73.9**	20.2	1.15	.86	.56
A1 base form items	**8**	**76.8**	17.2	0.98	.60	–
A2 derived items	**10**	**71.5**	24.7	1.37	.84	–
B Non-word-based test (n = 299)	**8**	**34.3**	26.4	1.53	.76	.62
C List-choice-based test (n = 327)	**12**	**39.3**	22.3	1.23	.78	.54
All three tests together	**38**	**54.6**	19.0	1.05	.90	.48

studied was the productive gap-fill test (mean score almost 74 per cent), although it required production rather than selection of the answers. Average scores in the two other tests was considerably lower and did not reach 40 per cent: the non-word-based test was the most difficult one, with the mean score of about 34 per cent, followed by the list-choice-based test (39 per cent).

The high scores on the productive gap-fill test can be explained in two ways. First, the base forms of all the words tested in it are based on Waystage (i.e., level A2) definitions for English (Van Ek and Trim, 1990), and the students could be expected to know many of them – the target level of proficiency for the mark 'good' in writing at the end of grade 9 is high A2; see NBE, 2004, p. 143). Second, about half of the items in the productive gap-fill test in fact measure the knowledge of the base, rather than derived, form of the word, which could be assumed to be easier than derived word forms.

The two other tests used in the study were both difficult for the target group, but for somewhat different reasons. The non-word-based test can be assumed to be demanding in several ways. Not only was the method unfamiliar, but general vocabulary knowledge was of a very limited use in completing this test. On the whole, being able to complete the non-word-based test would have required an ability to go beyond what had been taught at school and to apply in the abstract whatever derivation rules the students mastered by being exposed to the English language.

The difficulty of the list-choice-based test was somewhat surprising, although the input material in that test was not intended to be quite as easy as in the productive gap-fill test; for example, the vocabulary in the items was less frequent than in the Waystage. However, an attempt was made to keep the language of the items relatively easy – for example, by topic choice. Also, choosing from a list was a familiar test type to the participants. The test still proved to be difficult. The main reason for this seems likely to be the fact that, while the base forms of the words in this test were easy, many of the derived word forms turned out to be either abstract or rare words, or both. The result indicates not only that the frequency of the word and its derivational affixes differ (Mochizuki and Aizawa, 2000), but also that the frequency of the base and derived form of a word can differ substantially. There were also more choices than gaps in the test, which may have contributed to its difficulty.

For such short tests, ranging from eight to 18 items, reliability, as calculated by Cronbach's alpha, was satisfactory, being at least in the high .70s. The average item-total correlations are also quite respectable for all the three tests (.54 - .62). The fact that the overall item-total correlation for the combined test is lower than for any of the individual tests suggests that the three types of tests tap somewhat different aspects of knowledge of word parts.

Because of its unique nature, the non-word-based test (Appendix 1) deserves a closer look. It was the most difficult of the three tests with a mean score of only 34 per cent; the scores also spread more than in the other tests. For the most part, the short non-word test appears to be quite compact with relatively high item–total correlations (corrected for the brevity of the test by the Henrysson's correction formula; Heuvelmans, 2009, p. 18). A detailed analysis, however, reveals that the first and last non-word items behaved very differently from the others. The first item was quite easy (on purpose, since as a straightforward translation of the Finnish example, it was meant to provide an easy start to the test), whereas the last item was very hard. Both had only a modest correlation with the other items. The last item is something of a puzzle, as the reason for its low item–total correlation is not obvious. In a small-scale trial, with university students majoring in English, quite a few students had difficulty answering this particular item.

On the whole, the item and correlational analyses (see below) suggest that the new, non-word-based test format is at least as good as the other two, more traditional test types used in the study. This test provides, then, a good starting point for the development of other, longer and perhaps more diverse non-word-based research tools for the study of derivation skills.

We will next examine the structure of the derivation test battery used in the study. The three tests correlated strongly with each other, as indicated by Table 4.3: the disattenuated (corrected for unreliability/measurement error) correlations ranged from .699 to .784. However, the fact that the correlations are not higher gives further evidence that the three tests tap somewhat different aspects of English word derivation ability. It is also possible, of course, that some of this finding is explained by method effects, which, in the case of the non-word test, at least, can be expected to be quite substantial.

Table 4.2   Item characteristics of the non-word-based test

Item	Mean score (per cent)	Standard deviation (on 0–2 scale)	Item/total correlation (Henrysson's correction)	Item's correlation with the other seven items
1	74	.87	.35	.29
2	33	.94	.67	.60
3	48	1.00	.70	.64
4	31	.93	.53	.46
5	9	.56	.11	.36
6	16	.73	.64	.54
7	41	.98	.59	.52
8	22	.82	.31	.25

Table 4.3   Correlations between the three derivation tests

N = 281–325	A Productive gap-fill test			B Non-word-based test	C List-based test
	Total/all items (k = 18)	Base form items (k = 8)	Derived items (k = 10)	(k = 8)	(k = 12)
A. Productive gap-fill test	1.00				
A1 base form items		1.00			
A2 derived items		.778 (1.097)	1.00		
B Non-word-based test	.567 (.699)	.511 (.758)	.544 (.683)	1.00	
C List-based test	.618 (.754)	.566 (.830)	.596 (.740)	.601 (.784)	1.00

Note: Disattenuated correlations are in parentheses.

The highest correlation (.830) was found between the base form items of the productive gap-fill test and the list-choice-based test. The lowest correlations occurred between the productive gap-fill test (total score) and the non-word-based test (.699), and derived items and test B (.683). The overall pattern of correlations is not easy to interpret and there appears to be no straightforward relationship between the three main tests or the two different parts of the productive gap-fill test (base vs derived items) and the other tests. The focus of this study was on word part knowledge and its relation to overall language proficiency rather than to other types of word knowledge. Because of this – and not to overburden the learners – the students' general vocabulary knowledge was not measured. Interestingly, the base form items in the productive gap-fill test correlate somewhat more strongly with the other two derivation tests than the items based on derived forms. However, our current data are not optimal for shedding light on this question; further research, using different test instruments, is needed.

Consideration of the tests

The main feature that distinguished the tests from each other is whether they are based on real or invented English words. Any test based on real English words can be expected to be at least somewhat familiar to language learners, whereas non-word-based tests are probably totally unfamiliar to most students. Of the test methods used, the productive gap-fill is one of the most common methods used in both exercises and tests in Finland. The list-choice-based test is also a fairly common test format.

The suitability of a real-word-based vocabulary test to its target audience very much depends on the words used in the items, as was evident in the present study, too. The productive gap-fill test appeared to match the learners' level of proficiency quite well: it was designed to be an A2 level test and, indeed, all those who had reached A2, or exceeded it, did very well in the test. The list-choice-based test, on the other hand, turned out to be very difficult for the majority of learners largely because of the difficulty of the derived word forms. The real-word-based derivation tests, in particular, suffer from the difficulty of knowing to what extent they in fact measure word part knowledge rather than more general word knowledge – the learners may simply know the derived words because they have learned them one by one without understanding how they relate with the base form of the word or with other forms of the same word. They may be able to complete derived test items by memorizing the words rather than by applying any derivation rule.

The greatest strength of non-word-based tests in studies on derivational skills is that general vocabulary knowledge cannot interfere with test takers' performance on them, at least not directly. A learner cannot answer such test items without being able to know and apply the derivation rules of the language. Thus, a high score on such a test very likely indicates ability to derive words. This is an important consideration since one clear gap in research in this area is a single non-language-specific test that can produce comparable results for different language learners.

A low score on a non-word test is not as straightforward to interpret as a high score. It may indicate inability to derive words, but it is also possible that some low scores result from a strong (negative) test method effect. Test takers may not understand what to do in the test even when the instructions appear clear and they are also provided with an example, as was the case in this study. This is suggested by the fact that in the present study about 10 per cent of the learners failed to get any of the non-word items right despite trying at least one. In addition, another 10 per cent completely skipped the non-word test (these were removed from the analyses presented here). Simply having to think about and operate with non-words may be cognitively confusing and demanding to some learners (there may be a threshold age, for example, below which such tests are too complex to take).

Word frequency and word part knowledge

Since the frequency of the word is one of the key factors that affect the difficulty of a word, the relationship between the frequency of the words used in the derivation tests and the difficulty of the items that were based on these words, was checked. As the frequency of a derived form may differ from the frequency of an **affix**, and as there are other factors affecting the perception and potential difficulty of affixes, the frequencies of stems and derived forms rather than affix frequencies were used. The frequency of words in the non-word-based test could not be checked, of course, and it transpired too that most of the words in the list-choice-based test were sufficiently uncommon for them to be absent from the BNC. This fact, in itself, may hint as to why learners found mastering so many of these derivations so hard. The relationship between word frequency and item difficulty in the productive gap-fill test only was investigated. Information about the frequency was available for 16 of the 18 words used in the test items.

The rank order correlation between the item difficulty and the word frequency (rank) in the BNC was -.429, and not significant statistically (p = .097). Thus, word frequency was not related to item difficulty in the first test, or at least not very clearly. However, it was obvious that the infrequent words in the third, list-choice-based test contributed to the difficulty of that test, although that relationship could not be established statistically.

Word part knowledge and writing skills

The relationship between derivation skills and more general language proficiency was studied by correlating the vocabulary test results with the estimates of the learners' writing ability. These estimates were obtained from the part of the CEFLING project, in which the learners completed four different writing tasks rated on the six-point **CEFR** scale. Table 4.4 displays the correlations between the learners' average performance across the four tasks and the three vocabulary tests. It is obvious that word formation type of vocabulary knowledge is strongly associated with writing ability. The individual tests correlated at the level of .7, and the correlation of the combined derivation test battery with the writing skill was even higher. Performance on real-word-based tests was slightly more strongly associated with writing ability than performance on the non-word test (.733 and .759 vs .677), which makes sense as it is quite likely that the real-word-based derivation tests also tap more general vocabulary knowledge which is an important factor in writing as well as the other major skills – at least compared with the much more specific skill of mastering affixes.

Table 4.4   Relationship between derivation skill and more general language proficiency

n = 141–160	Writing skill (on CEFR scale)
A Productive gap-fill test (all items)	.733
A1 Productive gap-fill test (base form items)	.685
A2 Productive gap-fill test (derived items)	.713
B Non-word-based test	.677
C List-based test	.759
All three tests together (raw score)	.798
All three tests (only items testing derived word forms; IRT theta value)	.789

To cross-check the magnitude of the overall correlation, an ability index indicating derivation ability was computed for each learner with the item response theory (IRT)-based programme OPLM (Verhelst and Glas, 1995) and those were correlated with the ratings of writing ability. This correlation was almost the same as for the corresponding correlation based on raw derivation test scores. However, since the correlations between derivation tests and writing ability ratings are not perfect there is obviously no one-to-one relationship between the two areas of proficiency.

It is also possible to study the relationship between derivation and writing in more detail with our data. How do these young learners at different CEFR levels (in writing) perform in the word part tests? Do beginners (A1–A2 levels) master English derivation or does the ability to derive words develop only later?

Our results, as reported in Table 4.5, suggest that learners at level A2 – and even at A1 – know a reasonable number of derived English words when the words are fairly basic – that is, they are Waystage/A2 words. These are likely to have been taught, and learned, as individual lexical items rather than as a derivation of a base form. However, the results suggest that learners have to be at B1 or even at B2 before they can apply English derivation rules more systematically. This is indicated by the quite big gap between the performances of A2 and B1 learners on both the non-word- and list-choice-based tests. The mean score of the learners at A2 is around 30 per cent in both tests, but it jumps up to almost 60 per cent when the learners' more general (writing) proficiency is B1. The number of B2 level learners in our data was quite small so conclusions based on their results are tentative at best. The available evidence suggests, not surprisingly, that B2 learners outperform B1 learners when it comes to derivation: they scored over 70 per cent on the non-word- and list-based tests, which is over 10 per cent higher than the results achieved by the B1 learners.

Deciding when one 'masters' English derivation on the basis of test performance is not straightforward. Is the score of 50 per cent enough or should you reach 60 per cent or even 80 or 90 per cent before you can be thought to 'know' how to derive English words? And in what kind of a test should you

Table 4.5 Derivation test performance at different CEFR levels (based on writing)

Proficiency level (median across four raters and four writing tasks)	Mean test result (per cent correct)			
	Productive gap-fill test	Non-word-based test	List-based test	All three tests together
A1	49	15	14	26
n = 21–7				
A2	76	29	35	47
n = 53–7				
B1	90	58	58	68
n = 45–7				
B2	95	71	74	80
n = 7				

achieve that cut-off point? A wide range of mastery standards are reported in the literature on standard setting, and typical standards vary from 50 per cent to 80 per cent (Kaftandjieva, 2004, p. 17).

The most conservative estimate, based on mastering 70–80 per cent of the items, is, therefore, that English derivation skills are mastered by young Finnish learners only when they have reached level B2 on the CEFR scale. A less conservative estimate (50 per cent mastery) is that they do this at some point at level B1 – the CEFR levels are quite wide and it takes a considerable time to move from one level to the next, at least after the first one or two levels. Thus, there may be a distinct difference in performance between a low and a high B1 learner.

Practical implications and suggestions for further research

In this chapter we have discussed and reviewed studies on word part knowledge, and derivational knowledge in particular, from the viewpoint of L2 learners. On the whole, this area has received fairly little attention in second language acquisition (SLA) research and there have been few attempts at developing instruments to measure such knowledge. We have reported on our recent study of Finnish learners of English and their ability to recognize and apply different **affixes**. Three different types of (mainly) productive derivation tests were developed, one of them being a novel test type based on non-words. On the basis of this it is possible to add to the limited knowledge we have of the development of lexical knowledge in this field.

Previous studies have suggested that frequent and regularly inflected word forms are understood and largely applied quite early on in the L2 learning process. Our results suggest when and how the less frequent and less regular derived forms of words in English are mastered. They indicate that although learners at beginner levels (A1–A2) know quite a few derived forms, it is only at the intermediate level, perhaps at as high as B2 that learners start to grasp derivation as a method or a system. Assuming that derivation as a rule-based system is not explicitly taught to the learners then it might be suggested that the L2 lexicon needs to be relatively large before sufficient incidents of these derivations can be encountered and regular changes to a base word form inferred.

The analyses suggest that all the three tests used here have potential as word derivation measures, although they have different strengths and weaknesses and, thus, their combined use would make more sense than using any one of them as the only measure of derivation skills. The non-word task is included in Appendix 1 as an aid to future researchers in this area. However, the fact that these tests had to be created bespoke for this investigation reinforces the need for standard testing methodologies in this area. While a link between word parts and frequency of occurrence is common in the literature, it is not even clear yet how best frequency is to be addressed in relation to **morpheme** learning: as frequency of root form; of the individual occurrences of derived forms; or as an aggregate occurrence of a derivational rule. Clarification and a consistent methodological approach is essential for progress in researching this aspect of word knowledge so the utility of a test based on invented words may be significant in that a single test format might be applied to learners from different language backgrounds giving greater standardization in the approaches to testing we use in this area.

Considering the role derivation plays in English vocabulary and the multitude of affixes available, morphology learning is a challenge to the language learner. This is also true of languages other than English. It is not clear from this or previous research that L1 morphological ability impacts on the ability to develop this knowledge in an L2. It might make sense, therefore, to explicitly point out to learners how words have been constructed. At a beginner level, this would enhance at least learners' **receptive vocabulary**, and once the vocabulary size grows and language skills improve, would also be of assistance in building **productive vocabulary**. However, the advancement of learners' metalinguisic knowledge in this area appears not to be a feature of language teaching generally at the lower levels. In Finland, for example, derivation is not explicitly mentioned in textbooks and syllabuses until senior secondary school, when the students are supposed to already be at B1 level. A further avenue of research would be to test the impact on receptive and productive vocabulary knowledge of teaching interventions of this kind.

As far as instrument development is concerned, the next steps in our own research will be a qualitative interview and **think-aloud** study into the process of taking different kinds of word formation tests (cf. Nyyssönen, 2008). We need to understand better how learners arrive at their answers and whether they, for example, construct the derived word forms by consciously applying derivation rules, and how the test taking process differs in real-word vs non-word tests. We also need to construct somewhat longer versions of word formation tests and to study how to develop their content more systematically (e.g., how to balance different kinds of derivation in any one test). In addition, the frequencies of the affixes need to be addressed.

Questions for discussion

- What issues should be considered when using non-words in a test of **affix** knowledge such as the one described in this chapter?
- To what extent can knowledge of word parts be explicitly taught, and at what stage in a learner's development might this be most effective?
- How straightforward would it be to develop, for knowledge of word parts, 'a single non-language-specific test that can produce comparable results for different language learners'?
- What insights do you predict will be yielded by applying **think-aloud protocols** to the word formation tests described in this chapter?
- What reasons might there be which can explain the way learners often apply their knowledge of word parts so inconsistently in speech and writing?

Acknowledgements

We would like to thank Anna Zaborna MA for her valuable help with assessing and marking the test performances and Tuija Hirvelä Phil.Lic. for advice in the statistical analyses.

Knowledge of Form and Meaning

María Pilar Agustín Llach and
Soraya Moreno Espinosa

5

Introduction

Meaning	Form and meaning	R	What meaning does this word form signal?
		P	What word form can be used to express this meaning?
	Concepts and referents	R	What is included in the concept?
		P	What items can the concept refer to?
	Associations	R	What others words does this word make us think of?
		P	What other words could we use instead of this one?

This chapter will focus on the dimension of word knowledge that tries to establish the link between a word's form and meaning. Given that words are units of meaning and they are central in communication, it is believed that the form–meaning link is a basic dimension of word knowledge, and most probably the first to be acquired (cf. Laufer and Goldstein, 2004, p. 409). While the previous chapters have demonstrated that vocabulary knowledge can be measured in a way that does not require this knowledge of the learner, Laufer *et al.* (2004, p. 204) and Laufer and Goldstein (2004, p. 402) claim that most vocabulary tests involve demonstrating knowledge of the form–meaning link either in recognition or production. Moreover, many tests that do not apparently measure this knowledge, such as association tests or depth of vocabulary tests, also have implicit the assumption that the form–meaning link is known by the learner. These can be said to be indirect tests of meaning (Laufer *et al.*, 2004, p. 205; Laufer and Goldstein 2004, p. 403). Laufer *et al.* (2004, p. 205) argue that 'a good vocabulary test should measure the extent to which people can correctly associate word form with the concept the form denotes'.

60

Learners can have either receptive or productive knowledge of the form–meaning link. Receptive knowledge would involve linking an L2 form to the concept or meaning, whereas productive knowledge would require a link in the other direction, that is from the meaning or concept to its form in the L2. This second aspect will be the focus of the present chapter. Nation (2005, p. 594) argues that different test formats tap different aspects of vocabulary knowledge to different degrees, so choosing the test has important implications concerning the vocabulary knowledge aspect to be measured. To investigate knowledge of the link between form and meaning, the productive version of the Vocabulary Levels Tests, henceforth VLT, has been chosen. There are other tests that also examine the form–meaning relationship. For example, Laufer *et al.* (2004) and Laufer and Goldstein (2004), in the Computer Adaptive Test of Size and Strength, operationalize the form–meaning link in four different ways and demonstrate that some form of word presentation would be more difficult than the others.

Associating word form and meaning

Measuring knowledge of form and meaning

The receptive version of the VLT is probably the most widely used test in this area, even if there is no standardized test of the form–meaning link (Cobb, 2000; Cameron, 2002; Laufer and Nation, 1995; Laufer and Nation, 1999; Beglar and Hunt, 1999; Schmitt and Meara, 1997; Laufer and Paribakht, 1998). It is probably, as Meara and Fitzpatrick (2000, p. 19) state, 'the nearest thing we have to a useful tool'.

VLT tests words selected from the 2000, 3000, 5000 and 10,000 word **frequency bands** and, depending of the age and version of the test, from the Academic Word List (AWL) (Coxhead, 2000) or the University Word List (UWL) (Nation, 1990). It requires learners to link these words with definitions, which use language from the most frequent 2000 words. There are ten questions at each level, with three test words and six definitions per question. It provides a score out of 150, therefore, and Nation (1990, p. 76) has calculated a way of turning this into an estimation of vocabulary size. An example of the format is shown below.

1. business
2. clock _____ part of a house
3. horse _____ animal with four legs
4. pencil _____ something used for writing
5. shoe
6. wall

There is also a productive version of the test (Laufer and Nation, 1999) where the test structure takes the form of a **cloze test**, where the answer is primed so only the test word might reasonably be produced to fill the gap. Word selection and context sentence follow the same principles as the receptive version of the VLT. Tests words selected from the 2000, 3000, 5000 and 10,000 word frequency bands and AWL/UWL lists and the context words from most frequent 2000 words. There are ten questions at each level. An example of the format is given below.

> I'm glad we had this op_____ to talk.
> There are a doz_____ eggs in this basket.
> Every working person must pay income t_____.

While these tests are widely used as vocabulary size indicators, testing knowledge of words with a link to meaning, the VLT has also received some criticism on the basis of its construct validity. Read (2000, p. 125) writes that 'it is not clear just what the blank-filling test is measuring'. It is assumed that the VLT measures controlled productive knowledge – that is, words available for productive use. But Read (*ibid.*, p. 126) believes that the blank-filling version of the VLT 'may simply be an alternative way of assessing receptive knowledge rather than a measure of productive ability'. Webb (2008) argues in the same line, since as it is a test of cued recall, the presence of partial information could be sufficient to recognize the target word. This contradicts Laufer's (1998) findings that the productive version of the VLT obtained lower scores than the receptive version with its original matching format. This could be expected since the former required test-takers to supply a target word, whereas the latter required learners to select the target word from those provided (cf. Read, 2000, p. 125). The opportunity for guesswork may therefore lead to overestimation. Other criticisms revolve around the idea of the difficulty of inferring general **productive vocabulary** size from the scores of the VLT, because it tests only a small vocabulary sample (Meara and Fitzpatrick, 2000; Meara and Bell, 2001; Meara, 2005b), and the test draws target words from West's (1953) General Service List, which, as Nation himself acknowledges (2004), is now rather old. Notwithstanding these criticisms and the test's possible drawbacks, the VLT is widely used and is believed to be an appropriate test to investigate the relationship between word meaning and word form. There is, of course, no perfect vocabulary test (Meara and Fitzpatrick, 2000), but the VLT significantly distinguishes between different proficiency levels in L2 secondary school learners (Moreno, 2010) and the test has proven validity and reliability (Laufer and Nation, 1999).

Nevertheless, the word-recognition format characteristic of the VLT is not the only way to measure the form–meaning connection. Other measurement indicators of this link might include translation in the form of bilingual lists, such as L2 to L1 translation (form recognition), L1 to L2 translation (form production). Laufer and Goldstein (2004, p. 400) contend that most tests measure just one 'sub-knowledge' of lexical competence: form recognition (L2 to L1 translation), form production (L1 to L2 translation), meaning recognition (matching and paraphrasing, odd one out activity, providing definitions with target words), meaning production (filling the gaps, sentence completion), or **yes/no** tests, where learners have to indicate or tick the words they (think they) know. They refer to these as direct measures of the form–meaning link and demonstrating understanding or producing target words. Indirect measures of form–meaning links appear as **word association** tests, or in the Lexical Frequency Profile, which according to Laufer and Goldstein (2004: 403) is a measure that 'shows the proportion of frequent versus infrequent correct form–meaning links'.

What research tells us about knowledge of form and meaning

The form–meaning relationship is a complex one which can present itself in three different situations (VanPatten *et al.*, 2004, p. 3):

1. One form encodes one meaning
2. One form encodes multiple meanings in a single context or in different contexts
3. Multiple forms encode the same meaning.

Various studies (see, e.g., Jiang, 2002; VanPatten *et al.*, 2004) have tried to establish the steps that learners follow in making the form–meaning connection. After first making an initial connection essentially based on L1 knowledge and experience, learners subsequently process this connection, strengthening the link thanks to the different encounters in the input. They continue restructuring their L1 and the rest of their form–meaning connections according to the information they receive from the native input. Finally, learners access the connections for comprehension and production, thus consolidating the link. Understood in a broad sense, the form–meaning link can be extended to include not only referential meaning(s), but also abstract or metaphorical meaning(s), connotative meaning(s), sociolinguistic meaning(s), pragmatic and even syntactic meaning(s). The way a learner encodes a meaning into a form can reveal a lot of information about how the learners conceptualize reality and the world around them.

VanPatten *et al.* (2004, p. 16–17) contend that form complexity and form salience are relevant elements in the making of form–meaning links. In general, a form–meaning link will be established more easily if the form a) is linked to a single meaning rather than to several, b) is transparent, c) is regular and adheres to expected rules, d) is not easily confused with other forms, e) is easy to pronounce or spell and f) is salient – that is, noticeable.

Knowledge of the form–meaning link is not a straightforward issue and researchers identify different continua on which form–meaning connections can be placed (e.g., VanPatten *et al.*, 2004): a) partial to complete, b) weak to robust and c) non-target-like to target-like in nature. These dichotomies are extremely interesting in the case of low-proficiency learners, since evolution and progression along these continua can be examined. In line with this, Laufer and Goldstein (2004, p. 422) conclude that the knowledge of form–meaning connections is incremental and that before being able to produce a word's form, which is acknowledged as the final stage in the acquisition of the form–meaning link, learners first recognize the word's meaning, then the word's form and then produce the word's meaning. This is in keeping with Laufer's (1998) results and results from other forms of vocabulary knowledge which suggests that productive knowledge in this area is a sub-set of the recognition vocabulary. As with tests of recognition, learner knowledge is broadly linked with the frequency of occurrence of the words.

Current research work

This section will report the results of a three-year longitudinal study that explores the development of the productive knowledge of form and meaning of a homogeneous sample of EFL learners, by means of the productive version of the VLT (Laufer and Nation, 1995 and 1999). Results will be analysed from a quantitative and a qualitative point of view.

Research questions

The following research questions were addressed:

1. Does learners' productive knowledge of form and meaning increase as measured by the productive VLT along a three-year period?
2. Can any pattern in the evolution of that word knowledge be traced?
3. How does knowledge of the form–meaning link develop over the three years tested?
4. Which are the most and least frequently known words of the sample?

Research method

This is a longitudinal study with three points of data collection. The aim of the study was to establish learners' productive knowledge of the 2000 most frequent words as measured by the form–meaning link dimension, and how this knowledge developed over time.

Participants

A total of 197 students participated in the study. These were learners of EFL in the first, second and third grades of secondary education (ESO in the Spanish acronym). They averaged 11–12, 12–13 and 13–14 years of age. All learners were Spanish native speakers. The sample was taken in four urban middle-class secondary schools, so it can be argued that the sample is quite homogeneous.

At the first time of data collection, participants had received a total of 734 hours of instruction in the target language, which was a compulsory school subject for them. In the two subsequent data collection events with a one-year time span between them, learners had been exposed to 839 and 944 clock hours of instruction in English language, respectively.

Instruments

In order to test one dimension of vocabulary knowledge learners were given the productive VLT. This test measures the knowledge of the form–meaning link. According to Read (2000) this test measures discrete, selective and context-dependent vocabulary. The test was devised by Laufer and Nation (1999) on the basis of the receptive VLT. The original test is divided into five different bands: 2000; 3000; 5000; UWL and 10,000.

The original test measures the knowledge of 18 items per band. However, studies on the basis of the **receptive vocabulary** test (Schmitt *et al.*, 2001) have shown that 30 items are needed to get reliable estimates of the vocabulary size of testees at the targeted frequency levels. Thus, by taking into account Schmitt *et al.*'s (2001) findings, and following Laufer's personal advice, Version A and Version C (which are equivalent) from the Parallel version 1 (Laufer and Nation, 1995, 1999) were combined to create a 30-item test that could be given in a single administration. The first band of the test, providing a sample of the 2000 most frequent words in English, was created. Learners were presented with a set of 30 sentences including a blank and were required to write the missing target word of which a variable number of initial letters is provided to make sure that the learners supplied the correct target word, as well as to be insensitive to any word from the word family. The size of the underlined space at the end of the incomplete word does not indicate the number of letters needed in order to complete the elicited word, as in every single item, the underlined space has the same length. It should be noted that the VLT measures word families that consist of a base word and its inflected forms, together with derived forms which share a common meaning with the base word (Read, 2000). This is a diagnostic test which helps finding out how many high-frequency words learners know (Nation, 2005, p. 593)

Procedures and analysis

The tests were written in class. Students were given 15 minutes to complete the task. No dictionaries or other help was allowed. Tests were scored by one of the authors. One point was given for each correct answer up to a maximum of 30. Scores range from 0 to 30. Responses that formally resembled the target word were considered as correct, although they may have contained spelling errors. Responses belonging to the same word family as the target word were also considered correct and given one point. Other deviant responses were given a zero score.

Results and discussion

Table 5.1 gives the descriptive results indicating the development of the learners' productive knowledge of the 2000 most frequent words in English in each successive grade.

As can be observed in Table 5.1, descriptive values increase from one grade to the next. Learners in second grade of secondary education are, on average, able to produce more words than in first grade. Likewise, one year later, when they are in third grade, they obtain the highest mean scores. In order to determine whether the differences in mean **productive vocabulary** knowledge across grades were significant, a Wilcoxon signed-rank test was used. The results reveal that the differences in scores between grades are statistically significant. For the difference between first and second grade $Z = 7.29$, sig $<.001$, and between second and third grade $Z = -10.32$, sig $<.001$. Mean values of scores in the productive VLT reveal that most learners find themselves in the lowest quartiles. As they progress from one grade to the next, their scores also get higher, but for all grades the group of learners who score in the lowest half of the score-range is the most numerous.

Students' scores are also translated into a number of known words for each frequency level at each grade. In order to calculate the pupils' productive vocabulary size we applied Nation's formula (1990, p. 76) designed for the receptive version of the VLT. This formula reads as follows:

$$\text{Vocabulary size} = \frac{\text{N (correct answers)} \times \text{total N (words in dictionary/the relevant word list)}}{\text{N (items in test)}}$$

From these results, we can observe that learners show productive knowledge of fewer than half the most frequent 2000 words in English. According to our results, in the third grade of secondary education, learners are assumed to know around 820 words productively. Taking into account that the test requires learners to know the relationship/link between the form and the meaning of the target word, having productive knowledge of 820 words means that learners are able to establish a more or less accurate link between the target forms and their meaning of 820 English words when they appear in a particular context. These words belong to the most frequent 2000 words in English. The results also suggest that progress in word learning over the three years does not appear to be consistent. Learners gain on average 100 words from the

Table 5.1   Test results

	Mean	S. d.	Min.	Max.	Median	Mean estimated vocabulary size
First-grade ESO	7.26	3.01	0	16	7	484
Second-grade ESO	8.78	3.4	0	19	8	584
Third-grade ESO	12.30	5.05	4	27	12	820

most frequent 2000 words in the second grade, but more than double this, 236 words, in the third grade. A Wilcoxon signed-rank test reveals that this difference is statistically significant, $Z = 4.249$, sig. $<.001$.

This means that learners acquire significantly more words from the second to the third grade of secondary education than one year before. It can be concluded that not only do learners know significantly more words productively from one grade to the next, but they also learn significantly more words as they pass from grade 2 to grade 3. In other words, they incorporate more words into the lexicon in the interval from grade 2 to 3 than from grade 1 to 2. It is not clear that this is an obvious or expected result. It might be thought that, as learners acquire more words, then fewer words are available to learn and so lexical uptake would decrease over time. However, these results suggest the opposite, but since the learners in this study have such small vocabularies, and since the nature and quality of the lexical input is unknown, then the results are perfectly plausible.

In general, these results seem disappointing. Knowledge of less than 1000 words seems very low for learners who have received around 944 hours of instruction in English for nearly nine years. However, it is in line with results reported by Moreno (2010) in relation to a group of elementary learners, whose vocabulary size estimates were about 900 words at the end of compulsory secondary school education (i.e., fourth-grade ESO). Moreover, other studies (see Miralpeix, 2008; Moreno, 2010) have pointed out that Spanish learners of English end their secondary school education (i.e., second Bachillerato, 12th grade) with an estimated productive vocabulary size of about 1500 words, which, while larger than the estimates in this study, still appears small in relation to the time spent in instruction.

Studies of low proficiency or elementary level learners in other contexts outside Spain also suggest a low uptake of vocabulary in school. For example, in a study conducted by Laufer and Goldstein (2004), learners in grade 9 and 10 (equivalent to third and fourth of secondary education in Spain) obtained a lower number of known words productively than learners in the present study (around 434 words). By contrast, a previous study by Laufer and Paribakht (1998) showed that Israeli high school learners who had received similar amounts of instruction in the foreign language obtained much higher scores, with the productive version of the VLT giving a productive word knowledge estimate of 1655 words. This figure is more than double the vocabulary estimates obtained by learners in this study.

A study of receptive vocabulary size (Agustín Llach and Terrazas Gallego, 2009) revealed that in first-grade ESO learners have receptive knowledge of 817 words. If compared to the present results (484 words known productively) this confirms previous findings (Laufer, 1998) that productive word knowledge is lower than receptive. Given that research has established that learners need at least 3000 word families to be able to comprehend about 90 per cent of written and spoken text (Nation, 2006; Adolphs and Schmitt, 2004; Cobb and Horst, 2004; Laufer, 1997a; Hazenberg and Hulstijn, 1996) it can be concluded that our learners will perform very poorly in the foreign language. These figures suggest that, while there is some individual variation, the learners generally will struggle to communicate with so little vocabulary at their disposal. The rate of uptake is low, if compared to previous studies (Milton and Meara, 1998; Laufer, 2010) and it suggests that some vocabulary building might be useful. It is suspected that learners would benefit greatly from a foreign language teaching approach that puts special emphasis on explicit vocabulary instruction.

Table 5.2 presents the results of a between-groups comparison carried out to determine the number of learners who increased, decreased, or kept stable their word knowledge from one grade to the next.

This shows that while most learners increase their scores as they progress to a higher grade, there is a small percentage of learners who either obtain lower scores than in the previous grade or who obtain the same mark as the year before. These results may be evidence that the test of the most frequent 2000 words is not as reliable with learners at low levels as it is with learners at higher levels. Or it could be that the kind of knowledge being tested is not stable, but will vary as other kinds of vocabulary knowledge develop. Our interpretation is that the link between form and meaning is weaker at lower levels of proficiency and that it strengthens with time, language practice and exposure to input (cf. VanPatten *et al.*, 2004). Regressions of this kind reflect the fragility of knowledge at this level.

An analysis of the individual test words suggests that word knowledge is not scattered randomly across the test words. Words such as *private, temperature, sport, original* and *total* have the highest score totals in the tests and are known by three-quarters of learners from grade 1; this knowledge appears to remain stable in the group. These are all words of Latin origin and have great similarity with their equivalents in the learners' L1 (Spanish): *privado, temperatura, deporte, original* and *total*. As **cognates** perhaps it is not surprising that these words are the ones known by most learners. A more unstable picture appears if we consider the lowest-scoring words in the sample. Some words such as *lacks, tax, spoiling* and *roars* are almost unknown across the three grades. Two other words, *debts* and *charm*, increase after the first year, possibly due to the content of teaching material. All words in the lowest 25 per cent of the right-responses continuum are of Anglo-Saxon or Germanic origin, and thus non-cognate to the Spanish learner. These words bear no formal resemblance at all with the L1 equivalents, so their learning burden is higher than in the case of words of Latin origin, despite the fact that the latter are usually longer (cf. Laufer,

Table 5.2   Between-groups comparison of differences across grades

	Increase	Decrease	No change
From first to second	132/67 per cent	45/22.84 per cent	20/10.15 per cent
From second to third	156/79.2 per cent	17/8.63 per cent	24/12.18 per cent

1990). The results suggest that the learners in this study have more problems in remembering Anglo-Saxon words than Latin-based words.

A qualitative presentation of the ways learners develop over the three grades is presented in Table 5.3. Each of the 11 target words identified above is presented and the occurrences of the manner in which it is produced given in percentages.

It can be seen that learners show variation and inconsistency in the way they produce the target words. This implies that learners master only partially the form–meaning link of the target words. It is true that most learners display a correct spelling of the target words pointing to full knowledge of the form–meaning link. However, most target words are also wrongly spelled. Spelling problems remain as learners progress through grades despite the fact that the knowledge of target words increases. Spelling vacillation seems independent of learners' general proficiency level (co-occurring with grade) and with productive vocabulary knowledge. It would be interesting to observe whether learners at more advanced stages of language proficiency and displaying larger productive vocabularies still have spelling problems.

Nation's (2005) contention that linking a word form to its meaning will require a considerable effort, appears to be borne out. In this sense, deviations from the correct spelling are to be expected. Nation (*ibid*., p. 584) mentions two factors that can reduce the word learning burden: similarity of a word with the L1 equivalent (cognates or loan words), and predictability and regularity of the target word in relation to already known L2 words.

The results suggest that, curiously enough, target words from Latin origin with similarity to L1 words show a great variety of spelling forms. Deviations are located mostly within inflectional suffixes as in *introduced, admire, invite, elect* and *manufacturing*. It is remarkable since these are the most frequent, productive, regular and predictable suffixes (cf. Nation, 2005, p. 592). Although it has been suggested in the previous chapter that these inflectional suffixes are among the first to be learned in an L2, it appears that it still takes a little time before they are mastered. They deserve teaching time devoted to explaining the meaning and form of the different suffixes, as well as making learners aware of their productivity, frequency, regularity or predictability. Moreover, learners should note that by adding different suffixes to the stem, word meaning can also change. Suffixes are not interchangeable and which to choose is a relevant issue in word meaning.

Problems also appear in long words, which are often misspelled in a great variety of ways, as in *temperature* above, but also *manufacturing* and *birthday*. This finding concurs with Laufer's (1990) argument that word length is one of the intralexical factors that affects the learnability of a word. Among these, learners pronunciation influences the way target words are spelled. Learners tend to reproduce in writing the sounds of a word, and this is perhaps influenced by the learners' L1, where sound and symbol are more closely related. This may also be influencing the spelling of words which include two successive vowels or consonants – for example, *treasure* and *cream* – where spelling mistakes are also noted.

Table 5.3 Target word rendering across grades

	First ESO	Second ESO	Third ESO
Original	Original (97.45 per cent)	Original (99.38 per cent)	Original (97.76 per cent)
	Originale (1.27 per cent)	Originale (0.61 per cent)	Originaly (1.11 per cent)
	Originaly (0.63 per cent)		Originale (0.55 per cent)
	Oryginal (0.63 per cent)		Originate (0.55 per cent)
Private	Private (98.36 per cent)	Private (100 per cent)	Private (96.75 per cent)
	Privated (1.09 per cent)		Privat (1.08 per cent)
	Privrate (0.54 per cent)		Privated (1.08 per cent)
			Privatied (0.54 per cent)
			Privaty (0.54 per cent)
Total	Total (93.57 per cent)	Total (96.98 per cent)	Total (95.1 per cent)
	Totaly (2.85 per cent)	Totally (1.2 per cent)	Totally (2.17 per cent)
	Tota (0.71 per cent)	Totaly (1.2 per cent)	Totaly (1.63 per cent)
	Totale (0.71 per cent)	Totale (0.6 per cent)	Totale (0.54 per cent)
	Totall (0.71 per cent)		Totality (0.54 per cent)
	Totals (0.71 per cent)		
	Totoal (0.71 per cent)		
Spoiling	Spoiling (100 per cent)	Spoiling (100 per cent)	Spoiling (22.22 per cent)
			Spoils (33.33 per cent)
			Spoil (22.22 per cent)
			Spoiled (22.22 per cent)
Debts	–	Debts (28.57 per cent)	Debts (66.66 per cent)
		Debt (28.57 per cent)	Debs (23.33 per cent)
		Debits (28.57 per cent)	Debt (6.67 per cent)
		Debet (14.29 per cent)	Debds (3.33 per cent)
Roars	Roars (100 per cent)	Roared (100 per cent)	Roars (100 per cent)
Temperature	Temperature (98.14 per cent)	Temperature (98.84 per cent)	Temperature (100 per cent)
	Temperatur (0.61 per cent)	Temperamenture (0.57 per cent)	
	Temperatures (0.61 per cent)	Temperatures (0.57 per cent)	
Sport	Sport (98.85 per cent)	Sport (99.42 per cent)	Sport (100 per cent)
	Sporth (0.57 per cent)	Spoort (0.57 per cent)	
	Sports (0.57 per cent)		
Tax	–	Tax (100 per cent)	Tax (75 per cent)
			Tass (25 per cent)
Charm	Charm (100 per cent)	Charme (33.33 per cent)	Charm (78.78 per cent)
		Charmed (33.33 per cent)	Charming (15.15 per cent)
		Charming (33.33 per cent)	Charmy (6.06 per cent)
Lack	Lack (100 per cent)	–	Lack (100 per cent)

This study demonstrates many of the features of knowledge in this area that have been noted elsewhere in the literature. It demonstrates, for example, that L2 words with cognates in the L1 are likely to be better known than words without cognates. And it suggests that word knowledge in this form is not a binary,

known/not known quality. This research shows that word form can be very haz-
ily known. Learners know roughly what the form is like but not completely. So it
is not the case that the form is learned and then a meaning attached to it; rather,
the meaning is known (possibly for the learners in this study, because there is
such a meaning and a similar form in the L1) and then the form approximates
to the correct form(s). Our results also reveal that the process of establishing the
form–meaning connection is gradual, with learners first attaching the L2 concept to an approximate L2 form, and then slowly mapping the correct L2 form
to the L2 meaning. Similar L1 and L2 forms are acquired first. Often, spelling
errors are frequent in L2 forms at the beginning stages.

Results also suggest that knowledge of word and form combined may be
smaller than knowledge of form alone, since the estimates reported here are
on the small side compared with some of the other studies reported above. We
consider it astonishing that secondary school learners in Spain know so little
L2 lexis after so many of hours of instruction. These figures suggest that, on
average, the rate of learning is less than one word per contact hour of instruction and this is smaller than the three or four words per hour (Milton and
Meara, 1998) or one or two words (Laufer, 2010) reported for recognition
knowledge elsewhere in the literature. This lack of knowledge is all the more
surprising bearing in mind the importance of a solid lexical knowledge, understood as knowledge of the form–meaning link, to overall language success
(Laufer and Goldstein, 2004, p. 424).

Practical implications and suggestions for further research

One of the most important things these findings suggest is the importance of
promoting vocabulary knowledge among foreign language learners. Prevailing
methodologies can sideline the teaching of vocabulary (Milton and Alexiou,
2012) and many textbooks, it seems, can present for learning far less vocabulary than is needed for attaining even the most minimal of communicative goals
(Tschichold, 2012; Konstantakis and Alexiou, 2012; Alsaif and Milton, 2012).
But research is only now establishing norms for knowledge and progress that
allow judgements to be made as to whether learning in this area is satisfactory
or not. The research in this chapter has added to this store of normative data
on learning and progress, but more is needed. Further research might also usefully concentrate on investigating free **productive** and controlled productive
and **receptive vocabulary** size of learners and examine the evolution of lexical
knowledge over the years and proficiency levels. It would also be interesting to
find out whether foreign language lexical acquisition follows a parabolic function, with a peak of knowledge and a subsequent decrease in the number of new
words incorporated to the lexicon, such as happens in mother tongue vocabulary acquisition (cf. García Hoz, 1997, for Spanish L1). Future studies can
also address the relationships between the different aspects of word knowledge,
trying to relate knowledge of the form–meaning link with morphosyntactic

knowledge, pragmatic and sociolinguistic knowledge, or knowledge of word frequency, to mention some aspects.

In light of the present results, we advocate a teaching approach which explicitly provides instruction of the most frequent words in English. Consolidating knowledge of the first 2000 most frequent words can enhance greatly the communicative abilities of learners and also improve their academic skills (reading and writing in the foreign language). By means of bilingual lists, translations, matching exercises or synonym activities, teachers can present learners with the most frequently used words in the English language, in order to strengthen the form–meaning link by making the effort to acquire those words in a conscious way with study, memorizing, and practice activities.

Helping learners to establish the form–meaning link can be very beneficial, since this link contributes greatly to developing lexical competence as one of the most important aspects of word knowledge. The form–meaning link will develop and elaborate with increased exposure to input, new layers of meaning can be added and different meaning shades, distributional restrictions and **collocations** can be incorporated into the form–meaning connection. Exposure and practice seem crucial issues in establishing and consolidating form–meaning connections, so that these can advance from partial to complete, from weak to robust and from non-target-like to target-like (cf. Laufer and Goldstein, 2004; VanPatten *et al.*, 2004).

The test we have used to measure word knowledge through form–meaning associations is the productive version of the VLT devised by Laufer and Nation (1999); different versions of it can be accessed at Tom Cobb's webpage: www.lextutor.ca/tests/levels/productive

Questions for discussion

- Why might the actual vocabulary size of these learners be larger than the estimates calculated from the productive VLT scores?
- To what degree are **cognates** helpful to, and to what degree do they hinder, L2 vocabulary development?
- How can teachers help learners to overcome difficulties which arise from the fact that in English, one form can have multiple meanings, and one meaning can have multiple forms?

Acknowledgements

This study has been carried out under the auspices of a research project funded by the Spanish Ministerio de Ciencia y Tecnología and FEDER, Grant no. HUM2006-09775-C02-02/FILO. We also want to express our gratitude to the mathematician D. Ortigosa, who assisted us with the statistical analysis of the data. However, any remaining errors are the authors' responsibility.

Knowledge of Word Concepts and Referents

Parto Pajoohesh

6

Introduction

Meaning	Form and meaning	R	What meaning does this word form signal?
		P	What word form can be used to express this meaning?
	Concepts and referents	**R**	**What is included in the concept?**
		P	**What items can the concept refer to?**
	Associations	R	What others words does this word make us think of?
		P	What other words could we use instead of this one?

Nation's second element of his meaning section in 'Knowing a Word' (see Chapter 1) is knowledge of concepts and referents. At first glance it might be thought that this is different, especially for L2 learners, than the knowledge described in the previous four chapters. The previous chapters have described the addition of word forms in an L2 and the way these new forms are linked to meaning. It can be argued that the concepts and referents under consideration in this section are networks of knowledge and meaning which, once established in the L1, need not be re-established and recreated for L2 knowledge. The words involved might simply be relabelled. However, the creation of concepts and referents in the L1 takes considerable time and appears to be still in progress into adolescence; the time when many learners are beginning to learn their L2. At the very least, these learners are adding L2 capability in an emergent system, and it can be argued that elements of this system, at least, will need to be re-established for the L2.

The relationship between a word and what it refers to (referent) is a fundamental part of knowledge of word meaning. A referent can be a single entity (proper noun), a category (e.g., vegetables) or a concept (e.g., culture). In our ordinary and routine life, we never think, let alone ponder, about the words we use. In reality, we completely forget, if not ignore, the fact that words are arbitrarily used to label everything we have and know around us. We unconsciously use the word, or better say, the label 'cucumber' in English, 'concombre' in French and 'khiar' in Farsi to refer to a particular green vegetable, or in order to refer to a gas-filled bladder we use the label 'balloon' in English, 'ballon' in French and 'baadkonak' in Farsi, and so on. In other words, there is no inherent relationship between a word and its referent but it is rather arbitrary 'until formalized by the people using the word' (Schmitt, 2000, p. 23). In terms of 'formalizing' this arbitrariness, my 18-month-old, to-be-bilingual, son made up his own labels for the objects he very frequently referred to in his small toddler life. He also handled the formalization process well since everyone else tried hard to remember the new labels and communicate accordingly. Instead of saying 'balloon' (in Farsi baadkonak), he uttered 'beda beda' whereas for his favourite snack 'cucumber' (in Farsi khiar), he had created 'gauva'. Although this was a short-lived experience, it illustrates that the connection between a word and the concept it refers to must be bidirectional: 'the word must evoke the concept and the concept must evoke the word' (Carroll, 1964, p. 186).

The word–referent relationship is what Carter (1998) calls *referential meaning*. He points out that when we refer to the objects and entities in the external world, the feature is called 'reference' or 'denotation' and is therefore 'extralinguistic' (p. 17). The referential meaning is based on the assumption that children usually learn a language when the objects/items are pointed out to them and named in a certain appropriate vocabulary. Words, in this way, stand for the concepts that have been learned pre-verbally by the repetition of an experience – for example, seeing a balloon and hearing 'balloon' (Carroll, 1964). Also according to my introductory anecdote, the 'reference' can be (strangely) arbitrary. The powerful language experience behind this process provides an intuitive validity for the notion of a word as well as the relation between words and things (or referents). In terms of learning additional languages, some early authors – for example, Leopold (1939) – suggested that the bilingual child might have an ability to separate the word as a symbol from its referent since s/he deals with two or more languages at the same time. He called this the Abstract Thinking Hypothesis. This cognitive ability has recently been labelled as *metalinguistic awareness* (Bialystok, 1991). In support of Leopold's Abstract Thinking Hypothesis, Peal and Lambert (1962), in a landmark study on monolingual French and balanced bilingual French/English children, attributed the cognitive flexibility and creativity of bilinguals to their cognitive ability to form concepts through separating the label from its symbolic meaning (see also Cummins, 1978). This same notion is applicable to the many multilingual children around us nowadays.

The word–referent distinction and the referential meaning knowledge, however, make up only a small part of our knowledge of words, concepts and referents. An important aspect of 'knowing' a word or concept is that users of a language can, assumingly, 'describe' or 'define' the words/concepts they already know. Regardless of how simple this may sound, it is considered quite challenging, especially for L2 learners who, even if they have the conceptual knowledge may lack the vocabulary and structures to describe it. Some aspects of this descriptive knowledge can be very challenging. According to Schmitt (2000), it is particularly difficult to define a concept or category, rather than a proper noun, since concepts/categories are open-ended. Following this notion, I have focused in this chapter on bilingual and monolingual children's knowledge of words and referents and the relation it bears with lexical depth. It is probably easier to see in bilinguals how knowledge of concepts and referents emerges, separate from knowledge of other aspects of vocabulary. The first half of this chapter describes two processing models related to research in this area: one based on *semantic organization* theories (Cruse, 1986; Vygotsky, 1962) and the other an *information-processing* model (Bialystok, 1991, 2001a, 2001b). The second part of the chapter presents the account of my study on how the participating children demonstrated their word/concept knowledge by providing 'definitions'. Finally, I will discuss the findings in relation to the processing models.

Words, concepts and referents

Lexical organization

There are different ways of conceptualizing the spectrum of our knowledge of words or concepts (Phythian-Sense and Wagner, 2007). It can be conceptualized as continuum-based (Beck *et al.*, 1987), as a stage-based acquisitional knowledge (Aitchison, 1994; Graves, 1987), or as contextualized and decontextualized kinds of knowledge (Beck *et al.*, 1987; Snow, 1990). For example, Beck *et al.* place the knowledge of a word on a continuum that ranges from no knowledge to a context-bound narrow knowledge and, finally, a high level of knowledge that entails not only a rich, decontextualized understanding of a word, but also of its relationship to other words and metaphorical applications. By the same token, Wesche and Paribakht (1996) devised a Vocabulary Knowledge Scale (VKS) with which a language user self-assesses their level of (deep) word knowledge 'Figure 1: VKS elicitation scale – self-report categories (Paribakht and Wesche, 1997 p. 180)

I   I don't remember having seen this word before.
II I have seen this word before, but I don't know what it means.
III I have seen this word before, and I think it means___. (synonym/ translation)
IV I know this word. It means ____. (synonym/translation)
V   I can use this word in a sentence: _____. (If you do so, please do section IV)

The highest level of knowledge on this scale is considered to be a written sentence using the target word in addition to a definition or synonym. The conclusion drawn by the above researchers is that having a general sense of a word and what it refers to is not enough; even according to Harley (1996), it is possible for second language learners to know the core meaning of a new word *well enough* to produce it spontaneously, but they may not be able to use the word in a systematically appropriate way, or define it in terms of paradigmatically related words.

The most cited classification of word 'meaning' comes from Nation (2001), when he divided the word/concept meaning into three kinds of knowledge, each with a receptive and a productive level:

1. relationship between form and meaning;
2. relation between concept and **referents**; and
3. associations.

In terms of how much one knows about a *concept and its referents*, he poses two questions:

1. At the receptive level, one may wonder what a concept contains: the abstract or implicit level of knowledge we have.
2. At the productive level, one considers what items a concept can refer to: the concrete examples/items that represent the concept.

It must be emphasized here that there is consensus on the inter-relationship of the three kinds of knowledge and that we cannot isolate one from the others.

Another widely used conceptualization cited in the literature belongs to Aitchison (1994), who distinguished three connected but different tasks children do in their L1 vocabulary acquisition. Aitchison identified three stages in children's acquisition of word forms and associated word concepts: labelling, packaging/categorization and network building. Interestingly, Nation (2001) matches his three meaning categories mentioned earlier with Aitchison's classification in the following manner:

1. form and meaning = labelling
2. concepts and referents = packaging/categorization
3. associations = network building.

As mentioned earlier, the child learns to label objects, entities, etc. after the pre-verbal stage of learning about the world around. In the second and third stage, children try to organize, sort and relate the concepts in terms of lexical/semantic organization – for example, banana is a kind of fruit, or rose is a flower. What is of interest here is the way children cognitively develop and process semantic organization since it is a crucial stage in expanding and deepening of their knowledge of words/concepts. In fact, in the last two stages of word acquisition, depth of word knowledge depends on a shift from a contextualized idiosyncratic level (e.g., I like bananas/This flower smells good) to a more decontextualized quality of knowledge (e.g., banana/fruit; rose/flowers). This means that when semantically related words become part of the child's network, a '**syntagmatic–paradigmatic**' shift appears (Miller and Johnson-Laird, 1976) in terms of the way children relate the word/concept to its referent. Syntagmatic relations are linear (e.g., a rose grows in the garden and may come in red, white, yellow, etc.). On the other hand, paradigmatic relations, which are nonlinear, refer to hierarchical systems: part-whole and class-inclusion relations (e.g., rose is a flower that has a stem, petals, etc.). Therefore, **paradigmatic** relations signify decontextualized use of language as opposed to syntagmatic relations, which convey more contextualized or incidental information. At this point, I will pursue this discussion from a cognitive processing perspective.

Cognitive processing in lexical development

This section presents two cognitive processing models in children based on *semantic organization* theories (Cruse, 1968; Miller and Johnson-Laird, 1976; Vygotsky, 1962) and *information-processing* theory (Bialystok, 1991, 2001a). These two models are quite relevant to the task of 'word definition' in my study, which is presented in the second part of the chapter.

Starting from the first model, Vygotsky described how cognition aids, and inter–relates with, lexical development and organization in this way:

> At any age, a concept embodied in a word represents an act of generalization. But word meanings evolve. When a new word has been learned by the child, its development is barely starting; the word at first is a generalization of the most primitive type; as the child's intellect develops, it is replaced by generalizations of a higher and higher type – a process that leads in the end to the formation of these concepts. (1962, p. 83)

A good example for Vygotsky's view comes from Hatch and Brown (1995). They state that in first language lexical acquisition children start learning, for example, the name of their family dog before learning the word 'dog'. Later, they would learn 'pet' and eventually 'animal'. Accordingly, children learn the more specific 'sub-basic' (p. 55) term before the basic ('Napoleon' before 'dog/pet') or even the more general superordinate term (animal). Thus, the conceptual generalizations become more profound gradually and in a systematic way.

One important aspect of Vygotsky's theory (1962, 1986) deals with the distinction he made between *everyday (spontaneous)* concepts developing within practical community experience and *scientific (non-spontaneous)* concepts resulting from formal schooling. He characterized the former as empirical and situational and the latter as systematic, generalizable and detached from the concrete. According to Kozulin (as cited in Cummins, 2000), the organization of concepts is considered scientific when it has a formal, systematic and decontextualized structure. Vygotsky (1986) proposed that both concepts are inter-related because scientific concepts fine-tune everyday concepts to a level of conscious use, while spontaneous concepts serve as the basic framework for scientific concepts. In this sense, this distinction mirrors the paradigmatic–syntagmatic/paradigmatic dimension described earlier.

Vygotsky's 'systematic generalization' of concepts involves the formation of a *superordinate* concept, which includes the given concept as a particular case in a hierarchy. He exemplified this view with the concept of *flower*, which the child learns before learning the word *rose* (or 'dog' is learned before 'Spaniel', 'German Shepherd', etc). In a hierarchical format, a superordinate concept subsumes the existence of a series of *subordinate* concepts of different levels of generality. In this way, a given concept is placed 'within a system of relationships of generality' (Vygotsky, 1962, p. 92). In the realm of semantics, this is called **hyponymy**, one category of *meaning relations* or *sense relations*. Hyponymy consists of 'superordinate', 'coordinate' and 'subordinate' relations between words/concepts. From a cognitive developmental perspective, the scientific (non-spontaneous) concepts and their hierarchical inter-relationships would be the medium within which awareness first develops. Thus, through the portals of scientific concepts, higher intellectual functions will develop in the child with features such as reflective consciousness and deliberate control (in handling the concepts). For Vygotsky (1962), concepts can become subject to consciousness and control only when they are part of this system. We will see later that these features resemble those of Bialystok's information-processing model.

The second model belongs to Bialystok's earlier works on bilinguals and metalinguistic knowledge (e.g., 1991), particularly where children use their knowledge of mental representations (of referents, concepts) to solve linguistic tasks. Bialystok (1991, 2001a) refers to this ability as 'metalinguistic' as opposed to pure linguistic skills. Accordingly, there might be no awareness of the mental representations and their organization in order for the child to use them in conversations, interpretation of text, semantic judgements or giving definitions. To her, the base line for metalinguistic abilities is 'an information-processing description of cognition' (1991, p. 115). In her hypothesis (1991, 2001a, 2001b), there are two components involved in this model: *analysis* of linguistic knowledge and *control* of linguistic processing. The first component helps the mental representations to become more structured, and interconnected. This means that the semantic connections between various linguistic terms are organized in a hierarchical manner – that is, *animal–bird* or *bird–robin* as well as non-hierarchical ones: *robin–sparrow* (1991, p. 117). This component reflects the same idea mentioned earlier of the way children develop and organize the representations. The second component, control of linguistic processing, directs the child's attention to specific information for performing in a specific context – for example, attending to and selecting the information in problem-solving tasks. Furthermore, the analytic dimension entails mental representations having two aspects, according to Mandler's review (as cited in Bialystok, 1991). One aspect deals with the knowledge and its organization (see the above example) and the other refers to the use of symbols and the relation between a symbol and its referent. This means that in solving metalinguistic problems (e.g., providing definitions), 'the underlying mental representation must be organized around forms and structures and specifically indicate the nature of the symbolic relation, or how it is that the forms refer to meanings' (Bialystok, 1991, p. 117).

An important part of the information-processing model is another hypothesis that for various domains of language use – that is, oral, metalinguistic and literate; there are different processing demands along the analytic and control component continuums. For example, the metalinguistic domain needs high analysis and high-control mental processing in contrast to the oral/communicative domain with low demand on the analysis and control. In daily conversation there is less pressure to analyse the conceptions of language. Children pay only casual attention to the language itself to convey and interpret meaning (MacNamara, as cited in Bialystok, 1991). Thus, conversations are contextualized in nature, as opposed to definitions which are decontextualized, metalinguistic tasks in which the language is not presented through the empirical context it refers to. For bilingual and second language learners, she believes that there is an *increased* demand for analysis of linguistic knowledge because they have to rely heavily on their knowledge of language structure and analyse conceptions of a second language in a more organized and explicit way than in conversations (Bialystok, 1991).

In conclusion, both Vygotsky and Bialystok agree that since bilingual children have to express a thought in two or more language(s), this should help them with enhanced awareness of the analysis and control components of processing, especially when it comes to literacy tasks (reading and writing), which demand high control and analysis mechanisms (vs conversations). Bialystok (1986) found evidence that in solving metalinguistic tasks, bilingual children compared to monolinguals and irrespective of literacy or age, performed better in tasks with a high demand of control of processing. Those bilinguals who were also *biliterate* were better in tasks with high analysis skill. Also older and more literate children scored higher in general. She suggests that although bilingual children might solve the metalinguistic problems in the same way as monolinguals do, they approached them with a different level of mastery of analysis and control of processing depending on the task (Bialystok, 2001b).

Bialystok (2007) later comes to the conclusion that bilingualism is clearly a factor in literacy development of children, but its effect is not simple or straightforward. For example, bilingualism is advantageous in children's oral language competence skills but not with regard to the concept of symbolic nature of print. In terms of handling metalinguistic concepts, it indicates little difference between bilinguals and monolinguals. She believes that even the differences are to the benefit of the bilinguals since 'knowing more has never been a disadvantage when compared to knowing less' (p. 71).

Word definition: assessing word-referent knowledge

In the past few decades, many researchers have paid attention to the school task of 'providing definitions'. The task is considered as a specialized speech genre because it constitutes an example of decontextualized language use and is relevant to literacy skills development. Let me first exemplify 'word definitions'. The two examples are taken from Watson (1985, p. 182) and Snow *et al.* (1991, p. 91), respectively:

> Example (1)
> > Teacher: 'What is a lullaby?'
> > Child 1: 'It helps you go to sleep at night.' (a)
> > Teacher: 'But what *is* it?'
> > Child 2: 'It's a song.' (b)
> > Teacher: 'That's right.'
> Example (2)
> > 'What's a clock?'
> > 'That thing on the wall.'

'Word definition' as a task is simply asking a child 'What is an X [word/concept]?'. The interesting, and at the same time complex, part is children's answer to such a question, which is usually in forms similar to (a) or (b) in Example 1 above. Watson explains that the developmental shift form contextualized (syntagmatic) to decontextualized (paradigmatic) use of language typically happens from expressions like (a) to (b). Confirming Bialystok's model, Snow (1990) indicates that practically providing good definitions requires performing two tasks simultaneously:

1. Analysis of one's own knowledge of word meaning in order to distinguish 'definitional' from 'incidental' information about a word or concept.
2. Control of processing that includes the analysis and use of the linguistic form.

Therefore, the task of providing definitions also qualifies as a metalinguistic one. Litowitz (1977) gives a good example of an adult Aristotelian definition as, 'An X is *something* (superordinate class) which does/has (*function, attribute, composition*) (*somewhere*) (*somehow*)'. In Aristotelian definitions, words are presumed to be symbolic and separate from that to which they refer. From this point of view, a 'clock', that object on the wall, has rather a place in a hierarchy of non-living things as a device/machine that tells time and has some other properties. Also, the linguistic form of a good definition must conform to certain adult norms as in Litowitz's example.

An advantage of this task as opposed to formal vocabulary tests (picture tests, multiple choice tests, true/false type) is in its open-ended format. This feature provides an opportunity to study lexical knowledge in rather more depth, particularly in light of cognitive development. This means that by analysing word definitions, one can gain some understanding of the way word meanings and meaning structures are mentally represented.

Studies in L1 vocabulary acquisition (e.g., Anglin, 1985; Snow *et al.*, 1991; Watson, 1985) report that during the primary-school years, between the ages of six and eight, the child's semantic network becomes organized and

2nd Module

Name of Module —————————

Module start date(s) —————————

Module Level UG 1/2/3/4/Masters/MBA/Other

Number of Students on Module —————————

I am adopting the text as

- ☐ Essential/Sole text (i.e. students should buy a copy)
- ☐ One of Two course texts (i.e. students should buy one of the two books)
- ☐ One of Several(i.e.recommended for purchase)
- ☐ Background Reading

Name   Mr Mike Chick
Address   Schl Humanities & Social Scien
          University of South Wales
          Treforest Campus
          Pontypridd CF37 1DL

Signature:

Date:

Please return this section to your bookshop

Name of Module _____

Module start date(s) _____

Module Level   UG 1/2/3/4/Masters/MBA/Other

Number of Students on Module _____

I am ~~adopting the text as~~

☐ Essential/Sole text (i.e. students should buy a copy)
☐ One of Two course texts (i.e. students should buy one of the two books)
☐ One of Several/Recommended for purchase
☐ Background Reading

I am also recommending _____

Have you any comments on the book or suggestions for improvements in content or presentation?

With your permission, your comments may also be used by our marketing dept & editors and may be passed to the authors.

Can we use these comments in publicity material and/or pass them onto the author

☐ You can use my comments for publicity
☐ You can pass my comments to the author
☐ Please do not pass on my comments or use them for publicity

We are keen to keep all of our customers informed of new publications that might be of interest

☐ Please do not send me details of any other products
☐ Please keep me informed of new Palgrave/BFI publications
☐ Please keep me informed of new Palgrave/BFI publications by email

Email Address

Research Interests

Is there anything else we can help you with? If you have any general queries or comments please write them here

Please return this form to :
Lecturer services, Palgrave Macmillan, FREEPOST, SCE9735, Basingstoke, Hants RG21 6XS (01256) 302794
No stamp is required if posting within UK

AND CONDITIONS:

umer the consumer's statutory rights
s.

, injury caused by MDL's negligence
ised agent or representative of MDL,
an authorised agent or representative
quiet enjoyment, MDL shall not be
resentation or any implied warranty,
on law or under the express terms of
profit, loss of sales, loss of goodwill,
tial loss or damage howsoever caused
e supply of the goods or their use or
ovided in these terms and conditions.

omposition or arrangement with its
ion order, or (being an individual or
ny) goes into liquidation (otherwise
onstruction) or;
receiver is appointed of any of the

eases or threatens to cease to carry on

these events is about to occur then
dy available to MDL. MDL shall be
d any further deliveries under such
the customer, and if the goods have
shall become immediately due and

nditions is held for any reason to be
art this shall not affect the validity or
terms and conditions.

he agreement by the customer will be
of the same or any other provision.

ns will only be effective if in writing
each of MDL and the customer.

thorised to make any representations
in writing by one of its Directors.

ne or by fax, MDL has a statutory
customer in writing or other durable
atest at the time of delivery. This
vant invoice or in these terms and
e main characteristics of the goods
s) and delivery costs (if applicable)

clause 3 below, the customer has a
n (Distance Selling) regulations 2000
ich has been accepted by MDL by
n on the invoice and marked for the

Unless any other time limit applies under the Regulations, the notice must be
received with 7 working days following the day on which the goods which are the
subject of order being cancelled are delivered, unless the reason for such
cancellation is shortage, damage, defect in quality or condition, failure to
correspond with order or non-delivery in which case should be given and must be
received within 30 days following the day on which the goods are delivered.

9.2.   The customer may not cancel any order which has been accepted by MDL
where such order is for the supply of newspapers, periodicals or magazines. The
customer may not cancel any order which has been accepted by MDL, where such
order is for an audio or visual recording (including audio books) or computer
software if such recording or software has been unsealed by the customer.

9.3.   If an order is cancelled the customer must return the goods concerned to the
address shown on the invoice marked for the attention of the Customer Service
Manager within 14 days of giving notice of cancellation of the order. Where such
return is for reasons other than shortage, damage, defect in quality or condition,
failure to correspond with order or non-delivery this will be at the customer's
expense and liability.

9.4.   MDL will reimburse any sum paid by the customer for or in relation to the
goods as soon as possible following receipt of notice of cancellation given in
accordance with the appropriate time limit and in any case within 30 days of
receipt of such notice. Other than in the case of cancellation for shortage,
damage, defect in quality or condition, failure to correspond with order or non
delivery (where the reasonable costs of returning the goods by the mechanism
agreed with MDL will be reimbursed) this will not include reimbursement of the
costs of returning the goods.

9.5.   Any complaints should be sent in writing to the address shown on the
invoice marked for the attention of the Customer Services Manager.

10.   Payment
10.1.   Unless payment has been made at the time of order in a form acceptable to
MDL, orders received from consumers will be invoiced by MDL and payment
will be due immediately upon receipt of the invoice or goods (whichever is the
later). Where goods are ordered by a consumer for delivery to a third party the
invoice will be sent separately to the consumer and not with the goods to the third
party.

11.   Delivery
11.1.   Delivery of goods is at the customer's expense and liability, unless
otherwise agreed in writing by MDL or an authorised agent or representative of
MDL, delivery charges being invoiced at the same time as the invoice of the
goods.

11.2.   MDL will use its reasonable endeavours to deliver all goods within 30 days
of receipt of the order for such goods and will in any case deliver all goods within
90 days of receipt of such order. If for any reason MDL is unable to deliver any
goods within such 90 day period, it will notify the customer of this. Unless
otherwise requested by the customer the relevant order will be treated as cancelled
from the point of notification and MDL will reimburse any sum paid by or on
behalf of the customer for or in relation to such goods. MDL will reimburse any
such sum as soon as possible following notification to the customer and in any
case within 30 days following the day after the expiry of the 90 day period.

11.3.   If any goods ordered by the customer are to be delivered to a third party,
then delivery to such third party shall be treated as delivery to the customer and all
relevant provisions of these terms and conditions shall apply accordingly.

rrespondence or with returns.

MACMILLAN

Macmillan Publishers Ltd trading as Macmillan Distribution (MDL)

Order & Payments To:-
MACMILLAN DISTRIBUTION (MDL)
HOUNDMILLS, BASINGSTOKE,
HANTS, RG21 6XS, ENGLAND
Giro No. - 206 4057
Registered Number 785998 England

Telephone   +44 (0) 1256 329
Fax (Home)   +44 (0) 1256 81:
             +44 (0) 1256 81:
Fax (Export) +44 (0) 1256 84:

Bank - NATIONAL WESTMIN:
Code - 60-02-49
Account No. - 47301759
Email - mdl@macmillan.co.u
Swift Code - NWBKGB2L
IBAN - GB10NWBK60024947:

PLEASE REMIT TO THE ABOVE ADDRESS

013

CHARGE TO

Mr Mike Chick
Schl Humanities & Social Scien
University of South Wales
Treforest Campus
Pontypridd CF37 1DL

DESPATCHED TO

ED30010

Mr Mike Chick
Schl Humanities & Soc
University of South W
Treforest Campus
Pontypridd CF37 1DL

SEE REVERSE FOR TERMS & CONDITIONS OF SUPPLY AND FOR NET BOOK AGREEMENT.   ALWAYS QUOTE IN'

INTERNAL USE ONLY	ORDER REF.	QTY	ISBN	ED	C O M	C of O	PUB	TITLE
								Ref: 923265
8J6182		1	9780230275737	01	BK	GB	M4	Dimensions of

INTERNAL ONLY

BOOKS	1
LINES	1
WEIGHT	0.348
CARTONS	
INV. DISTR.	100000

KEYED BY	ZOX
BATCH	50971/058
BRICK	0117
TYPE	A ADIT
SPOOL FILE NAME	XWPOHA1389SI

www.macmillandistribution.co.uk

INSPECTION COPY

Inside

Swansea

NUMBER	76744400
DATE & TAX POINT	29-04-14
PICK LIST	61389/013 - ISI
PAGE NO.	1

759

300

l Scien
es

CUSTOMER INFORMATION:-

ACCOUNT NO.	097510009
CONTACT NAME	
DIRECT TEL NO. (DDI)	
PREFERRED DAY	Not Applicable
CARRIER / ROUTE	07 09
DESCRIPTION	2nd Cl. Post
VAT NO.	GB 199 4406 21

CE No. AND RAISE QUERIES IMMEDIATELY   **PRINTED BOOKS UNLESS OTHERWISE STATED**

	AUTHOR	TYP	PRICE	TRADE DISC %	VALUE	VAT	SOU
cabulary Kno	Milton J. et al	P	23.99		No Charge		

Items Zero Rated Unless Otherwise Stated	TOTAL	No Charge
	SUNDRIES	No Charge
	VAT	No Charge
	INVOICE TOTAL	£ No Charge

MACMILLAN TERMS

The following terms and conditions apply to all orders for goods that we receive from you, unless otherwise agreed in writing signed by an authorised representative of MDL, and supersede any previous correspondence or discussions between MDL or any authorised agent of MDL and the customer. Customers' terms of purchaser will not apply.

1. Orders
1.1. No order submitted to MDL shall be deemed to be accepted by MDL unless and until confirmed in writing (by invoice submitted with goods delivered, or otherwise) by MDL or by an authorised agent or representative of MDL.

1.2. By accepting delivery of any goods the customer acknowledges receipt of and agrees to be bound by these terms and conditions. All goods are supplied by MDL, unless the relevant invoice expressly states otherwise.

2. Risk and Title
2.1. Risk of damage to or loss of any particular goods supplied by MDL to the customer will pass to the customer on delivery of those goods or, if the customer wrongfully fails to take delivery of those goods, the time when those goods are tendered for delivery. Title and property in any goods, including full legal and beneficial ownership, shall not pass to the customer until MDL has received full payment (in cash or cleared funds) for all goods delivered to the customer under this and all other contracts between the customer and MDL. Full payment of the goods shall include the amount of any interest or other sum payable under the terms of this and all other contracts between the customer and MDL.

3. Charging and Selling
3.1. All books are sold subject to the condition that they shall not, by way of trade or otherwise, be lent, re-sold, hired out or otherwise circulated without our prior consent in any form of binding or cover other than that in which it is published and without a condition to the same effect as this condition being imposed on the subsequent purchase.

4. Payment
4.1. The price of goods is the published price as shown on the invoice less such discount (if any) shown on the invoice. The price is exclusive of any applicable value added or other tax which the customer shall be additionally liable to pay to MDL as shown on the invoice

4.2. No settlement discounts or other deductions may be made against amounts due on MDL's invoice(s) or statement(s).

4.3. If the customer fails to make any payment on the due date then, without prejudice to any other right or remedy available to MDL, MDL shall be entitled to charge the customer interest (both before and after any judgement) on the amount unpaid at the rate of 3% per annum above National Westminster Bank Plc base rate from time to time, until payment in full is made.

4.4. MDL reserves the right to withhold further supplies in the event of amounts payable being overdue, breach of any of the conditions of this agreement, or any other reason which at MDL's discretion warrants such action.

5. Liability
5.1. The agreement for the supply of goods shall be governed by the laws of England and these terms and conditions will be interpreted in accordance with those laws.

5.2. MDL shall not be liable for any failure in performing any of its obligations under the agreement if the failure was due to any cause beyond MDL's reasonable control.

5.3. Save as expressly provided in these terms and conditions all warranties, conditions or other terms implied by statute or common law are excluded to the fullest extent permitted by law.

5.4. Where the goods are sold to a c are not affected by these terms and condi

5.5. Except in respect of death or pers or the negligence of any employee or au any fraudulent misrepresentation by MDI of MDL or any implied term as to title liable to the customer by reason of any condition or other term or any duty at co the agreement or otherwise for any loss loss of business or any indirect or conseq which arises out of or in connection wit resale by the customer except as expressly

6. Insolvency
6.1. If:- (a) the customer makes an creditors, becomes subject to an adminis firm) becomes bankrupt or (being a cor than for the purposes of amalgamation or (b) an encumbrancer takes possession o property or assets of the customer; or (c) if the customer, being a trade custome business; or (d) MDL reasonably believes that any without prejudice to any other right or re entitled to cancel the agreement or sus agreement without incurring any liability been delivered but not paid for the pr payable.

7. General
7.1. If any provision of these terms an ineffective or unenforceable in whole or enforceability of the other provisions of t

7.2. No waiver by MDL of any breach treated as a waiver of any subsequent bre

7.3. Variations to these terms and cond and signed by an authorised representativ

7.4. MDL's employees or agents are no concerning goods unless confirmed by M

8. Information to be provided by MI
8.1. Where an order is placed by tel obligation to give certain information to medium in relation to such order at th information is provided either on the conditions. In particular a description being supplied, the price (including all will be set out on the relevant invoice.

9. Cancellations
9.1. Subject to the exceptions set ou statutory right under the Consumer Prote ("the Regulations") to cancel any order giving notice in writing to the address s attention of the Customer Service Manag

Always quote invoice number on

Inspection Copy Questionnaire

palgrave macmillan

Account ED300102130 0
Name: Mr Mike Chick
Address: Schl Humanities & Social Scien
University of South Wales
Treforest Campus
Pontypridd CF37 1DL

Book Details
Invoice: 76744400
Title: 9780230275737 Dimensions of Vocabulary Kno
ISBN: 9780230275737
Author: Milton J. et al

Dear Lecturer

Please find enclosed the inspection copy you requested. We hope that you will find it suitable for your teaching purposes.

We do not require you to adopt the book in order to keep it free of charge, but request that you **FULLY** complete this questionnaire.

To complete an on-line version, please go to www.palgrave.com/login/incidentlist.asp

If you decide to recommend this title, it would be most helpful if you could

* Send this completed form back to us
* update your reading list for your students
* forward the enclosed form to your local bookshop
* inform the library to ensure they have stock for your students.

The information you give to us is also used to allow us to keep bookshops informed of requirements, to plan needs for specific texts and to supply you with other relevant texts.

Palgrave/BFI Lecturer Services
lecturerservices@palgrave.com

1st Module

Name of Module ———————————

Module start date(s) ———————————

Module Level   JG 1/2/3/4/Masters/MBA/Other

Number of Students on Module ———————————

☐ I am adopting the text as

☐ I am NOT adopting the text for this module

☐ Essential/Sole text (i.e. students should buy a copy)
☐ One of Two course texts (i.e. students should buy one of the two books)
☐ One of Several/Recommended for purchase
☐ Background Reading

I am also recommending ———————————

2nd Module

☐ I am NOT adopting the text for this module

palgrave macmillan

Bookseller Notification

Dear Lecturer

We would like to ensure that copies of your recommended texts are available for students to buy. To that end, please could you complete the details and forward this form to your local bookshop.

Palgrave/BFI Lecturer Services
lecturerservices@palgrave.com

Dear Bookseller

I am pleased to let you know that I have adopted the following text for my modules.

Book Details
Title: 9780230275737 Dimensions of Vocabulary Kno
ISBN: 9780230275737
Author: Milton J. et al

1st Module

Name of Module ————————

Module start date(s) ————————

Module Level   UG 1/2/3/4/Masters/MBA/Other
————————

Number of Students on Module

I am adopting the text as

- [ ] Essential/Sole text (i.e. students should buy a copy)
- [ ] One of Two course texts (i.e. students should buy one of the two books)
- [ ] One of Several (i.e. recommended for purchase)
- [ ] Background Reading

the syntagmatic–paradigmatic shift happens. Vygotsky's distinction between *everyday* and *scientific* concepts refers exactly to this kind of developmental and cognitive change during school years, when scientific concepts appear more frequently in texts. As children progress in school, they need to learn technical and disciplinary vocabulary as well as concepts not found in their everyday spoken language. Therefore, the knowledge of decontextualized use of language becomes highly significant in educational contexts. To a great extent, a lack of knowledge of the low- and mid-frequency academic words that children usually encounter in school texts impedes the natural process of expanding word meanings during reading (Stanovich, 1986). During upper primary (ages 11–13) and secondary school, students are expected to use appropriate vocabulary, explain or define, and support solutions to problems in a logical way through oral interaction and writing. In maths, science and social science, abstract concepts (e.g., symmetry, precipitation, democracy) are expressed orally and in writing. Towards middle school, the nature of classroom instruction, texts and literacy practices becomes increasingly specialized, and the literacy ability that was functional in the primary grades becomes inadequate to deal with genre-specific demands (Carrasquillo *et al.*, 2004).

A literature review of the definitional skill of English monolinguals (Anglin, 1985; Johnson and Anglin, 1995; Kurland and Snow, 1997; Litowitz, 1977; McGhee-Bidlack, 1991; Watson and Olson, 1987) and European monolinguals (Benelli, 1988) shows that children as old as ten have difficulty expressing paradigmatic meaning relations in their L1. These researchers also reported that the conventions governing the linguistic form of definitions are opaque to children who had not yet developed the ability to analyse their word/concept knowledge. Another common finding of these studies indicates that the acquisition and recognition of superordinate membership for use in defining common objects is a 'late habit', occurring long after children refer to some evident sensory-object properties (Benelli, 1988, p. 229). McGhee-Bidlack (1991) found that the percentage of characteristics of a formal definition increased by age and in terms of abstract words; only 18 year olds could use more superordinate class names.

With regard to second language learners, it is not immediately apparent that these aspects of L1 conceptual knowledge are readily accessible in the L2. A number of studies in the past two decades have focused their investigation on the word definitional skill of bilingual and L2 language learners to explore the dimension of lexical depth knowledge. All studies have repeatedly referred to large differences between L2 learners and monolingual peers on measures of lexical depth, definitional skill and specifically superordinate production. They cover several educational settings: a series of studies on Hispanic children in the USA (e.g., Carlo *et al.*, 2004; Ordonez *et al.*, 2002; Snow, 1990; Snow *et al.*, 1991), immigrant children in the Netherlands (Verhallen and Schoonen, 1993, 1998a, 1998b) and the most recent, a study on immigrant Farsi-English bilinguals in Canada (Pajoohesh, 2007a), which is presented here.

Current research work

The data reported in this section is part of a larger data set on the definitional skills in a second language. In the original study, I elicited children's knowledge of words/concepts through a receptive as well as a productive task to assess the degree of their depth of word knowledge. In what follows, I have focused only on the productive task of 'word definition', which has a direct link to children's word-**referent** knowledge and the way they processed and performed the task. The details of the original study and the statistical analyses are reported elsewhere (see Pajoohesh, 2007b, 2008).

Participants and setting

Three groups of sixth graders (total of 49) attending Canadian public schools participated in the study: two bilingual immigrant groups (Farsi/L1-English/L2) and one English-speaking monolingual group of Caucasian background:

1. *Bilingual heritage language (BHL) group.* This group had some basic Farsi literacy skills (reading/writing) as a result of attending heritage language programmes of one three-hour class per week. They all had some accent when speaking in Farsi and lacked a high command of oral communication skills in that language. Some were even born in Canada and English was their dominant language.
2. *Bilingual content-based (BCB) group.* The children in this group had either some years of formal schooling in Farsi in their home country of Iran prior to immigration, or some years of content-based Farsi instruction at private Farsi schools in Canada. BCB participants had age-appropriate native language skills. These schools offer six to eight hours of instruction at weekends, and all school subjects are taught in Farsi.
3. *Monolingual English-speaking (MES) group.* All were born in Canada from English native-speaker parents who spoke only in English with their children at home.

The Farsi proficiency of the two bilingual groups was measured by the Farsi translation of the Bilingual Verbal Ability Test (BVAT) (Munoz-Sandoval *et al.*, 1998). For the English proficiency, the revised Vocabulary Levels Test was administered (Schmitt *et al.*, 2001). The length of residence of the bilingual children ranged from three to 11 years. All three groups had reached a similar level of English proficiency as measured with a proficiency tool; in this way English proficiency was controlled in the study. This result is based on the ANOVA findings showing no significant differences between groups at the .01 level of significance: $F (2,46) = 2.36$, $p = .05$. The Farsi proficiency of the two bilingual groups was measured as well but not controlled. The t-test results showed significant differences between the two Farsi-speaking groups: $t (30) = 2.44$, $p < .05$, with the BCB group outperforming the BHL group in Farsi proficiency by a statistically significant margin.

Methodology

The word definition task was used to measure the 'expressible' (productive) aspect of word knowledge of the participants in terms of definitional quality in English and Farsi. The participating children provided definitions for 16 words in answer to the question 'What is a ___?'. The target words were taken from a **word association** test designed by Verhallen and Schoonen (1998b) and used in my original study as a receptive (recognition) task. The words cover various semantic domains such as food, transportation, animals and profession. Also, they include content words: nouns (both concrete and abstract), verbs and adjectives.

The analysis of the elicited definitions, in terms of semantic and syntactic quality, is based on a scale adapted from the Formal Definitional Quality (FDQ) scale (Snow, 1990; Snow *et al.*, 1991; Ordonez *et al.*, 2002). The scale consists of four categories of syntax, superordinate, complement and definitional feature and distinguishes between high- and low-quality definitions as shown in Appendix 2. The relation between the definitional knowledge and word/concept processing models is also illustrated in Appendix 2.

To ensure the reliability of the FDQ scoring, inter-rater reliability was obtained with the assistance of a bilingual rater using 20 per cent of the definitions in each language. Inter-rater reliability for the syntax category was calculated at 90 per cent for English and 87 per cent for Farsi data. For the superordinate category, the reliability was 96 per cent for both English and Farsi data. The level of agreement for the definitional features was 89 per cent for English and 90 per cent for Farsi data.

Findings: English/L2

The results of definitional quality scales revealed various results for the four categories of syntax, superordinate, complement and definitional feature. The findings for the scale of syntax are illustrated in Figure 6.1. Overall, children of all three groups had similar performance on this scale, meaning that they had a fair knowledge of the syntactic conventions of a good definition and could follow almost the same format for all definitions.

On the other three scales of superordinate, complement and definitional feature, however, the groups showed differences in their performances. The differences in the superordinate knowledge of bilinguals and monolinguals are shown in Figure 6.2, indicating that the BCB group did not perform as well as the other two groups on this measure while the BHL and MES groups had similar performances. In fact, the largest statistical differences were found in this area in my study, as well as in other relevant studies (Ordonez *et al.*, 2002; Snow, 1990; Verhallen and Schoonen, 1993, 1998a). This finding is due to the fact that, in many cases, the BCB children either referred to a word/concept as 'something' or 'a thing', rather than a 'true' superordinate, or had a definition without 'an X is a Y' part. As a result, they obtained a lower score (or zero) on the scale. The implication is that superordinates can be rather 'infrequent' terms that need to be *relearned* in another language; for example, 'vehicle' is

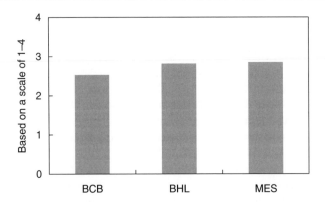

Figure 6.1 Mean average for English syntax measure of definitional quality scale

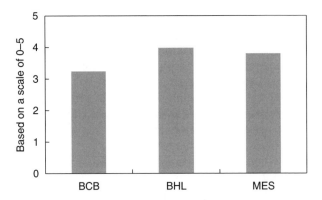

Figure 6.2 Mean average for English superordinate measure of definitional quality scale

the superordinate term for many transportation machines/devices; however, it may not be used in children's everyday use of language. This issue is discussed in more detail in the following section.

The same pattern of differences found for the superordinate category applies to the complement measure as shown in Figure 6.3. While no differences were observed between the MES and BHL group, the BCB group did not perform as well as the other two groups in providing restrictive and concise relative clauses that contain paradigmatic information about the target words/concepts.

The definitional feature scale evaluated the knowledge of syntagmatic meaning relations in terms of physical and situational attributes of objects/concepts. As illustrated in Figure 6.4, differences were found only between the BHL and MES groups, showing that the BCBs could not provide as many (correct) meaning relations in their definitions compared to the monolinguals. Again, the BHL and MES children were not different in their syntagmatic knowledge of words

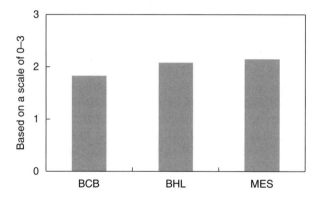

Figure 6.3   Mean average for English complement measure of definitional quality scale

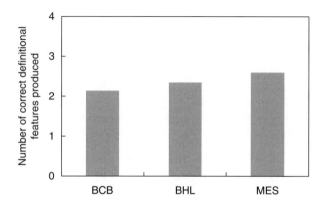

Figure 6.4   Mean average for English definitional feature measure of definitional quality scale

and concepts. Here, it is noteworthy that the longer a definition was, the more definitional features of syntagmatic nature were produced by the child. This implies that a long definition was not necessarily a standard well-formed one that contained the required decontextualized meaning relations. Based on the raw data, children produced a range of zero to six features per word; however, Figure 6.4 refers to a mean average of two to three features for all three groups. This means that while just a *minority* of children produced as many features as six or close to six, some must have had definitions without a relative clause and, therefore, without definitional features (e.g., 'equator is a place and … that's it'). In fact, some monolingual children provided very long definitions compared to some BCB children, who could only compose a rather short one and without a complement similar to the example above. This explains the differences found between the two groups on the scale. In comparison, the BHL children were able to include very few definitional features without composing long definitions.

Findings: Farsi/LI data

In the method section, I mentioned that, in terms of a measurement of Farsi proficiency, the BCB group outperformed the BHL group statistically. In the light of this information, the findings of the Farsi performance of definitions are certainly unexpected. As illustrated in Figure 6.5, the two bilingual groups had similar performances on all four categories of definitional quality. This implies that the BCB group, in spite of their dominance in Farsi and content-based experience in L1, did not use their academic/decontextualized Farsi repertoire in the definitional production. However, for the less-Farsi-proficient BHL group, it can be said that there were traces of transfer of knowledge and skills from English (the stronger language) to the Farsi production of definitions. An interesting point in the data that supports these findings is that for Farsi superordinate production, many among the BCB children switched to English (the weaker language), which resulted in a lower score on the scale for using translations. At the same time, they never switched to their stronger language (Farsi) when they searched for an English superordinate term that was unknown to them. This observation also implies the stronger role of L2 as the curricular language.

Discussion and conclusions

The focus of the report of this data has been on how bilingual and monolingual children demonstrated their knowledge of words/concepts in a definition task. To be specific, according to their semantic organization and development,

1. what the concept refers to (i.e., the meaning relation of superordination);
2. what the concept includes (meaning relations of coordination and subordination); and

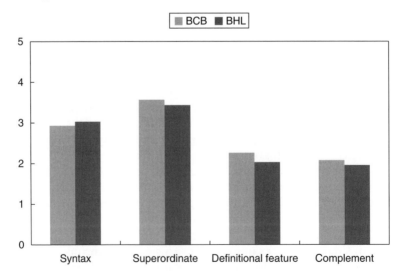

Figure 6.5 Mean average for measures of definitional quality scale in Farsi

3. how to fit all this information into the concise format of an 'X is a Y that … (relative clause)'.

The definition task also evaluated the degree of decontextualization of this knowledge on the definitional quality scale. The data were further viewed in terms of how participating children, especially bilinguals, used the analysis and control mechanisms, based on Bialystok's model, in providing definitions.

The main findings of the study show that the BHL children, those with longer residency and L2 schooling years in Canada and for whom Farsi was their less strong language, performed as well as their monolingual English-speaking peers on the English definitional measures. By the same token, in comparison to their bilingual counterparts, the BCB group, they either produced definitions with higher quality or had similar performance. The BCB group, on the other hand, with shorter residency and L2 schooling experience in Canada, showed poorer performance on the expressible measures (except for syntax) in English/L2 compared to their bilingual and monolingual peers. In fact they obtained the lowest mean scores on all four categories compared to the other two groups (Pajoohesh, 2007b) and similar Farsi/L1 production when compared to their bilingual counterparts who were less proficient in Farsi.

At this point, let me sum up the results, interpretations and issues for each language and category.

Syntax

The results of the syntax category in English showed no statistically significant difference between Farsi-speaking and MES children for the linguistic form of definitions. This supports, to some extent, the notion that bilingual children benefit from a control-of-processing mechanism when there is a great demand for linguistic control. As Bialystok (1991) posits, children dealing with two languages naturally pay more attention to language form (linguistic control) in conversation in order to decide which sources of information and which linguistic system is relevant to convey meaning. The fact that bilinguals did not outperform the MES children (and in none of the other definitional categories) suggests that there might not be any *particular* bilingual advantage for them over the monolinguals in using the control of processing mechanism. An interpretation can be that, according to Bialystok's theory, bilinguals may approach metalinguistic problems or tasks *differently* than monolinguals, but not necessarily excel in solving them (Bialystok, 2001a, 2007). On a different note, similar to Ordonez *et al.*'s Spanish/English bilingual sample (2002), it is possible that the bilinguals in my sample used a template, or followed a metalinguistic route, for their responses in the two languages. This explanation can be related to Snow's (1990) observation that non-native-speaking children need to *automate* the complex planning required for the syntax of definitions in order to speed up the process of genre identification and retrieve the linguistic form as a template. Generally speaking, although the scores of children on the syntax scale had not yet reached the highest possible rating, we can conclude that they all demonstrated a good knowledge of the syntactic requirements of definitions.

Superordinate

The superordinate knowledge is considered as an indication that the child has made the shift from the 'labelling' stage to the 'packaging/generalization' and 'network-building' stages of lexical acquisition. However, as children grow and develop in educational settings, they need to demonstrate and apply this knowledge to academic tasks; for example, in making a semantic map for the concept of 'eclipse' or 'rain forest', they need to know the superordinate terms as well as the associated meaning relations that compose the concepts. Apart from its cognitive aspect, the child needs a good 'analysis' of not only the *world* knowledge but also the *word* knowledge in order to perform well on such tasks. The findings of the quality of the superordinates children expressed in their English definitions of words/concepts show that the BCB group had a poor performance compared to the BHL group and the monolinguals. As mentioned earlier, in the main study I used definitions as a verbal task along with a recognition measure, the **word association** test, in which children were required to identify the superordinate of a target word from a list. The results of the recognition test revealed a very good performance by all three groups in *recognizing* the superordinates for the same words used in the definition task. However, as shown in Figure 6.2, that implicit knowledge was not used or *expressed* in their verbal spontaneous productions of definitions, especially for the BCB children. Other researchers have also reported similar evidence for L2 superordinate production (Ordonez *et al.*, 2002; Snow, 1990; Verhallen and Schoonen, 1993 and 1998a; Watson, 1985, Watson and Olson, 1987).

Several explanations may shed some light on this issue. Ordonez *et al.* (2002) explain that the transfer of superordinate knowledge from one language to another (Spanish to English for their sample of bilinguals) might have been due to a direct lexical transfer; the **cognates** serving as superordinate terms (vehicle/vehiculo; animal/animal; human/humano). The BCB children did not evidently have the same cognate transfer advantage as the bilingual sample in Ordonez *et al.*'s study. One explanation could be that in the case of dissimilar languages, the superordinate terms, even those already developed and acquired in L1, need to be learned again in L2 (Genesee, 1994). This task can be even more difficult for children in the case of *infrequent* superordinate terms. By examining the data, this notion might apply to *some* superordinate terms which are highly infrequent, such as 'means of transportation', or 'vehicle'. However, some superordinate terms which do not seem infrequent, were used by only a small number of children, such as 'bird' for 'duck' or 'a kind of doctor' for 'surgeon'. Another explanation comes from Pearson *et al.* (1995), suggesting that children can name some concepts in one language but not in the other, having no access to the lexical item. This is in line with the findings of Malakoff (1988) that, in solving difficult analogies, French-English bilinguals could retrieve and perform faster in one language (curricular), while they used their native language for easier tasks. In the case of superordinates, it is possible that the language imbalance (in this case for BCB group) becomes more visible with higher cognitive demand. In comparison, the BHL group clearly used a high level of the 'analysis' component to their advantage in their performance.

Complement

Formulating a restrictive complement in a word definition indicates that the child is successful in using the 'analysis of knowledge' mechanism by including the decontextualized information (Bialystok, 1991; Snow, 1990). Given the lower mean scores of the BCB group compared to the BHL and MES groups on complement category, one can conclude that the BCB group was not as successful in the 'analysis of word knowledge' mechanism identified by Bialystok (1991). Even if we assume that they have developed the knowledge of decontextualized use of language in such school tasks in their L1, their performance does not reflect a transfer of this knowledge. However, it is not clear whether it has ever been instructed or learned through L1 instruction. Another interpretation can be that these children need more length of residence and L2 instruction to perform better on academic tasks (in their L2) that are cognitively demanding. Based on findings from French-English bilinguals, Snow (1990) stated that even if children understand the demands of the genre in L1, they still need to achieve automaticity in the analysis component of giving definitions. In her study, children who had more practice in hearing and giving definitions in the curricular language, were able to produce better definitions.

Definitional feature

This category measured the knowledge of syntagmatic meaning aspects of words including information about the physical properties of an object, animal or person: size, shape, colour, composition, location, attribution and comparison. The production of definitional features in a definition relies on both processes of semantic organization and information processing. This means that children first need to distinguish between the paradigmatic and syntagmatic information and then identify and decide about the *type* of syntagmatic meaning relations to be included in restrictive clauses. To be more specific, they must analyse and control the inclusion of idiosyncratic incidental information that is not acceptable in a formal definition such as 'we grow *vegetables* in our yard', or 'my *bicycle* is a big red one'. The information in the examples is quite personally contextualized and not appropriate in a formal definition. A high number of definitional features do not qualify a definition as well formed and decontextualized.

As the findings show, there were differences only between the BCB and MES children in the number of correct definitional features provided for the target English words/concepts. It is tempting here to credit the monolinguals' advantage to their exposure to English in the home. However, this cannot explain the similar performance of BHL and MES children on the same measure, whereas BHL children reported the use of L1 as their home language. At this point, the influence of length of residence and exposure to L2 seems to account better for the quantity of syntagmatic knowledge of words. The definitional feature results can be also related to the way children revised their definitions spontaneously during the task. Based on my observations of the patterns of definitional revisions (Pajoohesh, 2007a), the BCB children were the least willing of all to revise their productions. In contrast, more revisions by the BHL and MES children led to the retrieval and production of more (correct) meaning relations by these groups.

Farsi definitions

There are several explanations for the unexpectedly similar performance of bilinguals on the definitional skills. In terms of the syntax measure, due to the similarity of form in both languages, children used the same metalinguistic route or template. Regarding the superordinate category, some BCB children switched to English, their weaker language, in trying to retrieve superordinate terms. This resulted in lower scores. On the other hand, BHL children, even without direct lexical access to these terms in Farsi (their weaker language), could fit vague superordinates into the structure and consequently scored higher. This finding implies that while, for the BCB group, L1 attrition is likely to occur, for the BHL group, maintenance of L1 is more evident. Regarding the complement and definitional feature categories, the interpretation might be that the groups used the same knowledge sources: practice effect from the English task, exposure to L1 at home or an L1-dominated social life, for both quality and quantity of the semantic content of definitions.

Alternatively, some of the L1 findings can be the result of their bilingual metalinguistic abilities, assisting them to use the same degree of control and analysis of processing on the Farsi definition task. At the same time, the findings of L1 definitions do not fulfil the prediction that BCB children would outperform the BHL group by taking advantage from their content-based schooling in Farsi. The similar performance of the BHL group might indicate that there is stronger evidence for transfer from L2 (as the stronger/curricular language) to L1 for this group than from L1 to L2 for the BCB group. At the end, some children might have benefited from a practice effect, since the Farsi task followed the English task.

Practical implications and suggestions for further research

This chapter reports that on certain measures of definitional knowledge, the bilinguals in the study had similar performance scores to the monolingual English speakers, or that the groups had a fair knowledge of a component such as syntactic form. It must be noted that the fair knowledge or similar performance does not necessarily mean that the children, regardless of bi/monolinguality, had a *high level* of the definitional knowledge (be it syntactic, paradigmatic or syntagmatic). It is said that the richness of knowledge of words/concepts or depth of lexical knowledge, develops gradually and that L2 learners are more likely to lag behind monolinguals of the same age. In this context, bilinguals and L2 learners, if biliterate, need to reach a threshold level in their L2 proficiency so that the transfer of the 'analysis skills' become possible across languages (Snow *et al.*, 1991). It would appear they would then benefit from more L2 instruction, although research to demonstrate this would be useful.

Furthermore, the role of curricular language and instruction becomes of prime importance in the development of decontextualized language skills. The findings on superordinate production in this study and other similar works (e.g., Verhallen and Schoonen, 1993, 1998a) strongly suggest that there is a need for raising 'a superordinate awareness' through focused instruction at school in subject areas such as science, maths and the social sciences. The sum of the findings presented here illustrate the fact that school-age children, regardless of their language background, need explicit instruction through techniques and guidelines that would help them notice, retrieve and apply the required information and format to academic decontextualized tasks.

Last, but not least, deep lexical knowledge as an underlying aspect of vocabulary is not always immediately perceptible and can be hidden behind other language skills and knowledge, such as the size of a learner's vocabulary, or their oral and communicative proficiency. Therefore, without accurate and sensitive measurement tools, it may not be possible in the first place, to identify L2 children's insufficient knowledge of lexical depth and, in the second place, fill the gaps in terms of instruction and teaching material. Research to develop reliable and valid methods for assessment in this area is of prime importance.

Questions for discussion

- How might word knowledge develop differently in the curricular language from the way it develops in the home language?
- Would you expect the findings of this study to be different if the participants were adults? If so, in what way?
- What sort of teaching interventions might enhance the definitional skills of bilingual children?
- From you own experience of foreign language learning, what differences have you noticed in the way underlying concepts and reference differ between language? Have the differences made the language learning task significantly more difficult?

Knowledge of Word Associations

Tess Fitzpatrick and Ian Munby

7

Introduction

Meaning	Form and meaning	R	What meaning does this word form signal?
		P	What word form can be used to express this meaning?
	Concepts and referents	R	What is included in the concept?
		P	What items can the concept refer to?
	Associations	**R**	**What others words does this word make us think of?**
		P	**What other words could we use instead of this one?**

Nation lists knowledge of associations as the third of three aspects of meaning which are 'involved in knowing a word' (Nation, 2001, p. 27). Evidence of this knowledge, he explains, lies in the answer to the question 'What other words does this make us think of?'. This apparently straightforward question forms the foundation of **word association** research, and the rubric for many word association tasks. Importantly, it does not ask what other words mean the same, or sound the same, or can be found in the same place, although the responses to the question might include words connected in all those ways and many others besides. Word association research is compatible with lexical models which use the metaphor of 'network' or 'web' to describe the organization of the mental lexicon (Aitchison, 2003, chapter 8; Wilks, 2009). The associative links elicited in word association tasks are assumed to represent the strongest and most salient links in individual lexical and semantic networks (Albrechtsen *et al.*, 2008, p. 32) and therefore allow us to identify similarities and variations in these networks between individuals. In Fodor's metaphor of 'the mental lexicon [as] a sort of connected graph, with lexical items at the nodes with paths from each item to the other' (1983, p. 80), word association analyses focus on the 'paths' chosen.

Developing word association networks

Work by Riegel and Zivian (1972), Politzer (1978), Read (1993), Söderman (1993), Sökmen (1993), Schmitt (1998) and others is indicative of a clear belief among second language researchers that **word association** patterns can inform us in some way about L2 word knowledge, and about the way in which the mental lexicon operates. However, there is some debate about how these patterns should best be interpreted. Meara (1996a) has described vocabulary knowledge as consisting of three dimensions: size (or breadth), depth and accessibility (or structure), and word association data have been used at various times to illustrate all three. Politzer (1978), for example, finds that the number of responses given to a cue word increases as an individual's proficiency increases, and so uses his data to glean information about vocabulary size. Word association tasks have also been called upon to shed light on the depth of an individual's vocabulary knowledge (see especially Read 1993 and 1997). Wolter (2001) discusses his word association study findings in terms of both breadth and depth of knowledge, but goes on to suggest that they indicate a difference in structure, too, between the L1 and L2 lexicons. This is a complex notion, though, and Wolter hypothesizes that the way in which the lexicon is structured is, in fact, a function of the quality of word knowledge.

The implication running through the research outlined above is that word association behaviour can tell us about such aspects of the lexicon as size, depth and organization. The extensive use of association tasks in investigations of the L1 in childhood (Entwisle *et al.*, 1964; Ervin, 1961) show that they can also be used to identify developmental changes in the lexicon. Perhaps it is a logical extension, then, to use the same tools to investigate the developing L2 language system, and in particular to draw inferences about proficiency levels from association behaviour.

With a few exceptions (e.g., Fitzpatrick, 2009; Riegel and Zivian, 1972; Wilks *et al.*, 2005; Wolter, 2006), word association tasks have been used in a very specific way in second language acquisition research: to investigate the proficiency of learners. This approach has grown out of the use of associations in first language acquisition research which, in turn, was developed from earlier psychology research and practice. A century ago word association tasks were used as a tool for psychiatric diagnosis, with research focusing very clearly and centrally on the way in which words are connected in prompt-response pairings, and, specifically, on the idea that some of these pairings could be considered normal, or frequent, or predictable (e.g., Kent and Rosanoff, 1910). From this developed observations about the ways in which association patterns evolve in early L1 development (see Nelson,

1977, for an overview), and the ways in which adult L1 users seem to have preferences for certain association types as illustrated by word association lists such as those in Postman and Keppel (1970). This body of research established standards of predictable word association behaviour, and led to the acceptance of certain word association behaviour 'norms'. These were, for example, that young L1 users tend to prefer **syntagmatic** responses, adult L1 users tend to prefer **paradigmatic** responses, and that, for many English stimulus words, adult L1 users will tend to give the same responses (e.g., *black > white, bread > butter*).

Given these established patterns, it seemed logical for second language researchers to look for ways of evaluating L2 proficiency by comparing response behaviour with that of the L1 user. In other words, if an L2 learner responds to the word *black* with *white*, we might consider him to be more 'native-speaker-like' than the learner who responds *yellow*. Measures of L2 proficiency not only examined the response items produced; the type of association made was also a focus for many studies. This focus was based on the hypothesis that L2 learners would mirror the observed L1 development pattern, with responses shifting from predominantly syntagmatic to predominantly paradigmatic as proficiency increased. If, as the previous chapter suggests, this knowledge is still developing among learners up to and even beyond the age of ten, then there may be good reason for expecting to see such a pattern of change in L2 knowledge and performance. Politzer (1978) was probably the first explicitly to test that hypothesis, and it is surely no coincidence that his paper appeared at a time when second language acquisition theory was heavily influenced by models of first language acquisition and development (Gass and Selinker, 2008, p. 30). As the hypothesis predicted, Politzer's subjects produced a higher proportion of paradigmatic responses in their L1 than in their L2, and he reports significant but weak correlations between the number of L2 paradigmatic responses and various measures of L2 proficiency. However, this finding was not consistent with previous research (e.g., Davis and Wertheimer, 1967), nor with many subsequent studies. Meara (1983), Söderman (1993), Fitzpatrick (2006) and Nissen and Henriksen (2006) have found that L2 users do not necessarily move systematically from syntagmatic responses to paradigmatic responses in the way that L1 users seem to. Other studies (e.g., Sökmen, 1993) found that not only response *types*, but also response *items*, did not become more native-like as proficiency increased, so that even the responses of quite proficient learners were less predictable than those of native speakers.

In many ways this is a surprising finding. Riegel and Zivian (1972) and Read, in his word associates test (e.g., 1993), suggest that **collocation** is an important determinant of response, and a tendency to define also influences association choice. We might expect that both these influences would result in increasingly native-like responses, as proficiency progresses; learners will become more aware of common collocations, and will become more and more likely to know the synonymous items needed for definition-type responses. However, the development of the L2 lexicon is susceptible to other influences too, which might cause it to deviate from L1 patterns of development. Sökmen (1993) and Politzer (1978), for example, consider association behaviour to be closely linked to classroom practice, with Politzer specifically suggesting that the use of drilling techniques in class will increase the tendency towards syntagmatic responses. A further confounding influence on association behaviour is that of cultural input. Kruse *et al.* (1987) emphasize this as problematic, and give the example of *apple > gravity* to illustrate the culture-specific nature of some responses. This suggests that observed differences in the response patterns of native and non-native speakers might have as much to do with cultural awareness as with proficiency level. In other words, the response patterns of the most proficient non-native speakers might still differ significantly from those of native speakers.

Frustratingly, it seems that association behaviour can be influenced by all and none of the above. Collocation may well be a strong factor in determining responses, but not to the degree that corpus collocation lists can accurately predict native or non-native-speaker responses. Responses often take the form of definitions, but in some cases, where a definition is almost certainly available to the task participant, it is not given. Wolter's mixed findings from his attempt to use word association responses to measure proficiency 'like those of past studies, do not support the notion that word associations in a foreign language are clearly linked to proficiency' (2002, p. 326). He adds, though, that 'the results do not seem to suggest that there is no relation at all ... I still believe that a word association/proficiency measure can be developed'.

Multiple attempts have been made, then, to measure proficiency by analysing association responses both by type (e.g., paradigmatic, syntagmatic, clang) and by item (identifying how stereotypical, or how native-like, responses are). Although none of these studies has conclusively identified a clear connection between proficiency and association behaviour, most conclude, like Wolter, that, if appropriately developed and designed, they have the potential to reveal important information about the developing lexicon. Schmitt's paper, in which he proposes an improved procedure for handling word association data, concludes 'The use of word associations holds a great deal of promise in the areas of L2 vocabulary research and measurement. This promise has been rather limited by somewhat unsophisticated methodology' (1998, p. 400). The main methodological components of a word association study are the choice of cue words, the mode of presentation and response (spoken or written, one response or multiple, etc.), and the way in which responses are analysed. The last of these is perhaps the most important in terms of experimental design, and the two main techniques for handling response data are described below.

The L2 word association studies which have their roots in the first language research of the 1960s focus on the types of association made, rather than on the specific items provided as responses. The properties of the associations can be categorized in a number of ways, but the most common categories, especially in earlier studies, are paradigmatic, syntagmatic and clang. In defining these categories we are, in fact, taken full circle back to Nation's aspects of word knowledge, which he broadly divides into form-based knowledge, meaning-based knowledge and use-based knowledge (2001, p. 27). Clang responses are form-based in that they are words with phonological similarities to the stimulus word, paradigmatic responses are meaning-based as they are from the same word class and with related meanings, and syntagmatic responses are use-based because they are commonly found alongside the stimulus word in a text. In some studies (e.g., Fitzpatrick, 2006, 2009) the link between classification methods and Nation's word knowledge framework is even more explicit, with categories and sub-categories matching exactly those in his framework, such as *collocation* and *word parts*, in addition to *form* and *meaning*.

Typically, studies compare the patterns and changes in these response types for different user groups (e.g., native or non-native speakers) and proficiency levels. Examples of this sort of study include Politzer (1978), Söderman (1993), Nissen and Henriksen (2006), Sökmen (1993), Albrechtsen *et al.* (2008) and Fitzpatrick (2006). Within this strand of study there is a degree of variation in terms of category definitions and parameters. Politzer, Söderman and Nissen and Henriksen, for example, use the standard three-way (paradigmatic, syntagmatic, clang) classification in their studies. Others, though, have criticized this system as being difficult to use and imprecise in nature. Meara, for example, notes that 'I have always found that this distinction is very difficult to work in practice, especially when you cannot refer back to the testee for elucidation' (1983, p. 30), and Wolter is similarly concerned that 'there are always some responses that may quite reasonably (and accurately) be classified in more than one category' (2001, p. 52). Maréchal addressed this problem by including a category (PS) 'to cover those cases where it is difficult to decide whether a response is paradigmatically or syntagmatically related to the stimulus' (Singleton, 1999, p. 234, citing Maréchal, 1995). Other researchers have attempted to devise more transparent and user-friendly classification systems. Sökmen (1993), for example, categorizes responses as *collocation, contrast, coordinate, synonym, classification (supra/subordinate), affective, word form*, or *nonsense*. Fitzpatrick (2006, 2007, 2009) models her system on the three-way meaning-based (≈ paradigmatic), position-based (≈ syntagmatic) and form-based (≈ clang) categories, but adds the following sub-categories: *defining synonym, specific synonym*, **lexical set**, *conceptual association, forward collocation, backward collocation, change of* **affix**, *similar in form only*. Choice of classification system is also dependent on the information the researcher wishes to elicit about the mental lexicon. Albrechtsen *et al.* (2008), for example, include a frequency dimension in their somewhat sophisticated categorization system, listing the following response types: *repetition/translation, form-related, chaining, high frequent non-canonical but semantically related, high-frequent canonical, low-frequent canonical* and *low-frequent non-canonical but semantically related* (p. 48). The *canonical* responses refer to a further dimension of response analysis, the stereotypy of response. Albrechtsen *et al.*'s study is unusual and innovative in that it combines a response-type analysis with a response-item analysis, the second main technique for analysis of association responses.

A second group of word association studies, then, focuses on the fact that certain lexical items have particularly strong connections in the lexicon, and that in many cases language users will share these strong links. Examples of such links in English would be *bread > butter, man > woman, black > white*. These studies typically use lists of native-speaker response norms – for example, the Postman and Keppel lists (1970), the Edinburgh Associative Thesaurus (Kiss *et al.*, 1973), the Florida State University norms (Nelson *et al.*, 1998) – to determine how 'native-like' is the association behaviour of learners. Studies which have compared this 'stereotypy' of responses with general measures of proficiency include Randall (1980), Schmitt (1998) and Wolter (2002), all of whom report findings which are inconclusive in themselves, but which, they claim, indicate the potential usefulness of this kind of test. Kruse *et al.*, however, finding only a weak correlation between response stereotypy and proficiency scores, conclude that 'word association tests do not show much promise for the specific role created for them in L2 research' (1987, p. 153). This paper had a rather negative effect on contemporary researchers working in this area, as Meara describes (2009, p. xii). Meara also observes, though, that with hindsight certain methodological features of the Kruse *et al.* study are revealed as problematic (perhaps this is an example of the sort of 'unsophisticated methodology' we have noted Schmitt referring to). In the remainder of this chapter, then, we review Kruse *et al.*, and report an original study which is based on theirs, but which attempts to address aspects of their methodology which may have adversely influenced their findings.

Adopting a methodology initially developed by Randall (1980), Kruse *et al.* (1987) investigate the viability of using a multiple response word association test to measure L2 learner proficiency. Their subjects were 15 third-year English majors at a Dutch university (Dutch L1) and a control group comprising seven native speakers of English. For the purposes of the study, a computer program was designed to display and collect a maximum of 12 responses to ten stimuli: *man, high, sickness, short, fruit, mutton, priest, eating, comfort and anger* (though data for *man* were erratic and therefore excluded from analysis). These stimulus words were chosen at random, one each from ten categories of stimuli of different strengths devised by Den Dulk (1985) according to the Postman and Keppel norms list (1970), and were intended to improve on the types of stimulus used by Randall. No restrictions were put on response type and informants were instructed to type in all the single English word responses they could think of, up to a maximum of 12 for each cue. The task was administered using a computer program which allowed participants 30 seconds to type their answers for each cue (excluding actual typing time).

The word association responses were scored in three different ways:

1. Number of responses. This is a straight count of the total number of responses entered for the nine cue words.

2. Non-weighted stereotypy score. This is a straight count of the total number of responses that match responses listed on the Postman and Keppel norms list (1970).

3. Weighted stereotypy. This is an order-related scoring system from 12 to 1. If a subject provides the response *low* as her first (or primary) response for the stimulus *high*, she scores 144 (12 × 12) because *low* is listed as a primary response on the norms list. If it is her secondary response then the score for this response would be 132 (11 × 12). If she provides *school* as her fifth response, her score would be 88 (8 × 11) since *school* is listed second on the norms list.

The validity of this test was assessed through a correlation analysis with two language proficiency tests: a **cloze test** and a grammar error monitoring test. The cloze was a 50-gap test where every sixth or seventh word had been deleted. To assess reliability, the non-native subjects completed the word association test on two separate occasions about two weeks apart, but the control group took the test only once. For the non-weighted stereotypy measure, native speakers scored higher than either of the non-native group scores, with 25.7 (compared to 23.4 and 22.9). For the other two measures, though, the non-native test time two mean score exceeded that of the control group, with 76.8 (tt1) and 82.8 (tt2) for the non-natives and 79.9 for the control group in the number of responses measure, and 1475 (tt1) and 1542 (tt2) for the non-natives and 1509 for the controls in weighted stereotypy (Kruse *et al.*, 1987, p. 150).

Test-retest correlations were significant, but not particularly high (.76, .66 and .55, respectively, for test measures A, B and C), indicating only a moderate consistency of performance across the two test sessions. In order to create a single set of scores for each non-native-speaker subject, the two test session scores were combined. Correlations between these scores and proficiency measures were then calculated, with all three test measures correlating significantly (p < .05) with the cloze test (number of responses r = .441; non-weighted stereotypy r = .547; weighted stereotypy r = .535), but only the number of responses measure correlating significantly with the grammar test (Kruse *et al.*, 1987, p. 151).

The authors describe their results as 'disappointing' for four reasons. First, they see no clear difference between native and non-native performance on the test. Second, correlations with the proficiency measures were low. Third, since the highest of those correlations was between the simple 'number of responses' measure and the grammar test, there would appear to be no need to measure responses for stereotypy, or quality of response in terms of native-speaker likeness. Finally, the test-retest demonstrated that test performance was not particularly consistent. They conclude by suggesting that factors other than language proficiency, perhaps the effects of cultural background knowledge and intelligence, affect association responses, and that therefore association tasks cannot be used to measure proficiency in a straightforward way.

As hinted at by Meara (2009, p. xii), it is possible that the conclusions of this study were premature and undermined by a methodology which was flawed in a number of ways. First, not only was the subject group small for a study based on quantitative analyses and aiming for results which could be generalized to a larger population, but also the non-native-speaker subjects had studied English through the Dutch education system, and had completed three years as English majors at tertiary level. They can, therefore, be assumed to be highly proficient. This fact somewhat tempers the authors' conclusion that there is no useful difference between native and non-native performance on the word association test. Kruse *et al.* show that the native speakers do, in fact, outperform non-native speakers in all three measures in test 1 (and also if the means of the two test times are used). However, they were not asked to take the test a second time, making it impossible to determine whether the higher test two scores for non-native speakers were due to increased proficiency or a test practice effect. The discriminatory power of the word association test is not, therefore, as fully explored as it would have been had the subjects represented more diverse, and less advanced, proficiency levels, and had all subjects taken the test twice.

Second, the format of the task was multiple response, with subjects instructed to provide up to 12 responses to each cue. Responses produced in this format often reveal evidence of 'chaining', where subsequent responses are prompted by previous ones, rather than by the cue word. The authors then score these multiple responses against normative data (from Postman and Keppel, 1970) drawn from a collection of single (i.e., primary) responses to 100 stimuli from 1000 subjects. Although the number of responses on the lists is large, it seems likely that these lists fail to tap more distant, or remote, associations in the native-speaker lexicon. It is precisely responses of this kind that subjects are more likely to provide when confronted by a multiple-response testing format. However, the validity of Kruse *et al.*'s test depends on the assumption that the lexical retrieval behaviours involved in producing single-word responses are identical to those involved in producing multiple responses. The apparently principled weighted stereotypy scoring system is therefore the product of an 'immediacy' score from the individual (represented by primary, secondary, tertiary etc. responses) and a 'popularity' or 'degree of commonality' score from the norms list (representing the percentage of people who produce that item as a primary response). The construct represented by these scores is in fact, then, somewhat opaque, and results in the awarding of a maximum 144 points for supplying a primary response which matches the most frequent response on the norms lists, while only giving one point for a low stereotypy 12th response.

The use of a weighted stereotypy scale (12–1) also belies the actual distribution of responses on a norms list. For example, a subject who in response to *high*, supplies *low*, *school* and *mountain* as first, second and third responses will score 144, 121, and 100 points, respectively, for each response on the weighted stereotypy scale. This does not reflect the response distribution of these items on the lists (675, 49 and 32). A further problem related to the use of these norms lists is that the norms lists were not contemporary to the study; they were published 17 years before the Kruse *et al.* study, and indeed were compiled some years before that.

A third issue with this study which requires further exploration is that results may be highly dependent on the stimuli chosen. Meara (1983) points out, for example, that (a) high-frequency words generally elicit very similar responses in both L1 and L2, (b) words such as *high* invariably produce their polar opposites such as *low* and (c) high-frequency stimuli produce high-frequency and rather obvious responses that are unlikely to discriminate between learners of different levels with any sensitivity. Five of the stimuli used by Kruse *et al.* are highly frequent (in the first 1000 of the BNC) and at least two have polar opposites, making them, according to Meara's analysis, susceptible to particular association behaviours.

Finally, the authors' interpretation of the low correlations between the proficiency measures and the word association test scores as 'disappointing' is perhaps misplaced. The three tests inevitably measure different aspects of language knowledge and use, and strong correlations should therefore not be expected. The cloze test is likely to measure more elements of linguistic competence than the grammar monitoring (Fotos, 1991), including lexical knowledge, and the finding of positive and significant correlations between it and the word association test measures could equally be interpreted as an argument for the validity of the latter.

In conclusion, the results of the study apparently question the usefulness of word association tasks in L2 research, and indeed seemed to dampen enthusiasm for L2 word association research for several years. However, the reservations listed above certainly give us cause to question the authors' interpretation of their findings and their conclusions and, importantly, there are still some useful characteristics of word association tasks revealed here, which may relate to levels of proficiency. In the final section of this chapter we will describe a study which attempts to exploit the strengths of this sort of word association test, while addressing some of its shortcomings, in order to reassess Kruse *et al.*'s rather negative conclusions.

Current research work

The study described here, then, aims to design and test an improved version of the measure used by Kruse *et al.* by devising an alternative list of prompt words, and using a different norms list for scoring. The degree to which the new version of the test can be used as an indicator of proficiency is assessed using three proficiency measures: a **cloze test,** a TOEIC test (listening and reading) and a single-word L1 > L2 translation test.

The development of cue words

As noted above, the nature of the cue words used by Kruse *et al.* mean that they provoke particular kinds of association behaviour (e.g., opposites such as *high* > *low*). One of the aims of our study was to see whether cue words which are selected in a more principled and informed way might help to differentiate more clearly between learners of different proficiency levels. Although there is some tendency for frequently occurring cue words to prompt frequent responses (Meara, 1983), we decided that it was important to select cues likely to be known by learners (as opposed to *mutton*, for example, from the original Kruse *et al.* cue list). Cue words were therefore all taken from the 0–1000 band of the BNC lists in order to maximize the likelihood that all learners, including low-level ones, were able to produce associations to all cues. Each of these 1000 words was screened to determine whether it met the following criteria:

- The word is not likely to produce a 'dominant primary' response; specifically, it does not have a polar opposite (e.g., *hot > cold*) and is not the first of a binominal pair (e.g., *food > drink*, *king > queen)*.
- The word is not likely to generate hyponyms or superordinates (in the way that, for example, *fruit* might prompt *apple*, or vice versa).
- The word is not a proper noun (some words on the 0–1000 BNC list are proper nouns such as *Germany* and *America*).
- The word is not likely to elicit proper nouns (in the way that, for example, *river* might prompt *Mississippi*, or *ocean > Pacific*).
- The word does not have a phonological equivalent in the L1 (Japanese in this case), or the potential to cause confusion because of the existence of a similar-sounding loan word.

Of the first 1000 BNC words, 125 met all the above criteria. In order to minimize the likelihood of similar responses being given for different cues, and of cue words being echoed in responses to other cues, we then discarded cue words with the same popular response, or with a popular response overlapping another cue on the list. To do this we used norms from the Edinburgh Associative Thesaurus (Kiss *et al.*, 1973). A popular response was defined as one which accounts for 6 per cent or more of the total responses. For example, *body* stimulates the response *soul* on 10 per cent of occasions, which means that the cue *heart*, producing *soul* on 7 per cent of occasions, cannot be used as a cue alongside *body*. This selection process resulted in the following list of 50 cue words:

AIR	CHOICE	GAS	MEAN	SCIENCE
BEAR	CHURCH	HAPPEN	MOVE	SET
BECOME	CLASS	HEART	NATURE	SHARE
BLOW	CROSS	HOSPITAL	PACK	SORRY
BREAK	CUT	KEEP	PART	SPELL
BOAT	DRAW	KILL	POINT	STAGE
CALL	DRESS	KIND	POLICE	SURPRISE
CASE	FAIR	LEAD	POWER	TIE
CATCH	FIT	LINE	READY	WORLD
CHANCE	FREE	MARRY	RULE	USE

Our task was now to identify the ten words from this list (to match the number of cues used by Kruse *et al.*) which had the greatest potential to discriminate between learners of different proficiency levels. To do this, we ran a preliminary **word association** test study with 82 participants (L1 Japanese). Their responses to the 50 cues were scored for stereotypy against a native-speaker norms list, and the results for each cue word were compared with their scores on a TOEIC test. The ten words with the strongest correlations with the TOEIC scores, and therefore selected for use in the main study, were *air, break, choice, church, heart, keep, lead, pack, police, sorry.*

Our purpose was now to compare the sensitivity (in terms of proficiency discrimination) of these cues with that of the original list from Kruse *et al.* In order to do this we administered a word association test, alternating cues from the two sets so that any order of presentation effect was minimized. Responses to the two cue sets were then separated out again for scoring and analysis.

Participants

The participants in the main study were 71 Japanese learners of English at tertiary level and included both first- and second-year students ranging in level from elementary to intermediate. They were presented with the **word association** test, and instructed to enter up to 12 English responses to each of the 20 stimulus words. They were requested to provide only single-word responses, to avoid using dictionaries, and to try to avoid proper nouns or chained responses (where the response is prompted by the previous response rather than by the cue). Participant scores from three additional tests were used as proxies for proficiency level. The first of these was a 50-gap **cloze test**, similar to that used by Kruse *et al.* The second was an L1 > L2 translation test adapted from Webb (2008), with 120 single-word target items, selected from three **frequency bands**. The third test comprised two parts of a TOEIC examination (listening and reading), which the students took as part of their university course requirement. These three tests were completed within a week of participants taking the word association test.

Results

Responses to the Kruse *et al.* cues and to the new set of cues were scored separately. Responses to the original set of cues were scored using the Postman and Keppel norms lists (1970), as in the original 1987 study. As detailed above, though, use of these norms is potentially problematic, both because they were compiled from a single-response task and because they are by now around 40 years old. A new norms list was therefore compiled for the new set of cues by asking 114 native speakers of English to provide five responses to each cue. The **word association** test was processed and scored in the same way as in the Kruse *et al.* study, except that the 'weighted stereotypy score' was excluded due to the problems associated with its calculation, which we discussed above.

So, for each cue and each subject, a 'number of responses' score was obtained by summing the number of responses given, and a 'stereotypy' score reflected the number of responses that matched words on the respective norms lists. The resulting scores were then compared with those from the three proficiency measures, and the correlations between these can be seen in Table 7.1.

Conclusions

Three aspects of these results are worthy of note. First, comparing the correlations between the two **word association** task measures using the Kruse *et al.* cues, and the **cloze test** with the equivalent correlations in Kruse *et al.*'s original study, we see that they are remarkably similar: .425 and .520 here, and .441 and .547 in the original study. This indicates that the relationship between performances on a cloze test and the word association test relate to each other in a broadly consistent way.

Second, all three proficiency measures correlate significantly with all word association test measures. The correlations with the stereotypy scores are consistently stronger than those with the number of response measure. This contradicts Kruse *et al.*'s rather tentative finding that 'the [number of] response tests would be the best overall predictor of proficiency' (1987, p. 150) and indicates that the quality of responses, as measured by norms lists (stereotypy), reveals more about a learner's L2 competence than the quantity of responses they produce. The implication here is that, with gains in proficiency, learners of English tend to move towards patterns of native-speaker-like organization in associative performance. The fact that there is also a positive correlation between the number of responses produced within a time limit and the proficiency measures suggests that learners become more fluent in their response behaviour with gains in L2 ability. This could be because learners at higher levels of proficiency are generally able to demonstrate more fluent, or efficient, accessibility to L2 vocabulary in their lexicons than their lower level peers. These tentative conclusions are consistent with claims that learning an L2 involves the gradual building of lexical networks that approach those of native speakers in terms of structure, dynamics and accessibility.

Table 7.1 Correlations between the word association test scores and the proficiency measures, for the Kruse *et al.* cues and norms, and the Fitzpatrick and Munby cues and norms

Cues and norms	Kruse et al.	Fitzpatrick and Munby	Kruse et al.	Fitzpatrick and Munby
Measures	A	A	B	B
Cloze	.425*	.310*	.520*	.662*
Webb	.533*	.394*	.606*	.676*
TOEIC	.459*	.371*	.534*	.700*

*$p < 0.01$.
Note: A = number of response measure, B = stereotypy measure.

The main aim of this study, though, was to develop a version of the test presented by Kruse *et al.* which could better differentiate between learners at different levels of proficiency. The correlations in the two stereotypy columns on the right of Table 7.1 indicate that by using a specifically selected set of cues, and a specifically compiled norms list, the test can indeed be improved to better reflect proficiency, whether the latter be measured in terms of vocabulary knowledge, listening/reading skills, or through a cloze test.

Practical implications and suggestions for further research

Taken together, the Kruse *et al.* study and the adaptation of it we present here illustrate well both the promise and the pitfalls of L2 **word association** research. We opened this chapter with the premise that knowledge of associations is a component of word knowledge, and the significant correlations we find between stereotypy of response and proficiency level support this and encourage us to echo Schmitt's optimism about the 'promise' of such studies (1998, p. 400). However, the differences between test results using the same cues and norms lists as Kruse *et al.*, and results using cues and norms lists compiled in a more principled and considered way, warn us of the potential pitfalls of such research. Schmitt goes on to say that the 'promise has been rather limited by somewhat unsophisticated methodology' (1998, p. 400). This perhaps understates precisely how sophisticated, careful and theory-driven the methodology for word association studies must be; cue words, task type and the compilation and application of norms lists can, as we have seen, all have a powerful influence on scores and findings. Nevertheless, by tweaking the design of the study by Kruse *et al.*, which had rejected word associations as unpromising to L2 research, we have, we hope, demonstrated that this strand of research is worthy of further investigation.

By understanding the nature of associational links we can identify their role in lexical processing and lexical retrieval. In this chapter we have investigated these links in the context of second language proficiency. This kind of study, though, helps us to hone methods and theoretical frameworks which can be applied to other conditions in which lexical retrieval is an issue, such as dementia, aphasia and even healthy ageing. Meara has commented that dimensions of word knowledge are 'not properties attached to individual lexical items: rather they are properties of the lexicon considered as a whole' (1996a, p. 37); this is perhaps most true of the dimension 'associative knowledge', and future research would benefit from using it to formulate a holistic representation of individual lexicons.

Questions for discussion

- Why might language learners develop networks of L2 **word associations** which are a) different from other language learners; and b) different from native speakers?

- Is it beneficial to target the building of word association networks in teaching activities? How might this be done?
- To what extent can word association responses be used as objective measures of L2 proficiency?
- How much word association information do you think can be usefully transferred from one language to another?
- Is word association information in a foreign language something you think could be usefully taught in class? If you wanted to do this, how would you set about it?

Acknowledgement

The authors are grateful to Paul Meara for designing software specifically to gather data for the **word association** study presented in this chapter.

Knowledge of Grammatical Use

Jeanine Treffers-Daller and Vivienne Rogers

8

Introduction

Use	Grammatical functions	R	In what patterns does the word occur?
		P	In what patterns must we use this word?
	Collocations	R	What words or types of word occur with this one?
		P	What words or types of words must we use with this one?
	Constraints on use	R	Where, when and how often would we meet this word?
		P	Where, when and how often can we use this word?

The patterns in which a word occurs form an integral part of what we know about a particular word, and it is not surprising that an important part of learning a language therefore involves learning about the patterns in that language. As has been known for a long time, children often use chunks such as *What do you want?* before being able to use grammatical structures which allow for the productive use of 'wh-' questions (Nelson, 1973, cited in Foster-Cohen, 1999, p. 130). In L2 acquisition, learning of unanalysed chunks is a common strategy of learners too, in that learners use the memory-based chunks to develop productive structures at a later stage (Skehan, 2003; Wray, 2002). L2 learners also transfer lexical patterns, such as sub-categorization frames, from their L1 to their L2 (Adjémian, 1983). Learners often assume that the patterns associated with a particular word from their L1 can be transferred to their second language, but this is clearly not always possible. Learners of French with English as their first language often assume, for example, that it is possible to say *entrer la pièce* 'to enter the room', instead of *entrer dans la pièce*, because in English a prepositional phrase is not part of the sub-categorization frame of *enter*. In standard French, however, *entrer* needs to be accompanied by the preposition *dans*, 'in' (see also Treffers-Daller and Tidball in press). Thus, part of the learning burden of a word – that is 'the amount of effort required to learn a word' (Nation, 2001, p. 7) – is to discover in which patterns it can be used and how these patterns differ from the patterns associated with the translation equivalent in L1.

The focus in the current chapter will be on a particular kind of patterns, namely grammatical use patterns. We will not deal with lexical collocations, as these are examined in Chapter 9. For the purposes of the current chapter we will use the term *grammatical use patterns* as a cover term for different types of grammatical knowledge that are associated with words. First of all, this refers to knowing about the grammatical **collocations** (Granger and Paquot, 2008) or colligations (Firth, 1957 [1968]; Hoey, 2005; Hunston, 2001; Sinclair, 1998), which can be formed with this word. As Carter (1998) points out, knowledge of the word *consent* involves not only having information about its lexical collocates, such as *mutual* or *common*, but also lexicogrammatical information: the noun *consent* occurs in prepositional phrases headed by the preposition *by* as in *by mutual consent*, and the verb *consent* belongs to a category of verbs which are followed by the preposition *to*, as in *he finally consented to go*, but cannot be used in combination with the *–ing* construction as in **he consented going*. Put differently, the verb *consent* forms a colligation with the complement construction *to + infinitive* but not with the *–ing* construction. But, in addition, it involves, as Richards (1976, p. 80) puts it, 'knowing a word means knowing the syntactic behaviour associated with that word'. Speakers of English know, for example, that *give* is normally used transitively and that the object of the act of giving is normally passed on to a receiver. More complex syntactic patterns are also part of the knowledge speakers have about *give*: they know that it is possible to move the receiver to different places in the sentence, so that *John gave a book to Mary* can also be expressed as *John gave Mary a book*.

The intention in this chapter is to illustrate just how many and how complex some of these patterns of use can be, and to consider what we know about the way these patterns of use are learned. While words from many different word classes occur in patterns, verb patterns have been chosen as the focus point here as verbs take arguments and are therefore involved in very complex patterns (Levin, 1993, p. 2). The focus will be on a specific group of verbs, namely motion verbs and, in particular, English *run* and French *courir*. These have been studied from a number of perspectives but less often from the perspective of the colligational patterns that they form part of. We believe a study of the colligations associated with motion verbs and a study of the grammatical properties of such verbs, based on the list of properties given in Levin (1993), may throw new light on the issue of the learnability of motion event expressions, which is widely discussed in the SLA literature (e.g., Inagaki, 2001). At the end of the chapter an example of recent research work in this field will be presented before final consideration is given to how this information might impact on classroom teaching and on the direction of future research.

Word patterns and use

The emergence of interest in lexical patterns

At least since the middle of the nineteenth century, researchers have been aware of the existence of fixed patterns in the lexicon. Hughlings Jackons (1866, cited in Wray, 2002, p. 7), for example, noticed that his aphasic patients were able to use rhymes, prayers and routine greetings but could not construct new sentences from scratch. Another early observer of the importance of lexical patterns is Bloomfield (1933), who notes that 'it is impossible to distinguish consistently, on the one hand, between phrases and words and, on the other hand, between words and bound forms' and points out that 'many words lie on the border' (pp. 179–80). The importance of patterns is also flagged up by Firth (1957 [1968], p. 179), who expressed this saying 'you shall know a word by the company it keeps!'. This is raised too by Hornby (1954), who identified 25 verb patterns and a few noun patterns and adjective patterns. In many ways, this study paved the way for later studies of patterns in language, such as that of Hunston and Francis (2000), who were able to analyse patterns in large electronic **corpora** which were not available at the time Hornby published his work.

Due to the rising popularity of generative or universal grammar (Chomsky, 1965), which focused almost exclusively on the creative power of syntax, at the beginning of the 1960s many researchers lost interest in fixed expressions and the ways in which these need to be accounted for in the lexicon. As Sinclair (2004, p. 25) puts it 'grammars are always given priority and grammars barricade themselves against the individual patterns of words'. This certainly applies to early generative models of grammar, in which there was a strict separation between syntax and lexicon; the latter was seen as a repository of idiosyncrasies which were largely irrelevant to the pursuit of abstract universal syntactic principles. In more recent versions of the theory (minimalism, see Chomsky, 1995), however, the number of syntactic rules has decreased to two or possibly three, which are located in the lexicon and operate on features specified on individual lexical items in the lexicon or syntacticon (Emonds, 2002). The role of syntax has become one of checking these features.

The minimalist view of the lexicon attributes a much more important role to the lexicon that previous versions of generative grammar. In this respect, it approaches the view of the lexicon, which emerges from Halliday's (1994) systemic functional grammar. Halliday does not assume the lexicon and the grammar can be separated. He uses the term *lexicogrammar* to cover both the syntactic and the lexical resources that are need to form meaning through language. To Halliday (*ibid.*, 15), 'grammar and vocabulary are merely different ends of the same continuum – they are the same phenomenon as seen from opposite perspectives'. According to Hunston and Francis (2000, p. 28), however, in Halliday's model single words rather than chunks or (partly) fixed phrases are generally the endpoint of the grammatical choices a speaker makes. Word patterns such as colligations are, therefore, not explicitly taken into account in lexicogrammar.

Strong support for the view that language knowledge cannot be strictly divided into lexical and grammatical knowledge comes from computational analyses of electronic text corpora. When large corpora became available for analysis in the 1990s, researchers revealed that patterns are indeed pervasive in all kinds of spoken and written language, and play a key role in the way we learn and process language (Nattinger and DeCarrico, 1992, p. 47). Most notably, on the basis of his analyses of large corpora, Sinclair (1991, p. 137) reaches the conclusion that 'when we have thoroughly pursued the patterns of co-occurrences of linguistic choices there will be little or no need for a separate or residual grammar or lexicon'.

Nattinger and DeCarrico (1992, p. 23) also draw attention to the importance of patterns and demonstrate that patterned phrases such as *the _____er the _____er* can be filled in with a wide variety of structures of different levels of complexity, such as *the earlier the better* or *the longer you wait, the sleepier you get*. Thus, patterned phrases are best seen as basic, intermediary units between the levels of lexis and grammar. Hunston and Francis (2000, p. 259) go even further and believe the omnipresence of patterns ultimately leads us to challenge many traditional assumptions in linguistic theory, such as assumptions about the existence of word classes and constituent units, because words can be shown to belong to many different word classes, and be seen to behave differently across a range of contexts. In addition, the units in which words are used often do not correspond to traditional constituents such as noun phrases (NPs) or verb phrases (VPs), but are chunks which cut across different constituent boundaries, as in *Can I have a* or *I thought that was* (Granger and Paquot, 2008). Hunston and Francis (2000, p. 14) even claim that corpus data reveal that the distinction between free phrases and non-free phrases needs to be abandoned because 'all language is patterned, ... [and] there is no such thing as a free phrase'. Finally, the analysis of lexical patterns shows us that words do not have fixed meanings: the meaning of an individual word can only be understood by looking at its behaviour in different contexts.

The increasingly sophisticated software that has been made available to study corpora has contributed, no doubt, to the fact that the study of lexical patterns, sometimes called phraseology, has been increasingly prominent since the 1990s. In fact, it is no longer the exclusive domain of linguistics in the narrow sense. The analysis of lexical patterns is equally important in natural language processing, machine translation and forensic science, to name but a few of the most obvious applications. Clearly much of this would not have been possible without the important contributions linguists have made to the ongoing debates as they have provided key insights in the form of typologies of lexical patterns and detailed analyses of their properties. However, what has not emerged from this variety of analysis is a set of descriptors of patterns of use which can be applied to language learners and users, and which can be used to explain, for example, the process of acquisition of these properties of word knowledge. Much may depend on the differences in pattern which language uses.

Describing patterns of use

Verbal patterns associated with run and courir

To illustrate some of the complexity and difficulty in describing the patterns of use, in this section we will present the results of an analysis of the verbal patterns found for one highly frequent manner of motion verb, namely *to run* and its French translation equivalent *courir*. These two verbs are chosen because they are very frequent in both languages and often referred to in the literature, which makes it possible to build on insights from other researchers about the semantic properties and the syntactic behaviour of these verbs. The main question we will try to answer is whether the analyses of *run* and *courir*, which are based on the different approaches sketched above, lead to the same insights into colligations or whether very different facts emerge from each analysis. The approach which will be illustrated here is the one which starts with grammatical patterns, as exemplified in the work of Firth (1957 [1968]) and Hunston and Francis (2000).

The patterns that will be investigated here represent a small sub-section of the patterns listed by Hunston and Francis (2000), namely intransitive patterns, transitive patterns (*V n*), *V prep/adv*, *V prep* and *V adv*. We have also included the causative patterns *let n V (pp) (adv)* and *make n V (pp) (adv)*, which are not listed in Hunston and Francis, but do occur in the data.

The **corpora** that are used for this study are the web-based French corpus on Sketchengine (126,850,281 words), and the BNC (112,181,850 words). Both these CORPORA were accessed through the Sketchengine website (http://the.sketchengine.co.uk/).

First of all, we have looked at the overall frequency of both verbs in the French and the English corpora by searching the verb **lemmas** in both corpora. Searching for verb lemmas makes it possible to exclude homographs such as French *court*, which can either be the third-person singular form of *courir*, or an adjective which means 'short'. For English, choosing the verb lemma made it possible to avoid nominal uses of *run*, as in *today's run was particularly difficult*. As can be seen in Table 8.1, the verb *run* is almost four times as frequent as the verb *courir*, which immediately raises the question whether particular uses of the verb run are more common in either language.

It is interesting to note that only a small proportion of the uses of *courir* and *run* involve literal meanings of these verbs. In total, 26 per cent of the uses of *run* and 29 per cent of the uses of *courir* involve a classic motion event in

Table 8.1   Frequency of the verbs *courir* and *run* in Sketchengine/BNC

	Raw frequency of each verb	*Frequency per 10,000 words in corpus*
courir	11,866	0.94
run	38,882	3.47

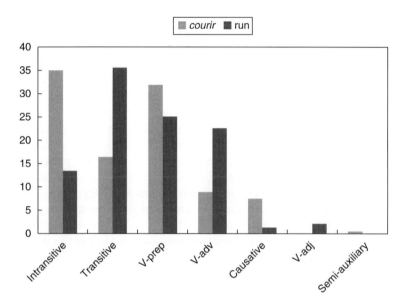

Figure 8.1   Patterns found with the verbs *courir* and *run*

which an animate figure moves through space, using its legs to move forward. All other cases consist of figurative and metaphorical uses of these verbs. The differences in the distribution of literal and figurative meanings of the verbs in the two languages are not statistically significant.

An analysis of the verbal patterns associated with courir *and* run

From the concordance lists for *run* and *courir* that were created with Sketch-engine, a random sample of 250 occurrences of both verbs for has been drawn with the help of the Sketchengine software. The different uses of *courir* and *run* were subsequently categorized in the following seven main groups, five of which are based on Hunston and Francis (2000). Usages that are listed under e) and f) emerged as separate minor patterns in the data that could not be grouped with the others. An overview of the different patterns found in English and French is given in Figure 8.1.

a) **Intransitive uses** of the verbs without any complements, as in *s/he runs* or *il/ elle court*. Any temporal adjuncts were ignored as they are not part of the complementation pattern of the verbs (see Hunston and Francis, 2000, p. 49).

b) **V prep**, as in *courir après qn* 'to chase after someone' or *to run for his life*. Locative adjuncts are included in this category.

c) **V adv/particle**, as in *courir vite* 'to run fast'; or particle usages in English, such as *run out/off/up* etc.

d) **V n**, that is **transitive uses**, as in *courir le cerf* 'to hunt the stag' or to *run a show* (but note that *courir* and *run* have very different meanings here).

e) **Causative uses** with *faire* 'to do' and *laisser* 'to let' (Faire/laisser n V and Make/let n V), as in *faire courir un bruit* 'to spread a rumour', or *make him run to win at the games*.

f) **Semi-auxiliary uses** of *courir*, as in *courir l'appeler* 'to go and call him straightaway' (see also http://atilf.atilf.fr/tlf.htm).

g) **V adj**, as in *still waters run deep*.

As can be seen in Figure 8.1, there are clear differences between the patterns in which *courir* and *run* are used. The main differences in the patterns associated with both verbs, namely between the use of **transitive patterns** and **V adv** patterns will be discussed below. Figure 8.1 reveals that some patterns are unique to either English or French: pattern f) **semi-auxiliary uses** of *courir*, is only attested in French, not in English. The English pattern which is closest to pattern f) is Hunston and Francis's (2000, p. 52) **V to- inf** pattern, as in *John began to laugh*. There are a few examples of that kind in the BNC which involve the verb *run*, cf. (1).

(1)   Kathleen called for help and *ran to meet* him.

There is also one pattern which is only attested in English, namely pattern g) **V adj**, as in *public expectations ran high* or *until the water runs clear*. In the next two sections, two of the differences between the patterns will be discussed, namely the differences in the **transitive patterns** and the differences in the **V adv** pattern.

Differences in transitive patterns

In English the transitive uses form the largest group, while in French the intransitive uses are most frequent. These differences are statistically significant $(X^2(1) = 33.2, p < .001)$. The transitive uses include a few causatives in both languages, as in (2) and (3).

(2)   Le dauphin savait tout juste monter à cheval que déjà *il courait le cerf* sur une petite haquenée.
      [As soon as the heir had learned to ride a horse, he hunted stag on a small palfrey.]

(3)   They never poached deer, or cut fences, or ran their dogs near in-lamb ewes.

Syntactic causatives with *faire* or *laisser* are recorded as a separate category, namely pattern e). As can be seen in Figure 8.1, syntactic causatives with *make* or *let* are much less frequent in the English sample.

According to the *Oxford English Dictionary* (*OED*), an intransitive (*rinnen*) and a weak transitive form (*rennen*) existed already in Old English, though the latter only occurred in the metathetic form *ærnen* or *earnan*, which usually had the meaning 'to ride'. Transitive usages of *courir* have been found from the early thirteenth century onwards (*Trésor de la Langue Française Informatisé*). Thus, there is evidence of early transitive usages of both verbs, but Table 8.2 shows that transitive uses are much more common in English than in French. This could be related to negative attitudes towards the alternate use of a verb in transitive or intransitive form. According to Rothemberg (1974, p. 134), Vaugelas condemned, for example, transitive uses of motion verbs such as *sortir* as in *sortir un chien* 'walk the dog'. We do not know whether Vaugelas also disapproved of transitive uses of manner of motion verbs such as *courir*, so further evidence regarding the attitudes towards such uses would need to be collected.

The meanings that are expressed in the transitive constructions in French and English overlap partially, but there are also some interesting differences. In the French sample, the transitive expressions fall into three main semantic groups, where *courir* is used in combination with:

a) nouns referring to a location or a distance, as in *courir les rues/le monde/la ville* 'to roam the world/the city'; *courir un kilomètre* 'run a kilometre';
b) nouns referring to dangers, risks or adventures: *courir un danger/risque* 'run a risk', *courir les aventures* 'to seek adventure';
c) nouns referring to animate beings which are the objects of a hunt: *courir le cerf* 'hunt deer', *courir les filles* 'chase the girls'.

Some of the meanings listed above under a) and b) for French are found in English too. Thus, we find, for example, *run a mile* and *run a risk*, but these usages are much less common in the English sample. In English we can also say *running the city*, but it does not mean 'to roam', which is the attested meaning in French, but 'to be responsible for organizing the city'. In fact, this meaning of *run* is the most frequent one in the current sample. *Run* is used most frequently in combination with nouns referring to events, organizations, pieces of equipment etc., where *run* means 'direct, conduct, look after, manage, control', as in *running an event, a business, a home, a car, a film*, etc., which originates in American English according to the *OED*. The list of nouns that can be used in this construction appears to be unlimited. This meaning is not attested for the French translation equivalent: constructions such as *courir une enterprise/un évènement/une voiture* etc. are not found in the French Sketchengine corpus at all.

Finally, as we can see in (4), some transitive usages of *run* undergo the dative alternation (see also Dang *et al.*, 1998). This is not possible for all transitive uses of *run*, as far as we have been able to establish, as the dative alternation is not grammatical in (5) and (6).

(4a)   John runs a bath for Mary/her
(4b)   John runs Mary/her a bath

(5a)   John runs a marathon for Barnardo's/them
(5b)   *John runs Barnardo's/them a marathon

(6a)   John runs the shop for Bill/him
(6b)   *John runs Bill/him the shop

Differences in V adv patterns

The differences in usage of the V adv pattern are also statistically significant (X^2 (1) = 15.6, p < .001). In English V + adv/particles are more frequent than in French, and this structural difference is also reflected in the differences in usages of *run* and *courir*: *run* can form phrasal verb combinations with a wide range of particles and locative adverbs, as is common in S-languages but not in V-languages (Talmy, 1985). The French locative adverbs which are combined with *courir* include *dessus, partout* and *non loin de X*, but the choice of locative adverbs that form colligations with *run* in English is much wider: *aground, (a)round, away, back(wards), down, forward, in, out, over, off, swiftly, through, up* and *upstairs*.

It is also interesting to look at the use of manner adjuncts with *courir* and *run*. The patterns found include: *(le plus) vite (possible) 'as fast as possible', à toute bride* 'flat out', *à son rhythme* 'at his/her speed' and *de toutes ses jambes* 'as fast as possible'. The English manner adjuncts are very similar and not much more diverse. The manner adverbs which pattern with *run* include *reasonably well, hard, a bit faster, smoothly, like hell*. The fact that there is about an equal number of manner adverbs in combination with *courir* and *run* is somewhat surprising, given the fact that S-languages are more likely to reinforce manner verbs with manner adverbs than V-languages (Slobin, 2004).

Differences in lexical **priming**

The differences in patterns can be interpreted in Hoey's (2005) framework as differences in lexical priming. Thus, we could say that *run* is typically primed to occur in transitive constructions, and also, but to a lesser extent, in constructions with prepositions and adverbs, whilst *courir* is primed to occur in intransitive constructions, with prepositional and transitive constructions in second and third place. *Run* is also typically primed to colligate negatively with intransitive or causative constructions with *make* or *do*, at least much more negatively than *courir* in causative or intransitive constructions. Conversely, *courir* is negatively primed to occur in V **adj** constructions.

According to Hoey (2005), the position a word occupies in a sentence is part of the colligational preferences for that word. We therefore investigated whether *run* and *courir* occupy different positions in the sentence. As French is a V-language and English an S-language (Talmy, 1985, 2000), we might expect *run* to occupy the main verb slot more often than *courir*, while *courir* could be primed to occur in the adjunct position more frequently than *run*. In order to find out whether the verbs are primed in this way, welooked at the literal uses of both verbs only, as only these involve real motion events, in contrast to the figurative uses which often involve metaphorical uses of the verbs. Both verbs turn out to be used mainly in the main verb slot of sentences. In fact, there are no occurrences of *en courant* at all in the sample, and only seven in the entire Sketchengine database. Similar results were obtained in a picture elicitation task carried out by native speakers of French, which revealed that only four out of 23 informants used the expression *en courant* as an adjunct in combination with a path verb (Treffers-Daller and Tidball in press). It was quite surprising to discover that the English translation equivalent *while/whilst running* is more frequent than *en courant*. There are 39 occurrences of *while running* and 12 of *whilst running* in the BNC, which is the opposite of what one would have expected. Interestingly, we found one example of a typical satellite-framed pattern in the French sample. In (7), the main verb slot is occupied by the manner of motion verb *courir*, whilst the adjunct contains the path verb *entrer*.

(7) J'ai *couru en rentrant* chez moi
    [I ran whilst returning home.]

Of course, (7) does not invalidate the typology proposed, because it is much less common in French than in English, but it illustrates the point made by Beavers *et al.* (2009), that most languages straddle the boundaries between the verb-framed and satellite-framed categories distinguished by Talmy (1985, 2000).

It appears to us that these three approaches lead to rather different results, although there are some overlaps as well. The list of verbal patterns offered by Hunston and Francis (2000) made it possible to categorize almost all the verbal patterns associated with *run* and *courir*. It is remarkable that, although Hunston and Francis's list was not developed for French, most of the patterns associated with *courir* were covered by the patterns the authors listed. Only the semi-auxiliary uses of *courir* (which is a pattern that does not exist for English) could not be described with the help of Hunston and Francis's list. The English data analysed in this paper also contained one very minor pattern that was absent from the list, namely the syntactic causative constructions **let n V (pp) (adv)** and **make n V (pp) (adv)**. The French translation equivalent of this pattern (*faire/laisser* **nV (pp) (adv)**) was much more frequent.

The patterns listed in Hunston and Francis (2000) were also helpful in revealing the similarities and differences in the colligational patterns associated with both verbs. The main differences found include the fact that transitive uses are most common for English *run*, whilst intransitive uses are most common for *courir*. The high frequency **of V adv** patterns in English, by comparison with French, was expected, given the fact that *run* can form phrasal verbs with a wide range of different particles, which is not common in French. With respect to the meanings of the patterns, an interesting difference between English and French emerged: *courir* is not used with the meaning 'to manage' in French. Thus, *courir la ville* can be used to mean 'roam the city', but does not mean 'run the city'. In carrying out a cross-linguistic comparison of patterns, it is therefore important not to assume that the same kinds of meaning are automatically to be attributed to patterns which on the surface appear to be structurally similar in both languages. The transitive verb patterns, for example, have at least partly different meanings in both languages. The meaning extensions of *run* provide some evidence for Slobin's (2004) claim that languages such as English, which possess a fine-grained manner of motion lexicon, will often continue to innovate in this domain, which leads to a range of extended and metaphorical uses.

The results obtained with Hunston and Francis's approach can be interpreted in Hoey's framework as evidence that *run* is primed to occur in transitive patterns, whilst *courir* is primed to occur in intransitive constructions. Given the fact that French is a verb-framed language (Talmy, 1985, 2000), one might have expected *courir* to occur less often in the main verb position and more often in adjuncts than *run*, but that turned out not to be the case. Examples of satellite-framed constructions in French were also found in the data. While this does not invalidate the typology proposed by Talmy (1985, 2000), the facts do illustrate the point made by Beavers *et al.* (2009) that in most languages both satellite-framed and verb-framed patterns are available.

The results illustrate that learning verbal patterns is a considerable task for L2 learners. It is very important for learners to be aware of the patterns in which a word occurs, and results from corpus-linguistic analyses can obviously help to establish which patterns need to be taught and learned. If there are large differences between the patterns associated with a particular word in a learner's first and second language, the learning burden of that word will be rather heavy for that learner.

The acquisition of syntax and grammatical use patterns

The way learners, of both first and second languages, acquire grammatical use patterns is not easy to describe succinctly and there is no concise summary of how this process occurs. As research has concentrated more on the analysis of creative syntax than on fixed grammatical patterns, we know more about the ways in which learners acquire the former than the latter. The research we have suggests that there can be distinct stages in the development of syntax.

Bartning and Schlyter (2004) identified the following stages of development for Swedish learners of French. They argue that transfer from the L1 is minimal and that these apply to all L2 learners of French.

Stage 1 – *initial*
Utterances mainly made up from nouns. Verbs are either in default forms or
    non-finite. There is no distinction between person forms (e.g., *je* vs *tu*).

Negation is formed using *non* + noun (e.g., *non lit*). Some use of the connectors *et*, *mais* and *puis*.

Stage 2 – *post-initial*

Very variable production but connectors like *quand* and *parce que* start to appear. Preverbal negation using *ne* and *pas* also emerges. The use of non-finite verbs in finite contexts continues, but the number of finite verbs increases.

Stage 3 – *intermédiaire*

Production becomes more systematic but still in very simple sentences. Post-verbal negation starts to emerge. Use of the past tense starts to emerge and object pronouns start to appear pre-verbally. Coordination and subordination of clauses appears.

Stage 4 – *avancé bas*

Structures start to become more complex with the use of auxiliaries, conditionals and some subjunctives. Negation is also expressed with *rien*, *jamais* and *plus*. Non-finite verbs in finite contexts are rarely found. The use of gender remains problematic, as does the use of object pronouns.

Stage 5 – *avancé moyen*

There is development in the use of inflectional morphology. The use of the subjunctive is more productive. There remain issues with gender agreement and concord. There remain some issues with third-person plural marking. The use of the gerund and *dont* emerge.

Stage 6 – *avancé supérieur*

The use of inflectional morphology has stabilized. *Dont* and *enfin* are used productively. A wide range of grammatical structures are used at near=native levels.

While these hierarchies provide important insights into the order in which syntactic structures are acquired, the key question is, of course, what drives the transition from one stage to the next. For L1 acquisition, according to Bates and Goodman (1997), it is clear that the emergence of grammar is highly dependent upon vocabulary size. Thus, for example, the best predictor of the grammatical structures a child can produce at 28 months is total vocabulary size at 20 months (*ibid.*, 514). These results, and those of Marchman *et al.* (2004), who studied the relationships between vocabulary and grammar in bilingual children, confirm that the lexicon and the grammar are not completely separate modules in the minds of speakers. Lexicalist approaches of language acquisition, which emphasize the strong interdependency of grammar and lexicon, are better able to explain these findings than theoretical approaches, which see these as separate modules.

Much less is known about the extent to which vocabulary size can predict grammatical development in L2 acquisition, although cross-sectional studies often reveal strong correlations between measures of vocabulary knowledge and measures of grammar (Droop and Verhoeven, 2003; Nassaji, 2003). In the following section we hope to shed more light on this issue by reviewing some recent work in this field, particularly in relation to French.

Current research work

Investigating the link between syntax and vocabulary

Recent research by David *et al.* (2009) investigated the possible link between syntax and vocabulary in second language acquisition from a generative (or universal grammar) perspective among learners of French as a foreign language in UK schools. In relation to this chapter two possible links were investigated:

1. between the development of the lexicon and grammatical gender on nouns,
2. between the development of the lexicon and the development of verbal projections.

The participants

Three groups of instructed English-speaking learners of French after one, three and five years of instruction were tested. The learners were therefore young adolescents who had received approximately 100 hours of instruction after one year of study, 240 hours after three years and a maximum of 525 hours after five years of study. There were 20 students in each group.

The task

The learners were tested on the acquisition of grammatical gender (DP), verbs (VP), the use of finite verbs with subject clitics (IP), embedded clauses (CP) and lexical density through a semi-elicited oral production task. In the first part of the task the learners were shown stimulus photographs showing people engaged in age-appropriate activities (the routines of daily life, pets, holidays etc.). In the second part of the task, the learners were questioned by researchers on a similar range of topics.

Data analysis

The oral conversations were transcribed using CHILDES guidelines in CHAT.

Results

David *et al.*, first, found a significant positive correlation between mean length of utterance (MLU) and lexical density as measured by Guirard (Pearson correlation, $r = .619$, $N = 60$, $p < 0.01$). Second, they found no significant development between the groups in the acquisition of gender as the learners used very few different nouns. There was, therefore, no correlation with lexical density. There was also no correlation found between the use of subject clitics with finite verbs and vocabulary. However, significant correlations between lexical density and the number of verbless utterances ($r = -.258$, $N = 60$, $p = 0.46$) – that is, the larger the lexical density, the fewer verbless utterances were found and between lexical density and the production of embedded clauses (Pearson correlation, $r = .633$, $N = 60$, $p < .001$) were found. The authors suggest that learners increase their syntactic complexity in relation to their vocabulary acquisition; however, the authors do not believe this extends to abstract syntactic (or uninterpretable) features (i.e., DP and IP).

Further investigation of the vocabulary and syntax link

However, in a new analysis of data from Rogers (2009), Rogers *et al.* (in preparation) used a more detailed measure of IP to examine the link between vocabulary and syntax. In David *et al.* (2009) the measure of the projection of IP was not satisfactory as it relied on a theory internal analysis of syntax to provide evidence of IP. Rogers (in preparation) takes a more theory external approach by examining the acquisition of IP in terms of word order – that is, by examining the placement of adverbs, object clitics and negation, it is possible to determine whether IP is projected as these items cannot be accommodated under a VP-only analysis. The differences in word order are shown in Table 8.2 below. This clearly shows that the word order in French is not possible in English and vice versa.

Participants

Five groups of 15 instructed English learners of French were tested through two semi-elicited oral production tasks. Ten native French speakers were also tested. The L2 participants are summarized in Table 8.3.

Task

Learners were tested through two semi-elicited oral production tasks. The first consisted of a set of cards with picture. Fifteen elicited negation by including a

Table 8.2 Word order differences between French and English

	French	English
Negation	Je ne regarde pas la télé	I don't watch TV
	* I watch not the TV	* Je (ne) pas regarde la télé
Adverbs	Je regarde souvent la télé	I often watch TV
	* I watch often the TV	*Je souvent regarde la télé
Object clitics	Je la regarde	I watch it
	*I it watch	*Je regarde la

Table 8.3   Summary of participants

Group	Age	Hours of instruction	Years learning French
Beginner	12–13	75–94.5	1
Low-intermediate	15–16	275–345	4
Upper-intermediate	17–18	521–708	6
Low-advanced	19–31	2nd year university	8
Upper-advanced	21–24	4th year university	10 + 6 months in a French-speaking country

Table 8.4   Calculations of overall measure of verb movement

Year	N	Median	Minimum	Maximum	Sum
Beginner	15	1	0	4	23
Low-intermediate	15	2	0	20	83
High-intermediate	15	30	4	41	408
Low-advanced	15	35	15	45	521
High-advanced	15	39	14	43	531
NS	10	47	26	51	436

cross through the picture and 15 elicited sentences with adverbs, as an adverb was included on the card and participants were asked to include the word in their utterance. There were also five distracters, which included neither a cross nor a word. The second task consisted of the participants being shown a picture book and being told a story about the pictures. At various points, the learners were asked questions about what was happening in the pictures. Fifteen of these questions targeted the use of object clitic pronouns. There were also seven distractors. In order to include the same evidence for IP as David *et al.* (2009), Rogers also analysed the object clitic task for the use of subject clitics with finite verbs, as for each of the questions posed to the participants, a subject clitic response was most felicitous. X-Lex was used as a measure of **receptive vocabulary** and students were given a paper version and asked to tick if they knew the word or not. X-Lex is a measure of receptive vocabulary knowledge.

Results

Rogers calculated an overall measure of verb movement, which contained the percentage of target-like verb placement in 15 contexts for each of the four structures providing evidence of the acquisition of verb movement in French. This is shown in Table 8.4.

A Spearman's correlation was performed between the learners' performance on the **receptive vocabulary** measure and their performance on the verb movement measure. The results showed a strong positive correlation $r = .836$, $p < .01$.

This result suggests that there is a link between vocabulary and syntax even at the level of the acquisition of uninterpretable features in IP contra David *et al.* (2009). However, the measure of vocabulary acquisition was limited to receptive vocabulary and future work involving a larger range of vocabulary measures and a wider range of syntactic structures in other languages as well as L2 French is needed to more fully examine this issue.

Practical implications and suggestions for further research

The results of recent research in second and foreign language learning support the relationship, already noted in first language learning, between **vocabulary breadth** and the knowledge and the use of the structural patterns of language. They lend support, therefore, to theories of acquisition in which syntactic development is driven by lexical development (Bates and Goodman, 1997). This has important consequences for the teaching and learning of foreign language, since it is no longer possible to minimize, as Wilkins (1972) indicated was occurring, the volumes of lexis in teaching syllabuses to only that which can usefully exemplify the structures being taught. If the structures are to be learned then it becomes imperative to learn a foreign language vocabulary of sufficient size for the various language structures to be appreciated and used.

Our understanding of the order and sequence in which learners acquire the structures of their foreign language is still opaque, however, and there is a huge research agenda opening to expand our understanding of this process. There are still questions of description to be answered: exactly what structures do learners find salient, notice and then add into their receptive and productive knowledge? What sequences then emerge? The sequences we do have, especially in second and foreign language learning, are rudimentary and incomplete and in the absence of good descriptions of structures, which match the learning process, it is difficult even to model this process to form the basis of principled research. Finally, if structure learning is driven by knowledge of vocabulary, then there are questions of the volumes of vocabulary which are necessary for particular structures to emerge. It is a big agenda where we are only scratching the surface at the moment.

Questions for discussion

■ Among the learners you know, yourself or those you teach, what structures have you noticed emerging and is there a particular order to the way these emerge?

- If future research does reveal a preference for certain structures to emerge in the minds of learners, how would you try to take advantage of this information teaching?
- If future research does manage to place these structures in a preferred order of acquisition, is it necessary to present and teach these structures in the same order. How would you try to link the presentation of structures with the input of vocabulary?
- In your experience, is the emergence of language structure linked to vocabulary size? If it is, does this remove the need to explicitly teach structures?

Knowledge of Collocations

Dale Brown

9

Introduction

Use	Grammatical functions	R	In what patterns does the word occur?
		P	In what patterns must we use this word?
	Collocations	**R**	**What words or types of word occur with this one?**
		P	**What words or types of words must we use with this one?**
	Constraints on use	R	Where, when and how often would we meet this word?
		P	Where, when and how often can we use this word?

Collocations has attracted considerable interest from researchers, both in its own right and as a prominent part of the wider issue of formulaic language. In Nation's (2001) framework, collocation has clear links with two of the other nine aspects in the scheme: associations and grammatical functions. Research into **word associations** considers collocations as one major type of association. Work on collocations and phraseology more generally has raised questions about where lexical description ends and grammatical description begins, leading to a blurring of the lines between the two and a view that they represent end points on a scale rather than separate entities.

Nation's framework outlines collocation in its receptive form as 'What words or types of words occur with this one?' (2001, p. 27) and in productive terms as 'What words or types of words must we use with this one?' (*ibid.*). Two points may be raised immediately about this. First, the framework positions collocation as an aspect of word knowledge, yet it has been argued that collocation should be viewed as an independent construct, with collocations considered lexical items in their own right (see, for example, Revier, 2009). From this point of view, if collocations are lexical items in their own right, the nine aspects of knowledge in Nation's scheme may be thought to apply to them. That is to say, we should be able to ask 'What does the collocation sound like?', 'How is the collocation pronounced?', and so on. It is, however, difficult to see exactly how all nine aspects could be applied to collocations as lexical items. Second, the use of the word *must* is of note, since, certainly in some traditions of collocations research, collocation is seen as an issue of probability, not of requirements. It is also of interest since it raises the question of who defines what words *must* be used, with critical approaches to applied linguistics questioning what they see as the assumption that native speakers can or should make those definitions, a point discussed in more detail below.

Knowledge of collocations

What are collocations?

Nation's questions provide us with a core definition of **collocation** as words occurring or used together, which would perhaps be accepted by many researchers. The questions are about the specifics of this. Nesselhauf (2004, 2005), Granger and Paquot (2008) and Barfield and Gyllstad (2009) discuss two traditions in research on collocation: the phraseological approach and the frequency-based approach. The phraseological approach can be traced back to Hornby's work on lexicology and has been heavily influenced by Russian scholarship, with key recent figures being Cowie, Howarth, Melčuk and Benson. This approach tries to define multi-word units linguistically – that is, it tries to set linguistic criteria by which one type of phraseological unit can be distinguished from another, and, in particular, determine how phraseological units can be distinguished from free combinations. Central to the approach is the idea of scales of opacity and of fixedness. Collocations are seen as occupying a certain space along the scales, being less restricted than idioms, which lie at one extreme, but more restricted than free combinations at the other. A distinction is also usually made between lexical collocations, in which two lexical words combine, and grammatical collocations, in which one grammatical and one lexical word are involved.

The frequency-based approach derives from the work of Firth and has been developed by Sinclair, Halliday, Kjellmer and Stubbs. This approach sees collocations as words that co-occur within a certain distance of each other. It has become closely linked with research in corpus linguistics and the development of a variety of statistical approaches to identifying collocation. In the frequency-based approach today, researchers use **corpora** and specialized software to find collocations, usually in one of two ways. One technique identifies recurrent sequences of words. The other uses one word as a node and searches for items appearing within a certain span, usually four orthographic words, either side of the node. Various statistical techniques are then used to determine the significance of the items found, the question essentially being to what extent the items appear together more often than we would expect given their individual frequencies.

The differences between the phraseological and frequency-based approaches are well illustrated by *The BBI Combinatory Dictionary of English* (Benson *et al.*, 1986) and *A Frequency Dictionary of Contemporary American English* (*FDCAE*) (Davies and Gardner, 2010). The former shows words, along with collocations, based on eight types of grammatical collocations – for example, noun + preposition or noun + *to* + infinitive – and seven types of lexical collocations – for example, adjective + noun or adverb + adjective. The latter includes words based on their frequency and range in a very large corpus, and then for each word shows collocates that have an MI score of around 2.5 or greater (MI, standing for mutual information, is a statistical measure of how strongly associated two words are).

Recent publications on collocation suggest that the frequency-based approach might be dominant at present, but it should not be seen as having replaced the phraseological approach, which remains in use and has strong advocates. Howarth (1998), for example, has stated that 'the approach followed here recognizes the enormous value of corpora large and small, but takes the view that phraseological significance means something more complex and possibly less tangible than what any computer algorithm can reveal' (*ibid.*, p. 27). Granger (2009; see also Granger and Paquot, 2008) has suggested the adoption of different terms for linguistically defined and quantitatively defined units, with *collocation* being reserved for the former and *recurrent sequences* or *co-occurrents* for the latter. However, it is also, of course, possible to combine the approaches. Several papers in Barfield and Gyllstad's (2009) edited collection, for example, begin with frequency-based techniques using a corpus to produce a list of collocations before then applying a phraseological approach to try to make sense of the items found. This combination is, in fact, seen in *FDCAE* (Davies and Gardner, 2010), discussed above, as, while the selection of collocations for inclusion relies on frequency-based techniques, the organization of each entry is more phraseological, with the list of collocates for each word organized by part of speech and a symbol used to indicate whether the collocate typically appears before or after the word.

Wray (2009) makes the point that there does not necessarily need to be universal agreement on one definition of collocation, 'but there is, I think, value in researchers reflecting on the implications of the definitions they use' (p. 239). She argues that there is a need for researchers to consider carefully the definitions of collocation employed and the definitions implied by the methods they adopt and that they should be wary of adopting definitions simply because they follow on from convenient methods of identification or convenient methods of data collection.

Collocations and L2 learning and teaching

Interest in **collocations** as an aspect of word knowledge stems in part from the seemingly widespread view that learners struggle with formulaic language in general and collocations in particular. Bahns (1993) suggests that the sheer number of collocations that need to be learned is overwhelming, but sees a solution in the fact that between many languages there are a considerable number of collocations that can be directly translated:

> It is necessary to distinguish (out of all the collocations considered worth knowing for the learner of English) such collocations which the learner with a particular L1 background 'knows already' (because they are fully equivalent in his or her L1 and in English), from those collocations which a contrastive analysis has shown to be language specific (in at least one of the components) and which the learner really has to learn. (pp. 61–2)

Bahns claims that 'the majority of collocational errors can be traced to L1 influence' and the problem is that 'learners seem to rely on a "hypothesis of transferability"' (Bahns, 1993, p. 61). This may be the case when the L1 and L2 in question are as closely related as German and English, but with other pairs of languages the situation may differ. Yamashita and Jiang (2010), on the basis of their research with Japanese learners of English, argue that learners probably need to encounter congruent collocations in the L2 in order to realize that they are in fact congruent. Yamashita and Jiang's study does, however, provide evidence of the important role the L1 plays in learners' knowledge of collocations, as do studies by Wolter and Gyllstad (2011) and Nesselhauf (2003 and 2005). In particular Nesselhauf found that L1 effects are the main source of difficulty for learners with regard to their use of collocations, and are a bigger factor than how restricted a collocation is.

From a different standpoint, the work of Michael Lewis (1993, 1997, 2000) gained particular prominence in the field of English language teaching (ELT) for a period with his strong advocation of a lexical approach that was largely founded on the idea of collocation. His starting point was not so much the problems learners face with collocations, but rather the view that there was an overemphasis on grammar which a focus on collocation could help to redress. Boers and Lindstromberg (2009), while aiming to build on Lewis's work, are also critical of his focus on raising learners' awareness of the importance of collocation, rather than on the actual teaching of collocations. Nesselhauf (2003) voices a similar complaint about publications on the teaching of collocations and argues that while awareness-raising is important, the teaching of collocations must go much further. Boers and Lindstromberg, in a series of publications of which their 2009 book provides an overview, suggest one way this can be done. They argue that while what they call chunks are often seen as arbitrary co-occurrences of words, a large number do, in fact, have non-arbitrary characteristics, by which they mean 'anything about the history of the chunk, its meaning and/or its form which has influenced the acceptance into conventional usage of its particular combination of words for the purposes of expressing a particular meaning'

(p. 15). That collocations are not, or at least not always, arbitrary combinations finds support in recent research by Liu (2010) and Walker (2011). Boers and Lindstromberg advocate an approach whereby chunks are selected for teaching on the basis of exhibiting non-arbitrary characteristics and that teachers or materials make use of these characteristics to make the chunks memorable for learners.

Other pedagogically motivated work has been towards the development of lists of collocations, based on varying corpus-based techniques. Much of this work has focused on the needs of English for academic purposes (EAP) learners: Simpson-Vlach and Ellis (2010) have produced an academic formulas list; Coxhead (2008) reports on ongoing work to provide information on the collocates and recurrent phrases involving the items in her widely used academic word list (Coxhead, 2000); while Durrant (2009) has produced an alternative list of collocations for academic purposes. Shin and Nation (2008) meanwhile have produced a list of frequent collocations in spoken English.

A completely different approach to the issue of learners' struggle with collocation challenges the assumption that native-like use of collocations is a desirable goal. Cook (1999), for example, questions the whole idea of the native speaker as the model for language learning and criticizes the deficit view that sees L2 users as failed L1 users, noting that any features of their language that differ from native usage 'are treated as signs of L2 users' failure to become native speakers, not of their accomplishments in learning to use the L2' (p. 195). Widdowson (2000) and G. Cook (1998), likewise, have questioned the use of **corpora** based on native-speaker usage in language teaching, with G. Cook making specific reference to collocation in this context, asking 'if a certain collocation occurs frequently among British or American English speakers, must it also be used by the Japanese or the Mexicans?' (p. 60). On the other hand, Nesselhauf (2005) points out the difficulty of replacing the native-speaker norm, since it is difficult to describe an alternative or even ascertain the existence of one. Wray (2002), meanwhile, argues that the prevalence of formulaic language is due not only to the processing advantages it offers speakers, but also the processing advantages it has for listeners. Speakers use formulaic language because it helps them to promote their interests by presenting the message in a form that facilitates processing for the listener. If this is the case, learners surely do need the opportunity to gain control over this language. But is it the case? Millar's (2011) recent study suggests that it may be, as far as native speakers are concerned. Millar identified two-word combinations in a corpus of learner writing that did not appear in the BNC, and which a native English speaker also confirmed to be non-standard. Then, using a self-paced reading task, he found that these non-standard collocations led to significantly slower reading by native speakers, and that the reading of words to the right of the collocation was also slowed down. Non-standard collocations do then seem to place a greater processing burden on native-speaker addressees. Nevertheless, a major element in the movement towards considering English as a lingua franca is the idea that for most learners of English it is interaction with other users of English as an L2 that is the priority, not interaction with native speakers. Whether the use of non-standard collocations has similar effects in these settings remains open to question.

Another question is why learners appear to struggle with collocations and formulaic language. Wray (2002) suggests teenage and adult L2 learners, having usually acquired literacy in their L1, have a strong bias towards word-sized units. One reason for this, she suggests, is that for adult learners saying the wrong thing has consequences for them socially and psychologically, while transparent, combinatory language is less risky. The bias towards word-sized units is true even of learners in naturalistic settings, while in instructional settings teaching practices additionally encourage a focus on words. In her words:

> Where the first language learner starts with large and complex strings, and never breaks them down any more than necessary, the post-childhood second language learner is starting with small units and trying to build them up. Phrases and clauses may be what learners encounter in their input material, but what they notice and deal with are words and how they can be glued together. The result is the classroom learner homes in on the individual words, and throws away all the really important information, namely what they occurred with. (p. 206)

Wible (2008) provides another perspective on this, noting that for the large number of foreign, rather than second, language learners around the world in traditional classrooms the main source of input is in written, not spoken, form. Written text (in many scripts) marks word boundaries very clearly with white space. The task for learners then is 'discovering that some sequences of the discrete units occurring between white spaces in text are in some respects best considered as bundled wholes despite the lack of typographical evidence that this is so' (p. 167). This point is also made by Bishop (2004), who refers to Schmitt's idea of noticing as a crucial condition for acquisition and suggests that **formulaic sequences** simply go unnoticed by learners. Regarding the learning of regular words, it is increasingly believed that secure knowledge of a word's form is a vital foundation on which other aspects of knowledge are built (Schmitt, 2008). Yet if formulaic sequences or collocations are not perceived as units, this crucial step cannot take place. In Wray's model, the result of learners throwing away 'all the really important information' is that the L1 and L2 lexicons contain very different balances of different types of units (2002). With particular reference to collocations, she suggests that for native speakers they are formulaic strings, but for non-native speakers they are not.

This question of the psycholinguistic status of formulaic language has prompted some research in recent years. Pawley and Syder's (1983) much-cited paper is often seen as the starting point for this work. They described the puzzle of native-like fluency: 'the native speaker's ability to produce fluent stretches of spontaneous connected discourse [despite the fact that] human capacities for encoding novel speech in advance or while speaking appear to be severely limited' (p. 191). The answer to this puzzle, they suggested, is that speakers possess a large store of memorized sequences and lexicalized sentence stems. A number of researchers (Conklin and Schmitt, 2008; Jiang and Nekrasova, 2007; Schmitt *et al.*, 2004; Schmitt and Underwood, 2004; Siyanova-Chanturia *et al.*, 2011; Siyanova and Schmitt, 2008; Underwood *et al.*, 2004) have attempted to find evidence for this 'large store' and investigate the extent to which this extends to second language learners, using a variety of techniques, including oral dictation tasks, self-paced reading tasks, eye movement tracking and online grammaticality judgements. These studies suggest that sequences of various types are psycholinguistically real for native speakers. For non-native speakers, however, the picture is unsurprisingly more nuanced, but it does appear that learners can and do achieve holistic storage of formulaic language. With specific reference to collocations, Yamashita and Jiang (2010) compared the processing of congruent collocations (i.e., having a direct L1 equivalent) and non-congruent collocations (without a direct L1 equivalent) among Japanese learners of English. They found that, if known, non-congruent collocations are processed just as quickly as congruent ones. Wolter and Gyllstad (2011), working with Swedish learners of English, also compared the processing of congruent and non-congruent collocations comparing their processing with that of unrelated word combinations to provide baseline data. They found that, if known, non-congruent collocations gain the same processing advantages over unrelated combinations as congruent collocations. These two studies did not aim to establish the psycholinguistic reality of collocations, but do provide indications of it.

A number of recent studies have also begun to reveal the types of collocations favoured by native speakers and L2 users respectively. Ellis *et al.* (2008, see also Ellis and Simpson-Vlach, 2009) first identified recurrent strings of words appearing significantly more often in spoken and written corpora of academic language than in a corpus of general English. They then randomly selected strings at three levels of frequency and three levels of MI score, and conducted a series of psycholinguistic experiments with native speakers and highly proficient non-native speakers to assess the psycholinguistic validity of the strings. The experiments showed that for native speakers the strings with higher MI scores were more easily processed, while the frequency of the strings did not have as large an effect. With highly advanced learners of English, the opposite was the case: the frequency of the strings affected their processing more than the MI score.

Siyanova and Schmitt (2008), on the other hand, compared the use of collocations in native and non-native written production. They classified the adjective-noun collocations found in essays in terms of five **frequency bands** in the BNC and looked at the proportion of those collocations over an MI score threshold of three. These analyses revealed no significant differences between the native and non-native writing. However, a difference in the type of strings favoured by native speakers and non-native speakers was found in a similar study by Durrant and Schmitt (2009). This study looked at all modifier-noun collocations in the writing of groups of native and non-native writers, and rated the collocations in terms of t-scores and MI scores in the BNC. (A t-score is another statistical measure of collocation, indicating how confident we can be that two words are associated, as opposed to MI which tells us about the strength of the association [Schmitt, 2010]. A list of collocations ordered by t-score is quite similar to a frequency ranking of the collocations [Durrant and Schmitt, 2009].) Interestingly, rather than use an MI score threshold, the study placed the collocations in a number of bands by MI score. The study found that native writers use more low-frequency collocations than non-native writers, non-native writers use at least as many or more collocations with high t-scores than native writers, and non-native writers use fewer collocations with high MI scores than native writers. Durrant and Schmitt thus suggest that learners do acquire many high-frequency collocations, yet their underuse of collocations with high MI scores gives rise to the intuitive feeling of many teachers and researchers that non-native writing is unidiomatic.

In related work, researchers have looked at intuitions regarding collocations. McGee (2009) investigated intuitions for adjective-noun collocations among 20 native-speaking teachers of English. Participants were asked to provide what they thought was the most frequent noun collocate for 20 common adjectives, and the participants' responses were compared to the most frequent collocates in the BNC. The study found that the participants' intuitions differed significantly from the corpus data in the majority of cases. Unfortunately, the paper considers only the frequency rank of collocations in the corpus, not their actual frequency nor other measures of their association, and so cannot be directly compared with the studies reported above. Siyanova and Schmitt (2008), already discussed in part above, also included an investigation of intuitions of collocations. Their study asked native and non-native speakers to rate adjective-noun collocations as to how common they were. Two groups of collocations were used: 31 collocations that reached both a certain frequency and MI cut-off in the BNC, and 31 adjective-noun pairs not appearing in the BNC at all. Both the native and non-native-speaking groups rated the frequent collocations as more common, but the non-native speakers were less willing to rate the unusual collocations as uncommon. A second analysis compared the ratings for ten high-frequency and ten medium-frequency collocations from among the 31 frequent collocations. Here too the native speakers were able to distinguish between the two, while the non-native speakers proved unable to do so. These two studies appear to show that native speakers are able to recognize collocations quite easily, but find it more challenging to produce the most frequent collocations for a word on demand. Non-native speakers seem to have a broad sense of frequent collocations, but struggle to distinguish finer differences between the frequency of word combinations.

Current research work

The research reported here is a follow-up to Barfield (2009). Barfield's starting point is a sense of dissatisfaction with previous work on learners' use of **collocations**. In particular, he makes three criticisms. First, the claims made by some studies were often based on small amounts of data: in many studies the number of collocations actually collected from learners was very small. Second, many previous studies focused on learners' errors with collocations while ignoring their often successful use of many collocations. Barfield characterized this as the deficit view. Third, many studies focus on advanced learners, which has meant that collocation has come to be characterized as a form of advanced knowledge. Barfield's solution was to adapt the Lex30 (Meara and Fitzpatrick, 2000) test format, a test of **productive vocabulary** size. Lex30 presents a cue to the test-taker and asks for three associations in a 30-second limit. Barfield's instrument, which he calls LexCombi, likewise presents 30 frequent nouns as cues and gives a 30-second limit for each cue, but asks for three collocations. Responses are then scored against a database of acceptable collocations for each cue. Referring back to his criticisms of previous research, Barfield claims that LexCombi: (1) allows the collection of a large number of collocations efficiently; (2) focuses on what learners know rather than on what they do not know; and (3) can be used with learners of varying proficiency.

Testing methodology

My own study, reported below, made use of LexCombi, but had a rather different focus from Barfield's. Rather than focus on the differences between learners, I looked at the characteristics of the responses produced by learners. In this sense then, the study has some similarities with McGee's (2009) work discussed above. My focus is on responses that recurred frequently among the participants as a group. A recurrent response was defined as a response to a particular cue produced by at least 10 per cent of the participants. The study included 78 participants, meaning that a recurrent response is one produced by eight or more participants. In accepting any and every response reaching this threshold, the study aligns itself with the frequency-based view of **collocations** and its interest in words occurring in the environment of each other.

This study sees these recurrent responses as having some sort of currency for the participant group and attempts to answer the broad question: what are the characteristics of the recurrent responses? More specifically, three questions are addressed:

1. What types of words are the recurrent responses? This question involves looking at the frequency of the words in English and their part of speech in order to establish the basic nature of the recurrent responses.
2. Are the recurrent responses acceptable collocations in terms of native-speaker use? As noted above, the acceptability of responses was a major part of Barfield's design and provides an insight into the state of the participant group's collocational competence. Also of interest are the responses deemed unacceptable by this criteria, given that these responses were provided by at least 10 per cent of participants.
3. What types of collocations, in terms of MI scores and frequency, are the recurrent collocations? The work of Ellis *et al.* (2008) and Durrant and Schmitt (2009) discussed above suggests intriguing differences between the types of collocations favoured by native speakers and non-native speakers. Can these tendencies be identified in the recurrent responses also?

Participants

The participants were Japanese university students of broadly low-intermediate proficiency (n = 78). All the participants were in the first year of their degree programme, pursuing degrees in subjects other than English, but all had at least two English classes a week. Data were collected at the end of an academic year in which their twice-weekly English classes had had a strong emphasis on vocabulary learning. In particular, the vocabulary component of their classes had emphasized the thorough learning of frequent vocabulary, with regular tests on their knowledge of the part of speech, syllable pattern, translations, key collocational phrases and word family of targeted items.

The participants produced 139 recurrent responses as defined above. As Figure 9.1 shows, the majority, 84, were only slightly above the threshold of being given by 10 per cent or more of participants. There were also some responses, however, that occurred with remarkable uniformity, with ten responses being given by half or more of the participants.

Results

The first question asked what type of words the recurrent responses are, with reference to their frequency as individual words in English and their part of speech. Regarding their frequency in English, based on Nation's (2006) BNC-derived wordlists accessed via Cobb (http://www.lextutor.ca), Table 9.1 shows that there are very few recurrent responses beyond even the first 1000 word families, and only two beyond the second 1000 word families. The recurrent responses are then of very high frequency in English. Figure 9.2 shows the

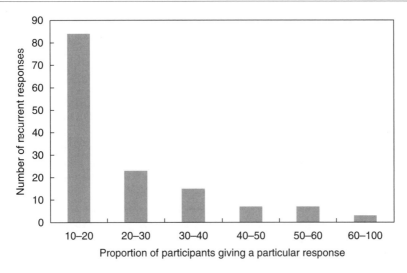

Figure 9.1 The number of responses given by various proportions of participants

Table 9.1 Frequency in English of the recurrent responses

	Number of recurrent responses	Percentage
First 1000 word families	128	92
Second 1000 word families	9	6
Other	2	1

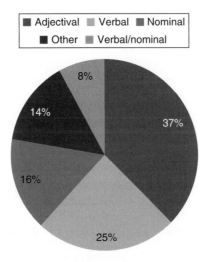

Figure 9.2 The part of speech of the recurrent responses

proportion of the recurrent responses of different parts of speech. With no context to aid in assigning responses to a part of speech, the responses were categorized according to their typical usage. Some words, of course, regularly occur as different parts of speech, notably words that are used variously as nouns and verbs, which necessitated the inclusion of a verbal/nominal category. The 'other' category consists mainly of pronouns and prepositions. Predictably, since all the cues are nouns, adjectives and verbs account for the largest proportions of the recurrent responses, but at least 30 per cent of the responses are of other word classes. There is, then, a wide range in the types of words provided by the learners as **collocations**.

The second question was concerned with the acceptability of the frequent responses in terms of native-speaker use. As mentioned previously, this was a major part of Barfield's work, and he created a database of acceptable collocations for each item using the *Oxford Collocations Dictionary* (*OCD*) (McIntosh *et al.*, 2009) and *Collins WordBanks Online* (HarperCollins, 2004). In this study, a somewhat cruder approach was taken, with the acceptability of the recurrent responses being determined by the appearance of the word in either the *OCD* or in *FDCAE* (Davies and Gardner, 2010). Here, the aim is not to determine definitively whether a response is an acceptable collocate or not, but simply to gain another perspective on the data. This analysis found that 90 of the 139 recurrent responses (65 per cent) were acceptable collocations. Figure 9.3 re-presents the data given earlier regarding the number of recurrent responses, besides which the same information is shown for the acceptable responses only. Here, then, we can see that many of the responses deemed unacceptable were those that only narrowly passed the minimum threshold,

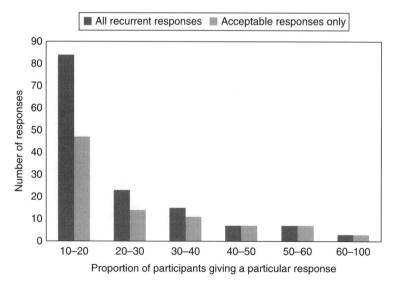

Figure 9.3 The number of acceptable recurrent responses produced by various proportions of participants

while all 17 of the responses given by 40 per cent or more of the participants were acceptable. Thus even by this fairly conservative measure of acceptability, it would seem that as a group these low-intermediate proficiency learners have some sense of standard collocations in English.

The question must be asked, however, whether the so-called unacceptable responses are really unacceptable. An examination of the 49 unacceptable responses showed there to be four types. First, some of the unacceptable recurrent responses simply reveal the limitations of the dictionary sources by which acceptability was judged. For example, the recurrent responses *my* for the cue *family* and *why* for the cue *reason* do not appear as collocates in either the *OCD* nor the *FDCAE*. Yet in both the Corpus of Contemporary American English (COCA) (Davies, 2008) and the BYU-BNC: British National Corpus (Davies, 2004) these responses appear as important collocates, occurring with both high frequency and high MI scores. Such responses presumably do not fit easily into the dictionaries' categorization schemes and so were omitted. The non-listing of *my* as a collocate for *family* is perhaps reasonable in that almost all approaches to collocation would agree that it is either not a collocation or an uninteresting one, but the omission of *why* as a collocate for *reason* does seem more questionable.

Second, some unacceptable recurrent responses seem to derive very much from the particular linguistic environment of the group of participants. This includes both the wider environment of English as it is used within Japan and the participants' experience of English in the classroom. One example of the former is the response *note* given for the cue *death*. The recurrence of this response will be easily understood by those familiar with contemporary Japan; it is presumed to come from the title of an extremely popular manga and film series *Death Note* (Japanese: デスノート *Desu Nōto*). An example of the latter is the response *word* for the cue *family*. As already noted, the data were collected at the end of an academic year in which the participants' main exposure to English would likely have been in their two weekly classes. The term *word family* occurred on a weekly basis in these classes and so this collocation was a prominent part of the recent English experience of the participants.

Third, some of the unacceptable recurrent responses seem to come from compounds that are usually written as single items in English. For example, two recurrent responses were *news* for the cue *paper*, and *man* for the cue *police*. These pairs of words appear very infrequently in **corpora** as combinations, but are of course frequent as single words. Given the variety in English with which compound nouns are written, and the existence of terms which are sometimes written as single words, sometimes as hyphenated words and sometimes as two separate words, and given that compounds may be acquired aurally in any case, it is perhaps not surprising that learners would struggle in this area. Alternatively, responses such as these could be seen as evidence not so much of the participants' unfamiliarity with conventions, but of their tendency to analyse items. This tendency has been much noted in work on phraseology, but responses of this type may be an indication that learners also analyse orthographic words at times. That is to say, even though a learner may have seen *newspaper* as a single orthographic word many times, they may have always thought of it as a two-word phrase. Indeed, it could be the case that while, for example, *news* and *paper* are strongly associated in a learner's mind, there may be no holistic storage of the item *newspaper*.

Granger and Paquot (2008) point out that while one of the foundations of the study of collocations and phraseology is that the units are made up of at least two words, the ambiguity and openness to interpretation of the concept of a word means that this foundation is not particularly clear. They point out that this issue is rarely discussed in the literature and that the way researchers treat compounds of different types – that is, whether they are included or excluded as phraseological units – varies a great deal. The data discussed above give some indication that the difficulties surrounding this issue for researchers may be matched in terms of learners' knowledge of these items.

Finally, there are some recurrent responses that from the perspective of native-speaker norms may be described as not acceptable. For example, the response *solve* for the cue *issue* and *keep* for *health*. The former does occur occasionally in COCA, but what seems to this author as the more conventional *resolve* appears with vastly greater frequency and produces a strong MI score. This may be a case of the participants mislearning the collocational phrase or perhaps viewing *solve* and *resolve* as equivalents as, indeed, both can be translated into Japanese as 解決する (*kaiketsusuru*). The latter example, *keep*, appears in the vicinity of *health* with even lesser frequency in COCA, and it seems likely here that the issue is translation from the L1, Japanese. *To keep one's health*, meaning to protect or look after one's health, is a literal translation of the Japanese phrase 健康を守る (*kenkou o mamoru*).

Considering all the above, the recurrent responses labelled as unacceptable seem in many cases to be quite reasonable responses. The cases that are due to the dictionary sources used are clearly acceptable, while it seems odd to describe the phrases derived from the local linguistic environment or the participants' knowledge of compounds as unacceptable. Even with those frequent responses that stand out as peculiar in terms of native English usage, all that we can really say is that they are highly unusual. It must also be remembered that native English usage is being judged here with reference to British and American sources.

The third question about the characteristics of the recurrent responses to be considered concerns the work discussed above regarding the types of collocations favoured by learners. As was noted, both Ellis *et al.* (2008) and Durrant and Schmitt (2009) found that native speakers of English favoured collocations with strong MI scores, while users of English as an L2 favoured those with high frequency. The aim here is to determine whether similar tendencies can be found in the recurrent responses data from my low-intermediate proficiency participants. We might expect that those recurrent responses which a greater proportion of the participants provided would occur more frequently as a word combination in a corpus while there would be no or a smaller correlation with MI scores. To investigate this matter, each of the 139 recurrent responses was checked in COCA. Specifically, searches were conducted for each recurrent response within a $+3/-3$ span of the LexCombi cue as node. The search was for the **lemmas** of both the response and the cue rather than exact forms, and specified the cues as nouns. Correlations were then calculated between the recurrence of the responses in the participants' data and the frequency and MI scores obtained via COCA. Since the data were not normally distributed, Spearman's Rho was used to calculate the correlations. As Table 9.2 shows, a correlation was found between the number of times the responses recurred and the frequency of those collocations in COCA, and an almost identical correlation was found with the MI scores in COCA. Also noticeable here, however, is the correlation between the two corpus-based figures. While we would perhaps expect a correlation between two measures of collocation, this correlation suggests that to a certain extent both frequency and MI score are measuring the same thing and thus it is not surprising that if one correlates with another measure (the recurrence of response), the other should too. Looking at scatterplots for the three variables, it became clear that a number of recurrent responses that just passed the threshold to be counted as such achieved both low frequency and low MI scores in COCA. The correlations were thus recalculated with only the 90 acceptable responses as defined earlier. Table 9.3 presents these results. The correlation between the COCA frequency and MI scores is now considerably smaller and non-significant, confirming the influence of those low-frequency and low MI score combinations. Removing those items has also led to smaller correlations between the recurrence of the responses and both the COCA-based frequency and MI scores for

Table 9.2 Correlations between the recurrence of the participants' responses and the frequency and MI scores for those collocations in COCA

	Frequency of collocation in COCA	MI score of collocation in COCA
Recurrence of response in learner data	.33*	.34*
Frequency of collocation in COCA		.41*

Note: * $p < .05$.

Table 9.3 Correlations between the recurrence of the participants' responses (acceptable responses only) and the frequency and MI scores for those collocations in COCA

	Frequency of collocation in COCA	MI score of collocation in COCA
Recurrence of acceptable responses	.24*	.21*
Frequency of collocation in COCA		.16

Note: * $p < .05$.

the collocations, there remaining little difference between them. In these data, then, there does not seem to be evidence of learners favouring collocations of high frequency. However, there are a number of limitations that may have influenced the results. First, as Figure 9.1 showed, there are many responses that only just met the criteria to be counted as recurrent responses and relatively few items that were given by a large proportion of the participants. The spread of items is thus highly uneven. This problem remains an issue even when considering only the acceptable items (Figure 9.3). Second, while the studies inspiring this analysis compared L2 English speakers with native-speaker performance, the data here only look at learners. It is thus attempting to find an absolute difference between the types of collocation favoured rather than a comparative difference with native speakers. It is possible that native-speaker data would reveal a contrasting pattern. It should also be remembered that those studies involved advanced learners of English, while this study looked only at learners of lower proficiency.

Pedagogical implications and suggestions for further research

This study set out to examine three questions concerning the characteristics of recurrent responses provided to LexCombi. All three questions can be seen as related to the issue with which this chapter began regarding the nature of **collocation** and how it can be defined. Regarding the first question on what types of words the recurrent responses are, the part of speech data highlight the fact that for these learners collocations come in all shapes and sizes. The noun cues not only prompted adjectival and verbal responses; a variety of parts of speech also were provided as collocations by the learners, including grammar words as well as lexical words. Focusing only on the lexical collocations, or only, as many studies have, on adjective-noun collocations would have narrowed the scope of the study considerably. The second question considered the acceptability of the recurrent responses in terms of native-speaker use. It was found that the majority were acceptable on these terms, but it was also clear that those responses that were not acceptable cannot be simply described as unacceptable. There is no simple way to decide what counts as a collocation and what is an unconventional combination of words. Neither the phraseological nor frequency-based approaches to collocation fully deal with this issue. The phraseological tradition has provided us with notions of scales, but struggles to demarcate the boundary between collocations and what it calls free combinations. In the frequency-based tradition, meanwhile, certain conventions have arisen for the various measures of collocation regarding what is classed as a collocation, but it is recognized that these are to an extent arbitrary and atheoretical. Finally, the third question asked whether the recurrence of the responses correlated more with MI scores or more with frequency in corpus data. Significant correlations were found with both, but they were weak and almost identical.

The data do not, then, appear to support the idea that L2 users tend towards highly frequent collocations rather than collocations with high MI scores. Regarding the nature of collocation, the tendency of native speakers to favour collocations with high MI scores that Durrant and Schmitt (2009) and Ellis *et al.* (2008) have identified suggests a psycholinguistic definition of collocation for native speakers as word combinations with high MI scores. This clearly needs confirmation, as does the finding that even highly advanced L2 users were found not to display this tendency, given the results of my study above.

This study also shows that even learners of relatively low proficiency have some sense of conventional collocations. Collocation is often viewed as a problem for advanced learners of English and research (e.g., Nesselhauf, 2005) does seem to show that advanced learners continue to struggle with collocational conventions. Nevertheless, there is a need for research into the collocational knowledge of less advanced learners to establish the extent of this knowledge and how it develops. It seems sensible to assume that collocational competence would develop in concert with general proficiency, but what exactly is the relationship between these two? A host of questions arise, all of which are currently under-researched. Does collocational competence lag behind proficiency in some way? Could it perhaps drive the development of proficiency as in ideas about the learning of chunks driving grammatical development? To what extent do learners vary? Do some show collocational competence beyond that of proficiency or vice versa? What factors could cause such differences? collocations has been a rich area of research for some time, yet the collocational knowledge of low proficiency learners remains largely absent.

With so many questions about the acquisition of collocational knowledge unanswered, it is not entirely clear how to fit this type of knowledge into a teaching syllabus. At present collocations are taught explicitly, and are formally tested, at the more advanced levels. However, it may be appropriate that the more frequent collocations, and collocations containing frequent elements, might usefully form a focus of teaching at a lower level of knowledge. But the impact of teaching such material at a low level is also largely unresearched and this could itself provide a useful avenue of research.

Questions for discussion

- What factors should be considered when deciding which **collocations** to teach in the classroom? To what extent does this depend on whether the class shares a single L1?
- How useful/practical is the concept of an 'acceptable' collocation?
- At what point in the frequency with which words co-occur does a collocation cease to be a collocation?
- How might the findings reported here differ if the participants were advanced learners of English?

Knowledge of Constraints on Use

10

Clarissa Wilks

Introduction

Use	Grammatical functions	R	In what patterns does the word occur?
		P	In what patterns must we use this word?
	Collocations	R	What words or types of word occur with this one?
		P	What words or types of words must we use with this one?
	Constraints on use	**R**	**Where, when and how often would we meet this word?**
		P	**Where, when and how often can we use this word?**

This chapter focuses on the 'constraints on use' element of Nation's presentation of word knowledge (Nation, 2001). 'Constraints on use' is the term used to describe the last element of the three sub-sections of the *use* aspect of Nation's description of what is involved in knowing a word, appearing alongside 'grammatical functions' and '**collocations**'. In some senses this is the 'Cinderella' component of Nation's framework – the poor relation to the other elements of the framework in terms of the attention that it has received in vocabulary knowledge research. We can begin to get a feel for this just by comparing the relative invisibility of constraints on use in the research concerned with developing tests of the depth of learners' L2 vocabulary knowledge – see for example Read (2000, 2004) and Daller *et al.* (2007) for discussions of assessing **vocabulary depth**. Whilst collocations, associations and grammatical functions figure prominently, constraints on use have little role to play. A paper by Webb (2007) provides a good illustration of the Cinderella status of the constraints on use dimension. Webb takes a systematic and highly controlled experimental approach to exploring **incidental vocabulary learning** in terms of the development of different dimensions of word knowledge. Using invented lexical items, he explores how different incidental learning conditions impact on learners' acquisition of ten aspects of word knowledge. What stands out in terms of our focus here is that, even though his ten tests do include productive and receptive tests of both associations and grammatical functions, there is no mention of the third element of the *use* category of the word knowledge framework. I am going to suggest that the relative lack of attention to constraints on use in the word knowledge research stems partly from the elusiveness and comparative fragility of the original elaboration of the construct in relation to the other aspects of word knowledge. The lack of a precise definition compounds problems in operationalizing the constraints on use construct in experimental protocols and has led to a rather narrow focus in research directly addressing learners' knowledge of constraints and what it can tell us about modelling and assessing L2 vocabulary acquisition.

I'll begin by trying to unpick what Nation means by 'constraints on use' and by exploring the issues that his presentation of the construct raises.

Constraints on use

What does Nation mean by 'constraints on use'?

The receptive and productive incarnations of the constraints on use component are encapsulated in the parallel questions: 'Where, when and how often would we meet this word?' and 'Where, when and how often can we use this word?'. These questions are clear and practical and are entirely in tune with the focus of a book whose raison d'être is to provide informed pedagogical advice to teachers and learners. However, matters become more problematic when we try to analyse in greater detail what Nation means by 'constraints on use' in order to understand the directions taken by, and implications of, subsequent research in this area.

Nation's initial presentation of terms foregrounds *frequency* and **register** as the most significant constraints, although, tantalizingly, also suggests that there may be other constraints that he doesn't specify: 'constraints on use (register, frequency ...)' (2001, p. 27). Indeed, he himself seems to imply that this is a difficult dimension of vocabulary knowledge to pin down. In the section headed 'constraints on use' of his chapter on the dimensions of 'Knowing a Word' (chapter 2), he states that: 'there are several factors that limit where and when certain words can be used'. However, unusually in a text which makes extensive and effective use of tables, he does not provide his own list. Instead he turns to work such as that of Hartmann (1981) on usage labels in dictionaries as 'one way of seeing the range of constraints' (p. 57). As he points out, however, this work just underlines how difficult it is to assign consistently the 'style value' of a given item, highlighting the lack of consistency between such taxonomies of constraints and showing how liable they are to become quickly outmoded.

In neither the 'constraints on use' section of his chapter 2, nor in any other part of the book does Nation offer a fully elaborated definition of how he interprets constraints on use – understandably given the encyclopaedic scope of the text and its focus on pedagogic applications of word knowledge research. Instead he expands the concept via a range of examples and additional details that emerge more or less indirectly in the course of discussions on a number of different topics. The list below picks out the most obvious points that he makes in relation to what constitutes constraints on vocabulary use (Nation, 2001):

- He states that constraints on use are linked to word meaning: 'The constraints on vocabulary use are most closely related to meaning and would benefit from explicit learning' (p. 34).
- He suggests that constraints on vocabulary use are limited: 'Most words are not constrained in their use by sociolinguistic factors' (p. 57). This contention is repeated later when he says: 'Most words are not affected by constraints on use. That is, they are neutral regarding constraints like formal/informal, polite/impolite, child language/adult language, women's usage/men's usage, American/British, spoken/written' (p. 106). Elsewhere, he refers to the importance of teachers deciding which aspects of a word to prioritize, including potentially: 'restrictions on its use through considerations of politeness, formality, dialect or medium' (p. 91).
- Although he suggests that most words are 'neutral', he nevertheless acknowledges distinctions between languages noting that 'some languages do have severe constraints on the terms used to refer to people, particularly in showing the relationship of the speaker to the person being referred to' (p. 57). He also refers to the importance of cultural differences in determining the appropriate usage of different words, as, for example, in the acceptability of referring to someone as fat when they are present (p. 58).
- As regards testing knowledge of constraints on vocabulary use, he identifies the key questions for evaluating receptive and productive knowledge as: '(R) Can the learner tell if the word is common, formal, infrequent etc? (P) Can the learner use the word at appropriate times?' (p. 374).
- In respect of frequency constraints, he homes in on the inappropriateness that results from using rare words in everyday situations (p. 57) and on the possibility that learners might be trained to estimate the frequency of words in the target language (p. 396).

What emerges from this piecemeal presentation of the constraints on use construct is a somewhat elusive picture. What can we extrapolate from these statements and what questions do they raise when we look at them from today's perspective and try link them to the developing agendas of vocabulary research? In the next sections we will explore a number of points that stand out in relation to the two major labels that Nation uses: register and frequency. We will consider, from a current perspective, Nation's interpretation of each of these aspects of word knowledge and the trajectory of vocabulary research that has built upon it.

Nation's presentation of register constraints

Nation's understanding of **register** is difficult to pin down from the statements we have listed above or from his indirect treatment of the concept elsewhere in the text. The notion of register was already at the time a complex and contested area beset by a lack of consensus over terminology (see, for example, Halliday and Hassan, 1976; Wardaugh, 1986). Nation's overall treatment of vocabulary learning acknowledges and makes use of these debates, as is evident, for example, in his discussion of 'Vocabulary in Discourse' where he uses the organizing principles of 'field', 'tenor' and 'mode' drawn from Halliday's (1994) conception of register to list the discourse functions of vocabulary (Nation, 2001, p. 207). However, this standpoint is not explicitly or consistently applied when Nation discusses the specific component of constraints on use. In these discussions he at times implies a narrow definition which more or less equates register with level of formality. At others, as we have seen, he implies a wider definition embracing concepts such as, 'politeness, formality, dialect or medium' (*ibid.*, p. 91) – each of which terms from a current sociolinguistic, pragmatic perspective could itself invite further detailed definition or interrogation.

The fact that Nation does not provide a clear, operational definition of register in relation to constraints on use may have been a factor in the comparatively slow development of a research agenda anchored squarely in the vocabulary research tradition around the acquisition of this component of word knowledge. Discourse-orientated research has, of course, looked at the role vocabulary has to play in 'general language constraints and discourse requirements' (*ibid.*, 205). In addition, a considerable body of research has been building since the 1980s into the acquisition of 'sociolinguistic competence' in second language learners, as attested, for example, by the special edition of the *Journal of Sociolinguistics* devoted to this topic in 2004 (Bayley and Regan, 2004). However, there seems to have been comparatively little work which takes register constraints on words and learners' knowledge of them as its explicit starting point. Even where this dimension of lexical knowledge is more central in sociolinguistic research into L2 acquisition, as, for example, in Dewaele's work on the underrepresentation of colloquial terms in the speech of learners of French L2 (Dewaele and Regan, 2001; Dewaele, 2004a), there is relatively little cross-referencing work exploring the potential and limitations of word knowledge frameworks. It seems that there are avenues still to be explored here that could more fully exploit the potential of bringing to bear other theoretical tools and frames of reference to the study of vocabulary acquisition.

From a contemporary perspective, for example, it seems legitimate to question the 'all or nothing' viewpoint that Nation seems to espouse in relation to register constraints on vocabulary use. He appears to assume a sharp distinction here between two different types of languages: the majority (including, by implication, English), in which most words are 'neutral', and a smaller set of languages with very 'severe' and highly codified constraints (e.g., in relation to vocabulary signalling relationships between speakers). For the former category Nation's description appears to assume that constraints on use exist only at the extremes (very formal or informal words, taboo language, English vs American usage). Whilst in places Nation acknowledges the significance of differences between languages and cultures, he doesn't do this routinely throughout his discussion of constraints on use. For example, the series of binary options cited above ('formal/informal, polite/impolite, child language/adult language, women's usage/men's usage, American/British, spoken/written' [p. 106]) is a somewhat odd mixture of oppositions, not all of which are of the same order or universally applicable. 'American/British', for example, obviously only applies to English. The distinction between 'women's usage' and 'men's usage' on the other hand, whilst possibly still clearly encoded in some languages, would be the subject of enormous controversy if applied to English (see, for example, the debates covered in Holmes and Meyerhoff, 2003).

This lack of clarity does encourage a number of questions. Through the lens that social linguistics disciplines offer it is, for example, legitimate to question the idea of lexical 'neutrality' even in languages which don't have rigidly codified patterns of address terms or relationship markers. The scope of the references that Nation draws on (Fairclough, 1989; Corson, 1995; etc.) makes it clear that he is sensitive to these perspectives, but their implications do not filter through to his treatment of register constraints at a more granular level. We might further want to question the tacit assumption that words in any language, including English, have a fixed 'identity' or fixed limits in terms of their appropriate usage. First, the constraints on the use of a given word are contested amongst native speakers and not only in the case of terms at the extremes of formality scales or taboo language. Lack of consensus is evident not just between different social groups in broad terms (as categorized, for example, by social class/socio economic status or education), but also at more subtle levels between different communities of practice. This is well illustrated, for example, in the sensitivities that surround the use of lexis that may be perceived as pejorative or discriminatory in relation to ethnicity or sexuality. Moreover, the register constraints attached to words are highly dynamic and may change over fairly short time spans. An obvious case would be the changing perceptions of acceptability in relation to different swear words. There may also be important differences in perceptions of constraints on use at the level of the individual native speakers and learners. Dewaele (2004b), for example, reports positive correlations between learners' use of colloquial words in French and individual levels of extraversion, in addition to other factors such as proficiency level and exposure to the target language. We might further argue that Nation underplays the importance of communicative (rather than purely linguistic) context when it comes to evaluating the register constraints attaching to individual words, particularly in relation to potential accommodation effects between interlocutors.

Given all of these complications surrounding the identification of fixed limits on appropriate usage for lexical items, Nation's advice, that 'the teacher and the learner should discuss where and when certain words should not be used' (2001, p. 34) may, in fact, be much harder to put into practice than he implies, except in limited or extreme cases. What we might think of as the hazy middle of the spectrum of register constraints may be much harder to cover and yet to ignore it may mean that some of the vocabulary learning needs of more advanced learners are not met. Although Nation makes a distinction between learning *items* and learning *systems of knowledge* (*ibid.*, pp. 58–9), he does not develop the implications of this distinction in terms of register constraints on vocabulary use. Recent research into pedagogical approaches to developing sociolinguistic and stylistic variation in classroom settings (Van Compernolle and Williams, 2009; Van Compernolle, 2010) suggests that explicit instruction can help learners to develop their **declarative knowledge** of language variation, but that it is not yet clear how this knowledge affects their sociolinguistic performance. There may also be room for further explicit vocabulary research exploring whether developing sensitivity to context and to the subtleties of register constraints leads to improvements in learners' ability to derive knowledge about appropriate usage from input. The fact that this is a tremendously difficult challenge for learners is neatly illustrated by a personal observation. A French friend who has lived and worked in England for some 15 years and is married to a native English speaker recently reported that in a formal business meeting she had objected to a proposed project with the words: 'I can't be [a:sd] to do that'. She was acutely embarrassed when we told her that she had used a highly colloquial expression ('I can't be *arsed* to do that = 'I can't be bothered …') having believed that she was saying 'I can't be *asked* to do that' – that is, 'It's unreasonable to make this request to me.' When I reported this anecdote to two Greek colleagues, academic linguists, they both confirmed that they had been under exactly the same misapprehension. This observation sparks a number of questions about: (1) lexical storage in relation to the register constraints dimension of vocabulary knowledge; (2) its relative status against the *form* and *meaning* components of word knowledge; and (3) the influence of L1 transfer in shaping implicit learning. Since we can assume that all three very advanced non-native speakers had only ever encountered this expression in very informal spoken contexts, and since we can assume that they did know the word 'arse', we must speculate that a highly frequent known phonetic form ('asked') and the absence of a parallel colloquial expression in L1, overrode the register cues available from the input and led them to internalize an entry with a plausible, if incorrect, meaning. Although methodologically very challenging, these questions of the relative weight of different components of word knowledge in L2 vocabulary would merit formal research in the future.

Nation's presentation of frequency constraints

Not surprisingly, given Nation's prominence in the use of frequency data for test development, frequency seems to be a more straightforward constraint to capture. It is worth noting that the focus of frequency knowledge seems to be centred entirely on teaching learners to distinguish between very common and very rare words and not on any finer-grained acquisition of knowledge of frequency constraints. This position is, of course, consistent with the first principle of Nation's standpoint on teaching vocabulary – that is, that teachers and learners should play a percentage game – identifying which words it is most useful to learn and which aspects of word knowledge should be prioritized (2001, p. 373). He does not clearly map out the differences and overlaps between frequency and **register**, although the two often seem to be conflated (as in the question 'Can the learner tell if the word is common [frequency], formal [register], infrequent [frequency]?').

In contrast to register, there has been a significant amount of directly vocabulary-based research into learners' knowledge of the frequency constraints on word use. One of the most persistent strands of such research centres on investigations into speakers' intuitions about the frequency of lexical items. There exists, of course, other important research which looks at how word frequency correlates with learnability, lexical development and production (e.g., Milton, 2007) but this work deals with speakers' overall vocabularies rather than with the development of knowledge in relation to individual items and is beyond the scope of the present chapter. Nation alludes to the question of frequency intuitions when he claims that: 'With a little practice and feedback it may be possible for learners to develop a feeling for what is high frequency and what is low frequency' (2001, p. 396). He touches on some factors which may make this a more or less difficult task (such as the linguistic and cultural similarity/distance between languages) and notes that the major problem for learners lies in distinguishing the relative frequency of near synonyms. He suggests, however, that: 'This area of developing learners' intuitions about word frequency is unresearched' (*ibid.*, p. 396).

In the decade since Nation wrote this, the question of how to *develop* learners' word frequency intuitions has still not attracted a great deal of attention. There has been, on the other hand, a considerable amount of research into word frequency intuitions that concentrates on the accuracy of speakers' frequency estimates and on comparisons between learners and native speakers. It's fair to say that this area of research has proven to be somewhat frustrating and contentious terrain. The valuable insights into learners' acquisition of word frequency knowledge that once seemed to be promised by studies of word frequency intuitions have been obscured to a certain extent by the implications of the varying methodological approaches adopted by different researchers and by controversy over the theoretical positions (explicit or implied) that underpin their work. The brief outline of some key work in this area in the next section gives an insight into some of the debates and differences in theoretical and methodological approach that characterize the territory.

Current research work

Earlier work

Research in this field is, in fact, of long standing and runs parallel to psychological studies of general frequency estimation (e.g., Tversky and Kahneman, 1973). In the 1960s and 70s research concerned specifically with the estimation of word frequency at first focused principally on native speakers of English, but then broadened to include speakers of other languages and L2 learners (Shapiro, 1969; Carroll, 1971; Richards, 1974; Arnaud, 1990; Ringeling, 1984). Most of this work involved correlating informants' estimations of the frequency of words, their subjective frequency estimate (SFE), with an objective frequency (OF) measure, a baseline built on word frequency lists derived from the available **corpora**. Informants' intuitions about the frequency of test items were elicited via a range of methods. These methods fall into two broad categories (Arnaud, 1990, p. 1): *absolute frequency rankings*, in which informants give judgements on how common/rare a word is in English in general or in their own usage; 2) *relative frequency rankings*, in which informants are asked either to rank order a random list of items according to their frequency, or to estimate the frequency of a set of words in relation to an 'anchor word'. Broadly speaking, although correlation figures varied, the findings of these early studies showed a strong correspondence between speakers' estimates of word frequency and the objective frequency of the items. Researchers took this as an indication of the accuracy of informants' intuitions.

More recently, however, the findings of this earlier work have been debated in studies which engage both methodological and theoretical disputes across a somewhat wider range. We can see this played out, for example, in a sequence of studies including: Schmitt and Dunham (1999); Aizawa *et al.* (2001); McCrostie (2007); Alderson (2007); and McGee (2008). In the next section we will summarize these studies briefly in order to point up their different approaches and conclusions.

More recent work on frequency intuitions

Schmitt and Dunham (1999) conducted a study prompted by their perception of the methodological failings of earlier work claiming that 'Research into frequency intuitions reached its peak in the 1960s and 1970s but petered out before any truly useful conclusions were reached' (p. 390). In addition to the fact that earlier work had tended to use only small numbers of informants and had focused largely on native speakers, they identify two other major shortcomings. First, they highlight the fact that informants in earlier studies were often asked to rate unrelated words – a task which Schmitt and Dunham see as 'rather unnatural' and lacking in psycholinguistic validity (p. 393). We will return to this claim below. Second, they contend that earlier studies used deficient **corpora** as their baseline for assessing the objective frequency of the words used in the studies. In their attempt to remedy these deficiencies, they explored the frequency judgements of 160 native speakers of English and 209 non-native speakers with a range of L1 backgrounds. Their informants were given sets of five near synonyms in which one 'anchor word' was picked out. They had to rate the relative frequency of all of the items against the anchor word by giving a numerical score indicating how much more or less frequent the item was than the anchor word. Their main findings were that:

- Native speakers were able to identify the 'core' (most frequent) word in a set about 85 per cent of the time. This was also true of advanced non-native speakers, at least for those word sets that they completed (i.e., where they knew all of the words in the set).
- Both groups were, however, inaccurate in their judgement of the 'absolute frequency' of words.
- Native speakers were less homogeneous in their judgements than non-native speakers and differences in level of education appeared to be a factor in this lack of homogeneity amongst the L1 informants.

By the authors' own admission, this study did not provide the 'clear statements' about native and non-native intuitions of frequency that they had anticipated (p. 407). However, whilst acknowledging certain methodological problems which may make it difficult to interpret their results, Schmitt and Dunham are nevertheless hopeful that their work will 'aid future vocabulary research and provide the basis for a renewed discussion into the practical applications of frequency intuitions' (pp. 407–8).

Certainly their study did spark fresh interest and re-engage the debate around word frequency judgements (Aizawa *et al.*, 2001; McCrostie, 2005, 2007; Alderson, 2007; McGee, 2006). It must be said, however, that this was in part because of some significant problems in Schmitt and Dunham's work – mostly, but not exclusively, to do with their methodology and the way in which they extrapolate from the data gathered by their 'anchor word' method to claims about informants' ability to do things that they were not in fact asked to do (for example, rank the frequency of words in a set, or judge the absolute frequency of individual items). Aizawa *et al.* (2001) and McCrostie (2005, 2007) pick these points up and are stringent in their criticism, particularly of the elicitation method used by Schmitt and Dunham, pointing to its unnecessary complexity and to the level of numerical skill that it requires on the part of the informants. McCrostie, indeed, suggests that these flaws undermine the value of the study overall: 'Needless to say this design is overly complex, requiring a certain degree of mathematical sophistication, and as a result the study's conclusions must be considered as suspect at best' (McCrostie, 2007, p. 56).

What is surprising, perhaps, is that other aspects of Schmitt and Dunham's study received less attention in the studies that followed. The introduction to their paper contains a number of unacknowledged theoretical assumptions that do not seem to have attracted the level of consideration that has been afforded to other aspects of their work and which seem to have been buried in the ensuing controversy around methodological issues. One of Schmitt and Dunham's claims, for example, is that the elicitation method they used, in which informants are presented with a set of near synonyms, represents a task that they describe as a more 'natural' or 'life-like' task than other experimental protocols. Their justification for this claim raises some interesting questions. They argue that:

> To form a task which is more valid psycholinguistically, we must ask ourselves how frequency intuitions are used in real language. In cases where several synonyms from a lexical set could be chosen there must be some determining factor or factors which affect the eventual choice. Frequency is very likely among these factors, since it has close relationships with the register constraints which also affect lexical choice ... Thus rating near synonyms within a lexical set may be a more natural task in frequency experiments as we often have to choose from a number of near synonyms in our daily communication. (Schmitt and Dunham, 1999, p. 393)

There are a number of issues here that warrant closer inspection. First, of course, their use of the label 'daily communication', undefined in terms of mode or communicative context, makes it is hard to evaluate whether or not choosing between synonyms can be seen as a 'natural' activity. This rather vague use of terminology is a good illustration of the lack of cross-fertilization between social linguistic and lexical research traditions that we discussed above. We might, in any case, question the implication that there is a straightforward relationship between 'real language use' and 'psycholinguistic validity'. More importantly, we should query the tacit assumption that they seem to be making about storage and retrieval within the mental lexicon. If we presume that Schmitt and Dunham are referring to choice between synonyms below the level of the speaker's conscious knowledge, then their argument would seem to rest on a model in which synonyms or near synonyms are always co-located and co-activated *regardless of their frequency or **register**.* Such an assumption a) would not be uncontroversial and b) seems to lead us into a somewhat contradictory argument in which frequency/register are at the same time 'determining factors' in word selection and yet not relevant in determining the structure of the mental lexicon.

Subsequent research, however, was, as we have indicated, more interested in resolving the methodological problems associated with collecting data on frequency intuitions. Aizawa *et al.* (2001) developed a simpler methodology in which native speakers of English and Japanese learners completed two tests which required them to rank words in frequency order. The first test contained sets of three synonyms, and the second sets of three random words. All of the items in the tests were drawn from Nation's 1K, 2K and 3K word lists (Nation, 1996). They found that the native speakers were not significantly more accurate than the learners, who in some cases outperformed them. Furthermore, they found no correlation between vocabulary size and

the accuracy of the frequency ratings. They concluded, unlike the earlier studies, that native-speaker judgements do not always match the objective data
from corpora and that this may depend on the particular items used in tests.
McCrostie's 2005 study replicated Aizawa *et al.* (2001) using the same tests,
administered on this occasion to native speakers of English who were teachers
and to Japanese learners. His findings matched those of Aizawa *et al.* – that
is, that there was no significant difference between the accuracy of frequency
judgements of native and non-native speakers, and that there was no correlation between learners' vocabulary size and their performance. In a further
study, McCrostie (2007) pursued his interest in EFL teachers' frequency intuitions in a study which set out to compare their judgements with those of
average [*sic*] native speakers (undergraduate students). The study also focused
particularly on teachers' ability to estimate the frequency of words falling into
the middle range **frequency bands**. Participants completed two tests in which
they had to rank 24 words in order of frequency. In the first test, he used the
same items as Ringeling (1984), which were drawn from a wide range of frequency, and in the second items selected from a narrower frequency range. He
found that all participants were accurately able to rate the frequency of items
in lists which contained very high- and very low-frequency words, but that
the EFL teachers were not significantly better at this than the undergraduates.
He further reported that teachers had greater difficulty accurately ranking the
frequency of words in the middle range, regardless of their training. His conclusion is that 'teachers cannot always identify the most frequent words in the
English language and should consult frequency lists in conjunction with their
intuitions' (McCrostie, 2007, p. 62).

Other recent studies of frequency intuitions have focused more directly on
this issue of the relative primacy and value of teacher intuitions versus corpus-
based data. Papers by Alderson (2007) and McGee (2008) encapsulate the
main grounds of the debate. Alderson's starting point is the contention that
earlier studies (from the 1960s to the 80s), which found strong correlations
between subjective frequency judgements and objective frequency data, may
have been compromised by the inadequacies of the corpora that they used. He
reports three investigations of frequency judgements using different methodologies and with varying sizes of word samples. The degree of inaccuracy and
of individual difference that he finds leads him to suggest that:

> either judgements of word frequency, even by highly educated native
> speakers of a language, may not be very accurate estimates of the fre-
> quency of words in their language, or that even large, modern corpora
> are inadequate indicators of word frequency as experienced by individu-
> als and groups of individuals. (Alderson, 2007, p. 383)

In an explicit response to this paper, McGee (2008) takes issue with
Alderson's conclusions and with the grounds on which they are based. He
refutes Alderson's claim that earlier work is undermined by the deficiencies

of the corpora used: first, he notes that modern re-rankings of earlier SFE data against objective frequency counts based on much larger corpora find very similar correlations to those reported in the earlier work (McGee, 2006); second, he points out that even very large general corpora are not always consistent in the frequency rankings they throw up, even for very common words (McGee, 2008, p. 510). He accuses Alderson of dismissing too lightly the care which early work on frequency estimations had invested in trying to set legitimate parameters for comparing intuitions with corpus data, and of himself failing to consider certain variables (such as the grammatical class of the words used and the range of relative frequencies of the words in the sets). He concludes by suggesting that researchers need to adopt a more careful and detailed understanding of the frequency estimation data if they are to be useful in the development of teaching materials and tests, and urges a change of approach that would regard SFE data as *different from*, rather than *inferior to* the frequency information provided by corpora: 'The first step in developing this understanding requires a mind-set change – treating SFE data not as inferior but as useful data. Unless that step is made, then there is little benefit in comparing intuitions and corpus data' (*ibid.*, p. 513).

What, then, are the main messages that emerge from this review of key points in the development of research into the intuitions about word frequency of native speakers and learners in terms of the 'frequency' element of Nation's dimension of 'constraints on use'? First, that it is an area which presents really substantial challenges in terms of research design and methodology. These concerns have tended to dominate the debate, making it difficult to undertake secure comparisons between different studies and perhaps also hampering the evolution of sustained reflection about how L1 and L2 frequency intuitions might inform our thinking about models of word knowledge and of the mental lexicon in general. McGee (2008) is something of an exception in this respect and does, in fact, allude to the lack of theoretical underpinning in Alderson (2007) as a further flaw which compounds what he perceives to be the study's methodological flaws. Indeed, his exploration of some possible theoretical explanations as to why there may be differences between SFE data and corpus-based frequency data is one the most interesting aspects of his paper. He brings to bear the notion explored in psychology research that frequency estimations may rely not just on the *availability* of items in the mental lexicon, but also on their *saliency* for the participants. Thus, informants may, for example, underestimate, the frequency of some polysemous items because they are focusing on less common meanings of a word and overlooking its more frequent but less noticeable acceptations (McGee, 2008, p. 512). McGee also offers a welcome reflection on what the data from frequency intuition studies may suggest about the organization of the mental lexicon. He proposes that the inaccuracy of estimations might lend support to models which emphasize the importance of formulaic chunks of language within the mental lexicon (e.g., Wray, 2002). If the mental lexicon contains multiple entries for the same item, as both an individual word and as part of one or more formulaic strings, then we might expect a mismatch between intuitions and objective data if, in some of the occurrences which account for the high frequency of a given word, that word is buried within a common **collocation**. However, as we have noted, this kind of theoretical reflection seems relatively underdeveloped in the other work on frequency intuitions reviewed above.

Practical implications and suggestions for further research

This discussion of Nation's presentation of the 'constraints on use' dimension of word knowledge and of some of the vocabulary research that has built upon it has brought to light a number of issues. We have seen that 'constraints on use' is a slippery construct that has proved hard to pin down. If we are to bring this aspect of lexical knowledge out of the shadow of the other elements of Nation's framework, future research may need to take on board a number of considerations. As a starting point, it will be important to develop a more precise operational definition of **register** and to be much more explicit about how register and frequency overlap and interact. In addition, our discussion suggests that there is still untapped potential for vocabulary researchers to refine their understandings by adopting insights from social linguistics disciplines that might inform research design and analysis. Future research designs could usefully give greater emphasis to context in terms of the types of language under investigation and the language users themselves. Interdisciplinary methodological approaches looking at very specific types of language used by specific groups of speakers may well produce new insights into how lexical knowledge develops. For example, it would be interesting to explore in detail the development of both **declarative** and **procedural word knowledge** in relation to the lexis of the representation of argument in native speaker and non-native speaker undergraduates and academics. In a recent newspaper article ('The Lost Art of Essay Writing', *Guardian*, 26 April 2011), Professor Wayne Martin noted the need for essay-writing skills to develop over time. Interestingly, what he says implicitly emphasizes the critical importance of knowledge of constraints on vocabulary use in this context: 'some very smart students can write, but they get to university and they overreach themselves using phrases like "hegemonic dialectical superstructure"!' Vocabulary studies using the theoretical resources of language attitudes and sociolinguistic identity research might illuminate the processes by which learners and native speakers develop stable intuitions about register and frequency in relation to academic and other types of language.

There is also room for future research to look more closely at how knowledge of constraints on use is affected by the linguistic and cultural differences between languages and language users. Nation's framework implicitly takes English as a baseline for understanding the different components of word knowledge and the relationships between them. However, more detailed case studies of other languages, especially those which are linguistically and culturally relatively close to English, might lead us to question the generalizability of some of these assumptions. For example, structural differences between languages, such as the existence of grammatical gender, might have important consequences for the way in which the different elements of the *use* aspects of word knowledge relate to each other. The intense and well-documented debate surrounding the attempt to feminize professional terms in France (see, for example, Wilks and Brick, 1997; Gervais-le Garff, 2002; Van Compernolle, 2009) provides an interesting illustration of the instability of the relationship between grammatical features and register/frequency constraints with the high-profile controversy over the (un)acceptability of grammatically cohesive but lexically novel formulations (e.g., the *La première ministre* followed by the pronoun *elle*, vs *le premier minister* also followed by the pronoun *elle*.) Such instances raise interesting questions about individual variations in respect of the intricacies of word knowledge even amongst native speakers and about the relative pre-eminence in the mental lexicon of frequency (familiarity), register and grammatical constraints in respect of different languages.

In conclusion, then, whilst Nation's (2001) comprehensive presentation of the elements of word knowledge has been hugely influential in establishing an understanding of vocabulary learning as a highly complex, multi-faceted phenomenon, we are a still a long way from achieving the hoped-for precision as regards the way in which elements of word knowledge interrelate, at least as far as constraints on use are concerned. Perhaps, also, this reflection on the 'Cinderella dimension' of word knowledge acts as a salutary reminder of the dangers of expecting too much from any one attempt to capture what it means to know a word. We should be wary of the temptation to reify something that began as a descriptive list whose prime purpose was to establish the idea that the learner's challenge in respect of vocabulary acquisition is a multidimensional one, and to act as a practical template which can be used to evaluate the efficacy of teaching materials and pedagogic approaches.

Questions for discussion

- Is it possible to teach, effectively, knowledge of constraints of use, or is this aspect of vocabulary knowledge acquired incidentally?
- Given that native speakers of a language exhibit incomplete knowledge of constraints on use of some words, how important is it for learners to acquire this knowledge?
- Why does native speaker intuition about language use not always match objective evidence?

Confidence in Word Knowledge

Jim Ronald and
Tadamitsu Kamimoto

11

Introduction

Nation's (2001) framework of vocabulary knowledge has served in many ways as a valuable guide for researchers and language teachers interested in understanding and promoting second language vocabulary acquisition. At a basic level, it reminds us that knowing a word cannot simply be equated with knowing, for example, a word's meaning, and draws our attention to other facets of word knowledge, such as written or spoken word forms, **collocation** or word grammar, and **register** or associations.

The productive/receptive dimension of Nation's framework draws attention to two further essential features of vocabulary knowledge. First, it alerts us to the fact that someone's knowledge of a word, or of a facet of a word, may be partial; it is not limited to a dichotomous *know/don't know*. Second, the productive/receptive dimension makes a clear and important link between the extent of a person's grasp of a word, or facet of a word, and the manner and extent to which they are able to use it.

At word level, rather than facet level, the question of how to measure extent, or depth, of word knowledge has been addressed by Wesche and Paribakht (1996). Their Vocabulary Knowledge Scale (VKS) aims to measure depth of word knowledge by locating a learner's knowledge of each of a set of words along the five points of a scale, from not recognized to demonstration of productive knowledge by using the word in a sentence. To give the meaning of a word or to use the word in a sentence certainly does demonstrate productive knowledge of a word, but to perform these tasks also requires confidence about that knowledge. A measure of ability to use a word such as VKS, then, inevitably tests both word knowledge and confidence about that word knowledge.

Beyond vocabulary teaching or testing environments, it remains true that our ability to use a word, whether receptively or productively, depends to some extent on the confidence that we have about our knowledge about that word. In a language learning context, as in a test or classroom activity, we may consider our confidence about our knowledge of a word in a fairly abstract sense, and our ability to use a word as basically stable; this may, for example, be demonstrated through being able to give or select the right answer. In some classroom contexts, however, confidence about vocabulary knowledge will vary according to the context, such as using a word with one classmate, in a small group, or to a whole class. Outside the classroom it may be more usual to think of confidence about word knowledge in terms of being confident *to*: confident to use productively in an essay, in an email to a friend, or in a presentation at a conference; or confident to use receptively to follow directions or to take medicine based on our understanding of the words on the label.

Confidence about word knowledge is not mentioned in Nation's framework as an aspect or dimension of word knowledge, nor is it found in Henrikson's (1999) influential description of dimensions of vocabulary development. Neither does it receive even passing attention in major books on L2 vocabulary or the mental lexicon (e.g., Nation, 2001; Schmitt and McCarthy, 1997; Singleton, 1999) except, indirectly, in relation to guessing or risk-taking in tests. It can be argued, however, that the influence and importance of confidence about vocabulary knowledge extends far beyond issues relating to language learners' responses in vocabulary tests. This lack of recognition of the importance of confidence to vocabulary knowledge may, in part, be because of its fluctuating and context-related nature, because it is closely related to these aspects of actual language use that are typically excluded from experimental conditions for investigating vocabulary knowledge, and also perhaps because confidence does not fit easily into established models or frameworks for describing vocabulary knowledge or development. Since, however, research related to confidence about vocabulary knowledge does appear to be limited to questions of guessing and risk-taking in vocabulary tests, this, too, is the main focus of this chapter, which will review recent research (Shillaw, 2009; Iso and Aizawa, 2008) and a commentary related to these issues (Read and Nation, 2009), before going on to report two recent studies relating to confidence and vocabulary testing.

Confidence in word knowledge

One focus of attention that relates to guessing and risk-taking concerns the use of the **yes/no** format (Meara and Buxton, 1987) in L2 vocabulary testing (as described in Chapters 2 and 3 of this volume). This is a format in which learners are asked to look at, or listen to (Milton and Hopkins, 2006), individual words and simply to record whether or not they think they know the word. As Read and Nation (2009) note, since this is a test format in which learners rate their own knowledge of words and because test-takers are penalized for claiming to know items which do not exist as words in the target language, test scores are affected by confidence-related factors such as guessing, confusion (mistaking test items for other words), or optimism.

Shillaw (1999, 2009) has devoted much attention to the yes/no format and the issues of guessing and risk-taking in test-takers' responses, and how to deal with these. He describes (2009) a study in which he sets out to investigate whether the presentation of yes/no test words in the context of dictionary example sentences would increase learners' confidence in rating the items, as compared to a conventional yes/no test in which words are presented in isolation. This study was conducted with the help of 95 Japanese second-year university students majoring in English, with 48 taking a conventional non-contextualized yes/no test (the NC group) and 47 taking a contextualized form of the test (the C group). Overall, for the 30 test items the C group rated a significantly higher number of items as known than did the NC group; presenting words in context did appear to slightly increase test-takers' confidence that they knew the words. However, results for a subsequent translation test for the same 30 words showed no significant difference between the two groups, suggesting that any confidence that C group test-takers may have gained from seeing the test words in context may often have been misplaced.

Shillaw's study, which he describes as small-scale, is important in that it directly addresses an important issue in this under-researched area: how the presentation of test words in context may affect both recognition of the words and confidence about the rating of words as known or unknown. Although the results may appear somewhat contradictory, in that while context appears to increase confidence about rating of word knowledge, it does not increase accuracy in word knowledge rating, these results do conform to findings in previous research. Nagy (1997), for example, summarizing research in this area, notes the difficulties that learners often have in accurately inferring word meaning from context.

One further recent study that has been conducted in this area is Iso and Aizawa's (2008) investigation into the relationship between learners' vocabulary size and confidence regarding test responses. A number of Japanese EFL university students (159) were given a 240-item computer-administered vocabulary size test using Nation's Vocabulary Levels Test-style matching format (Nation, 1990, p. 264) consisting of sets of three test words with six definitions. They instructed the students to indicate their confidence level regarding responses on a three-point scale of 'high', 'medium' and 'low'. They counted the number of 'high' confidence ratings and correlated these data with the learners' vocabulary sizes. The result showed that the two factors of vocabulary size and rating confidence about responses had a correlation of medium strength, with $r = .59$, $p < .001$. It was suggested on the basis of these findings that the larger a subject's vocabulary size, the more confident were they likely to be about the answers they provided.

Iso and Aizawa report a conscientious attempt to examine the relationship between vocabulary size and confidence about test answers. Their research method and data provide a promising first step in this area, although the coefficient of correlation between vocabulary size and confidence about responses does seem somewhat low, probably due to some of the shortcomings of the VLT format (Read, 1988). Perhaps because this is a preliminary study, they did not go on to consider the important question of how the data regarding confidence about responses might be used to increase accuracy in estimating participants' vocabulary sizes.

Current research

The two studies described in this section address confidence-related issues in vocabulary testing.

Using confidence estimates to improve accuracy in assessment

The first, focusing on the VLT, employs and evaluates a method for using data from self-evaluation of confidence regarding test responses, to produce results that are more reliable. There is also a related issue concerning the assessment incorporating confidence – that is, when learners are asked to judge how confident they are of test responses, some reveal overconfidence in the accuracy of their responses while others tend to have too little confidence. To deal with these personal traits, Shizuka's (2004) approach has been adopted. By this method, clustered objective probability scoring (COPS) is expected to yield scores that are practically free from personality factor contamination. COPS scores are calculated using the following four steps. The first is to group items according to ratings of confidence level. The second step is to add up items sharing the same confidence level respectively. The third step is to divide the sum of the correct items in each confidence level by the number of items in that level. The resultant values can then be applied to correct responses as their scores. In this manner, the COPS scoring is capable of reducing the effects of personal traits of overestimation and underestimation of confidence regarding vocabulary knowledge. The purpose of this research is to apply confidence rating and COPS to a vocabulary test and to evaluate the extent to which the new scoring method can improve test results which employ dichotomous scoring (DS).

Method

A group of 84 Japanese EFL university students participated in the study. Their English proficiency level was considered intermediate. The second form of the revised VLT (Schmitt et al., 2001) was used. Among the five word levels available, four levels (2000-word, 3000-word, 5000-word and academic word level) were used. Two changes were made to the form. First, English definitions were translated into Japanese to prevent the reading ability of English definitions from influencing scores. Second, to collect data concerning the learner confidence level of responses, 'low', 'medium' and 'high' were given in parenthesis, adjacent to a cluster of words and definitions. Participants were asked to circle a corresponding confidence level regarding their response every time they matched a word to a definition.

Results

In order to compare differences in scores between the two scoring methods, descriptive statistics will be shown. Then two types of data will be compared from item facility indices. Third, data concerning the validity of the new scoring method will be presented.

Table 11.1 shows descriptive statistics on the scores based on the two types of scoring: DS and COPS. There are some points to be noted. First, the COPS means were consistently lower across the four word levels than the DS means; the difference in total mean score was 16.45 out of a possible 120. About 20 per cent of the DS total decreased when the same data were scored by COPS. However, an overall difficulty order of the items between the two types of scoring was the same with the 2000-word level the easiest, followed in order by the 3000-word level, the academic word level, and the 5000-word level. Second, the COPS standard deviations were larger across the four word levels than the DS ones. This suggests that COPS is capable of spreading test-takers more widely than DS. Third, the COPS reliabilities were higher across the four word levels than the DS reliabilities. None of the DS reliabilities achieved 0.80, but even the lowest COPS reliability achieved 0.80, with two COPS reliabilities in 0.90s.

Item facility indices

In order to show what effects the COPS had on items in terms of item facility (IF), Table 11.2 provides mean IF indices of target words according to DS and

Table 11.1   Descriptive statistics: DS vs COPS ($N = 84$)

	Mean				SD		Reliability (α)	
	DS	COPS	Diff	(per cent)	DS	COPS	DS	COPS
2000	25.50	23.16	2.34	(9.2)	3.08	4.20	0.73	0.88
3000	22.36	19.11	3.25	(14.5)	3.88	4.93	0.78	0.90
Academic	19.49	13.93	5.56	(28.5)	4.51	5.34	0.76	0.91
5000	15.07	9.77	5.30	(35.2)	3.68	3.84	0.63	0.85
Total	82.42	65.97	16.45	(20.0)	13.16	16.27	0.91	0.96

Note: A possible maximum of 30 at each word level.

Table 11.2   Mean item facility indices ($N = 84$)

Word level	DS	COPS	Diff
2000	0.85	0.77	0.08
3000	0.75	0.64	0.11
Academic	0.62	0.46	0.16
5000	0.50	0.33	0.17

COPS. Two points should be noted. First, mean IF values decreased as difficulty level increased regardless of the scoring method. The DS IF means were 0.85, 0.75, 0.62 and 0.50 as the word level went up, whereas the COPS IF means were 0.77, 0.64, 0.46 and 0.33. Broadly speaking, the COPS IF means were roughly equal to the DS IF means of one word frequency below. Second, as the frequency level went up differences in IF means between the DS and the COPS increased, despite the fact that the two types of IF means became smaller. To examine whether the differences between them are significant, pairwise t-tests were conducted. The differences at all four word levels were statistically significant at the .01 significance level (2K level: $t(29) = 9.763$, $p < .01$; 3K level: $t (29) = 7.506$, $p < .01$; academic level: $t (29) = 14.304$, $p < .01$, 5K level: $t (29) = 11.656$, $p < .01$).

IF differences and word levels

The finding above leads us to question how big are IF differences of the same items between the two scoring methods. Table 11.3 shows the distribution of all the 120 target items according to the IF differences and the word levels. It can be seen from the table that all the IF differences varied from 0.00 to 0.40. Target items with IF differences between 0.00 and 0.10 accounted for 43.33 per cent of a total of 120 target items. Target items with IF differences between 0.10 and 0.20 accounted for 38.33 per cent of the total. When these two categories of IF differences were put together, the number of items accounted for a little more than 80 per cent of the total. Items with an IF difference of above 0.20 accounted for a little less than 20 per cent of the total.

The table also shows that the majority of the items with IF differences between 0.00 and 0.10 were clearly distributed on the less difficult word levels of 2K and 3K. Concerning the items with IF differences between 0.10 and 0.20, a relatively large number of items were distributed on the more difficult word levels of the academic and the 5K levels. This tendency seems to be natural because the learners need not guess on the 2K and 3K word levels as frequently as they do on the academic and 5K word levels. In short, it can be said that most of the IF differences of the same items between the DS and the COPS fall within an IF difference of 0.20, and the degree of IF differences depends on the word levels.

Table 11.3 Frequency of IF differences by word level

	2K	3K	Ac	5K	Total	(per cent)
0.00 < IF diff < 0.10	22	17	6	7	52	(43.33)
0.10 ≤ IF diff < 0.20	8	8	18	12	46	(38.33)
0.20 ≤ IF diff < 0.30	0	4	6	8	18	(15.00)
0.30 ≤ IF diff < 0.40	0	1	0	3	4	(3.33)
Total	30	30	30	30	120	(100.00)

Validity of new scoring method

If confidence rating and COPS work in an effective and reliable way, we would expect that the following two assumptions hold true. The first assumption is that, as confidence level increases from low, to medium and to High within each word level, accuracy rate is expected to increase accordingly. Accuracy rate should correlate positively with the degree of confidence. The second assumption is that, as the word frequency level gets higher within each confidence level, accuracy rate is expected to decrease. Accuracy rate is expected to correlate negatively with the word level. If such implicational scaling is observed, that would mean, first, that participants indicate their confidence levels in a consistent manner and, second, that COPS is indeed an effective scoring method. In order to find out if these assumptions are the case, mean correctness was calculated.

Table 11.4 shows mean scores according to the confidence level and the word level. It can be observed that the mean score increased as the confidence level went up at each word level. For instance, at the 2K word level, it increased gradually in the increasing order of the confidence level. The same numerical changes can be observed at the other word levels. In short, the mean scores fell into an implicational scale. Therefore, it can be said that the first assumption holds true.

Table 11.4 also shows that the mean score decreased within each confidence level as the word level decreased. At the low confidence level, the mean score decreased gradually as the word frequency level declined. At the medium confidence level, there existed a gradual decrease according to the word level. At the high confidence level, the mean score decreased in a similar manner. As a result, the second assumption turned out to be the case too. The mean scores decreased gradually within the confidence level respectively as the word frequency level got higher.

Frequency count

There is another way of checking whether the combination of confidence rating and COPS works. It can be assumed that if test-takers express confidence consistently, the frequency count of the confidence level is also expected to

Table 11.4 Mean score (per cent) (N = 84)

Word level	Confidence level		
	Low	Medium	High
2000	0.48	0.82	0.99
3000	0.45	0.78	0.98
Academic	0.37	0.67	0.94
5000	0.33	0.63	0.90

systematically change. Table 11.5 shows that the frequency count of the low confidence level increased gradually as the word level gets higher. Conversely, then, the frequency count of the high confidence level decreased gradually.

In sum, the findings have shown the new scoring is extremely promising in the search for a more accurate measurement tool, and have increased the likelihood of measuring vocabulary knowledge more accurately than the DS.

Discussion

The findings showed that participants' scores decreased by 20 per cent when their responses were scored again, incorporating confidence rating and the COPS. We interpret this difference in scores between the DS and the COPS as the extent of guessing attributable to the matching format of the VLT, in which there are six words and three definitions (see Figure 11.1) and test-takers are expected to match words to definitions. This format is more efficient than the MC format in terms of the number of items that the tests can present at a time: three versus one. In addition, this format is claimed to offer very low chances of guessing correctly (Nation, 1990, p. 261). However, little research has been conducted into test-takers' performance in this test format and whether Nation's claim concerning guessing is fair.

It can be suggested, therefore, that the two claimed advantages of the VLT's format are not as profitable as suggested. In fact, they may be regarded as disadvantages of the VLT, which are not found in MC tests – in other words, that putting three test items in a cluster has caused more harm than good and created problems. The three items in a matching format are not independent,

Table 11.5 Mean frequency count (N = 84)

Word level	No of items	Confidence level		
		Low	Medium	High
2000	30	6.51	6.74	16.75
3000	30	10.68	5.23	14.10
Academic	30	14.08	5.99	9.93
5000	30	18.25	5.51	6.24
Sum	120	49.52	23.46	47.01

```
1. business
2. clock        _____ part of a house
3. horse        _____ animal with four legs
4. pencil       _____ something used for writing
5. shoe
6. wall
```

Figure 11.1 Sample question
Source: Nation, 1990, p. 264.

unlike items in the MC test. It is a principle of measurement that the success or failure of any item should not depend on the success or failure of any other item (Brown and Hudson, 2002). This assumption of local independence seems to be unsustainable with the VLT. Nevertheless, Schmitt *et al.* (2001, p. 61) assumed a noncommittal stance by saying that test items are independent when they are known to test-takers, but that they are not when they are not known. They concluded that this problems needs to be investigated further (for a similar view, see Beglar and Hunt, 1999).

It can be claimed that the combination of confidence rating and COPS adopted here can make items in the matching format behave as if independent. The reasoning behind this claim is that when test-takers are asked to express their confidence level concerning responses, they are most likely to concentrate on one match at a time and rate the confidence level for that match. For instance, if test-takers are not very confident about a match, they would probably choose the low confidence level. Therefore, the new scoring method lets dependent items work as independent items. Small differences in test scores are accumulated, yielding a total of about 20 per cent reduction of the DS scores.

This implies that COPS is a more accurate scoring method in that it can address a question of personal trait in expressing confidence level. It is not susceptible to test-takers' individual predisposition to be optimistic or pessimistic about matches. The COPS has successfully turned dichotomous scoring into polytomous scoring, allowing the VLT to measure their partial knowledge. This would require VLT scores to be interpreted as representing not individual words but an accumulated whole of vocabulary knowledge ranging from very little to perfect.

This study adopted three levels of confidence, but with hindsight test-takers might be able to differentiate in more detail (for more distinctions, see Pugh and Brunza, 1975; Rippey, 1970). If this is the case, it might be beneficial for both test-givers and test-takers to increase the confidence level to four or more. More confidence levels may improve the accuracy of vocabulary measurement. This is a field for further research.

Confidence rating and the COPS method were shown to be successfully incorporated into the VLT. The study argued that the matching format makes items in a cluster dependent and owing to this, the DS scores overestimated test-takers' vocabulary knowledge. The findings have indicated that the combination of those two elements can lessen the degree of item dependence, consequently controlling for guessing and estimating vocabulary knowledge more accurately than the conventional DS method.

Assessing confidence in reading with and without a dictionary

The second recent study reports a case study which served two main purposes in terms of research. One objective of the study was to compare the two second language vocabulary learning conditions of reading with the aid of a dictionary and reading without a dictionary. The second objective was occasioned by the relevance to confidence about word knowledge highlighted by the use, in conjunction, of the two instruments used for the study: V_States (v.03, Meara, 2001) and a test in which the participant was required to give translation equivalents for target words. A report concerning the first general objective may be found in Ronald (2009), and it was there that questions regarding the issue of confidence about word knowledge and the use of V_States were posed.

As we have suggested above, demonstration of word knowledge and, specifically, productive use of word knowledge require not only knowledge of a word, but also a certain degree of confidence about that knowledge. In this regard, Wesche and Paribakht's VKS (1996), by requiring a demonstration of word knowledge for higher points along the scale of vocabulary knowledge, may be seen as not simply a measure of a test-taker's knowledge but also implying an indication of his or her confidence about that knowledge. V_States, as a self-rating tool, does not require any demonstration of word knowledge, and test-takers' responses cannot be said to reflect confidence about word knowledge in the same way as those from the VKS. If we look at the wording of the descriptions of each state of V_States, however, it does appear that confidence regarding knowledge is an integral, even central, component of learners' rating of words with this instrument:

I don't know this word	I'm **not sure** I know this word	I **think** I know this word	I **definitely** know this word

The words shown here in bold print, essentially the words that distinguish one state from the others, appear to relate more directly to degree of confidence about knowing a word than to extent of knowledge about the word. If we accept that confidence is an important component in the rating of word knowledge using V_States, this leads us to two questions that should be investigated. One issue is whether learners' confidence about their word knowledge is justified; do they, for example, actually know the words they rate as 'definitely known'. A further question is the extent to which the accuracy of learners' rating of words may be affected by the vocabulary learning condition. In other words, are some learning conditions more likely than others to leave language learners with either a misplaced confidence in their knowledge of targeted words or insufficient confidence about words they actually do know? We will now go on to a case study which seeks to address these two questions.

Procedure

The case study was conducted as part of a six-week study abroad and TOEFL preparation course for a total of nine Japanese learners of English, with ages and educational levels ranging from 19-year-old first-year university students to postgraduate students in their middle or late 20s who are majoring in English. This study will focus on data from two of the students. One was a first-year student, Hiromi: a highly motivated intermediate level learner, with a TOEFL score of about 510 at the time, who was preparing to go to Canada as an exchange student for one year. The other, Yoko, was a postgraduate student, at the end of the first of a two-year MA course: also highly motivated, and with a TOEFL score close to 550 at the time of the study.

The learning materials were a set of 12 introductory academic texts, in each of which 24 words from the academic word list (AWL) (Coxhead, 2000) appeared, in bold print, between one and three times. These articles were printed in a vocabulary-building textbook (Schmitt and Schmitt, 2005); participants were only provided with the separate articles during the study, and the complete book was presented to them on completion of the course. Through the texts, 288 target AWL words were presented to the course participants. Of these, 287 were selected as target words (one was mistyped and so had to be excluded), together with 30 words of similar difficulty which served as control items.

The course and the study extended over six weeks. For each week, the participants were given the same set of 12 passages, with target words highlighted. Participants were instructed to read two passages per day for six days then to not do any of this reading on the seventh day of each week. A set of ten comprehension questions was also given for each passage. For the first three weeks, they were told not to use a dictionary at all while reading the passages, but to try to work out the meaning of important highlighted words by guessing their meaning from context. For the second three weeks, participants were told that they could use the English–Japanese dictionary contained in their hand-held electronic dictionaries while reading. The participants did not all use the same model of electronic dictionary, but all the dictionaries used contained the same English–Japanese dictionary, *Genius*, third edition (Konishi and Minamide, 2001), which was the most widely used dictionary of this type at university level. They were instructed to spend a similar amount of time for each reading, both day by day and over the six weeks: about 30 minutes per text, averaging one hour for each day of reading and a total of around six hours per week.

The looked-up words were automatically recorded by the electronic dictionaries, with the data deleted each week by the researcher following the noting down of looked-up words. Participants were also instructed to record looked-up words on slips of paper which would be handed in on the first day of each week. The two reasons for requiring participants to keep a written record of looked-up words were to provide a checklist for the words automatically recorded on the electronic dictionaries and, because these were conscientious students who specifically wanted to learn the target AWL words, to allow them to keep a record of looked-up words and to take away access to that list beyond each week of reading.

The participants were asked to rate their knowledge of the 287 target AWL words at the beginning of the course, and following each week of reading. In total, there were seven self-rating sessions using V_States. In this study, participants took an average of about four seconds to rate each item, totalling around 20 minutes per testing session for the total of 318 items. Following the final V_States session, participants were asked to give Japanese translation equivalents for all 288 target words. This was done to ascertain the accuracy of the participant's self-rating of targeted word knowledge. To avoid fatigue and its effect on participants' responses, this test was conducted in four 20-minute sessions with four sets of 72 words. As a break between testing sessions (and also as a valid ending to the course), participants were introduced to a range of self-study materials and resources.

The computer program V_States (v.03, Meara, 2001) was used as the principal instrument in this case study. The program presents the target words on a computer screen, one by one, in random order and records the participant's responses. For each word that appears, participants rate their knowledge of the word by clicking on one of four buttons 0–3 on the screen, representing the following states of word knowledge:

0 – I don't know this word
1 – I'm not sure I know this word
2 – I think I know this word
3 – I definitely know this word

As an instrument for recording changes in vocabulary knowledge, V_States meets three important requirements of this study:

1. It enables the rapid rating of vocabulary knowledge of large numbers of items.
2. It is more sensitive than an instrument that suggests a binary *know/don't know* representation of learners' word knowledge.
3. As an instrument to be used for repeated testing of knowledge of the same set of items, the use of large numbers of test items, the very rapid rating of items and the random presentation of items all reduce any possible effect that retesting itself may have on word knowledge.

In addition, as described above, V_States is of special value for this study because of the combination of word knowledge and confidence about word knowledge contained in the description of each state and, presumably, in test-takers' assignation of target items to the four states.

A further important feature of the data produced by this instrument is that they enable the creation of transitional probability matrices which can be used to produce projections for one learning condition to be compared with actual data for a second condition. However, as this was not the focus of the research described above, the data for this will not be reported here.

The following two hypotheses were formulated:

1. There will be a clear correlation between the participants' rating of target words in the final V_States session and their provision of accurate translation equivalents in the test that follows.

2. The participants will give a greater proportion of accurate translation equivalents for looked-up state 3-rated words than for state 3-rated words that were not looked up.

The reason for the first hypothesis relies on the simple assumption that L2 learners are more likely to know words that they are confident of knowing. The second hypothesis is based on the following two assumptions: 1) that guessing meaning from the written context of a word is more likely to lead to mistaken conclusions than is the consultation of a bilingual dictionary and 2) that as language learners may not be aware of their limited ability to correctly guess word meanings from single L2 contexts as compared to their ability to understand L1 equivalents for L2 words looked up in a dictionary, they may be overconfident of their knowledge of these words.

Results

These results will illustrate the relationship between the words allocated to the four states in the final V_States session with the numbers of correct or partially correct translation equivalents given for the target words. V_States and translation equivalent data for target words that were looked up in an electronic dictionary and target words that were not looked up, will be compared.

The overall data for the final V_States session and the meaning test for the two participants are shown in Tables 11.6 and 11.7.

Table 11.6   Accuracy rates of translation equivalents as compared with V_States ratings (Hiromi)

Word level Final V_States	No answer	Wrong	Partially correct	Correct	Totals
State 0	11	16	1	3	31
State 1	4	15	2	4	25
State 2	10	13	8	12	43
State 3	6	58	26	98	188
Totals	31	102	37	117	287

Table 11.7   Accuracy rates of translation equivalents as compared with V_States ratings (Yoko)

Word level Final V_States	No answer	Wrong	Partially correct	Correct	Totals
State 0	0	1	0	0	1
State 1	1	1	0	0	2
State 2	4	4	6	16	30
State 3	0	16	20	218	254
Totals	5	22	26	234	287

Although numbers of items in each state differ between the two partici-pants as we might expect, with the postgraduate student both reporting and demonstrating a rather larger vocabulary than the first-year undergraduate, in other respects they are very similar. Regarding V_States rating, neither of them rates many words as state 0 or 1: about 10 per cent for each of these states for Hiromi, and only one or two words in each state for Yoko. The vast majority of items were rated as state 3, definitely known, by both participants: almost 90 per cent of items for Yoko and close to 70 per cent for Hiromi.

To a large extent, both participants also rated their vocabulary knowledge accurately: they were able to give the greatest proportion of correct responses for the words they rated as definitely known, and the largest proportions of no response or wrong response for words they had rated as state 0 or 1: don't know or not sure. On the other hand, clear differences emerge when we note that the postgraduate student Yoko was able to give correct translation equiva-lents for almost 86 per cent of state 3-rated items, as compared to just over 50 per cent for the first-year student Hiromi, who gave around 30 per cent of wrong answers and 14 per cent of partially correct answers for these words she rated as definitely known. We see a similar pattern for words rated as state 2, *I think I know* ...; the postgraduate student gives correct answers for over 50 per cent of these items, as compared with 28 per cent for the first-year under-graduate.

We will now go on to look at how dictionary use affected both confidence about knowledge of the target words and knowledge of the words themselves. We will start by considering data for all looked-up and not looked-up target words, as shown in Tables 11.8 and 11.9.

As we can see, both participants were able to give a greater proportion of correct answers for words that were not looked up (45 per cent for Hiromi and 84 per cent for Yoko) than for words that were looked up (Hiromi, 28 per cent; Yoko, 76 per cent). It will be recalled that many of the target words were words that the participants knew, or believed they knew, prior to the study. This is confirmed by participants' responses from the first V_States session,

Table 11.8 Results for all looked-up and not looked-up target words (Hiromi)

	No answer	Wrong	Partially correct	Correct	Totals
Looked-up	16	33	3	21	73
Not looked-up	15	69	34	96	214

Table 11.9 Results for all looked-up and not looked-up target words (Yoko)

	No answer	Wrong	Partially correct	Correct	Totals
Looked-up	4	13	6	74	97
Not looked-up	1	9	20	160	190

in which both participants rated around 50 per cent of the target words as definitely known. Further, we may assume that language learners, including the two participants, are more likely to look up words that they do not know, or about which they do not feel confident, than they are to look up words that they already know, and that this too would be reflected in the above data. For this reason, it may be worthwhile focusing on words which participants rated as unknown or probably unknown in the first V_States sessions.

Before doing this, one aspect of the data that does stand out is that for both participants a greater proportion of not looked-up words were only partially known: 16 per cent for Hiromi and 11 per cent for Yoko, as compared to 4 per cent and 6 per cent, respectively, for the two participants for words that were looked up. We will consider the implications of these results below.

It will be noted from the data from Hiromi in Tables 11.10 and 11.11 that her V_States rating is largely accurate for both looked-up and not looked-up words for states 0 to 2; she either gives no answer or a wrong answer for well over 80 per cent of looked-up words in these states, and 75 per cent for words which were not looked up. The situation for words she rated as definitely known, however, is rather different: she was able to give correct answers for 60 per cent of the state 3 words that were looked up, but only for 14 per cent of the state 3 words that were not looked up. Another interesting aspect of the data is the number of state 3 words for which Hiromi gave only partially correct answers: 21 per cent (nine words) for words which were not looked up, as compared to none for words that were looked up.

Table 11.10 Initially unknown (0/1-rated at T0, T1) looked-up target words (Hiromi)

Word level Final V_States	No answer	Wrong	Partially correct	Correct	Totals
State 0	6	7	0	3	16
State 1	2	6	0	0	8
State 2	4	3	0	1	8
State 3	0	6	0	9	15
Totals	12	22	0	13	47

Table 11.11 Initially unknown (0/1-rated at T0, T1) not looked-up target words (Hiromi)

Word level Final V_States	No answer	Wrong	Partially correct	Correct	Totals
State 0	3	5	1	0	9
State 1	0	4	1	1	6
State 2	4	5	3	1	13
State 3	4	14	6	4	28
Totals	11	28	11	6	56

In the data for Yoko, in Tables 11.12 and 11.13, there is evidence of a clear ceiling effect in that she looked up almost every word which was initially rated as not known or probably not known, with almost all these words ending the study both rated state 3 and correctly translated. This was also true for the small number of words which were not looked up, with only one state 3 word having a partially correct answer.

Discussion

Two hypotheses were formulated regarding the case study results. They were:

1. There will be a clear correlation between the participants' rating of target words in the final V_States session and their provision of accurate translation equivalents in the test that follows.
2. The participants will give a greater proportion of accurate translation equivalents for looked-up state 3-rated words than for state 3-rated words that were not looked up.

Generally speaking, the results for the two participants confirm that their levels of confidence regarding knowledge of the target words were in line with their demonstrated knowledge of the words. Both participants gave the highest proportion of correct translation equivalents for the words they rated as state 3, definitely known. As for words assigned to the two lowest states, worded as *I don't know ...* and *I'm not sure I know this word*, participants either gave

Table 11.12   Initially unknown (0/1-rated at T0, T1) looked-up target words (Yoko)

Word level Final V_States	No answer	Wrong	Partially correct	Correct	Totals
State 0	0	0	0	0	0
State 1	1	1	0	0	2
State 2	0	0	0	4	4
State 3	0	3	0	20	23
Totals	1	4	0	24	29

Table 11.13   Initially unknown (0/1-rated at T0, T1) not looked-up target words (Yoko)

Word level Final V_States	No answer	Wrong	Partially correct	Correct	Totals
State 0	0	0	0	0	0
State 1	0	0	0	0	0
State 2	1	0	0	0	1
State 3	0	1	1	7	9
Totals	1	1	1	7	10

the wrong answer or no answer for all or most of these words. In other words, they were justifiably lacking in confidence about words they did not know.

One important difference noted between the two participants was that Yoko, the postgraduate, was able to give correct or partially correct meanings for over 90 per cent of words she rated as definitely known, as compared to just over 60 per cent for Hiromi, the first-year undergraduate, for whom one third of the meanings given were wrong. Hiromi, then, was clearly overconfident in her rating of words as definitely known. This overconfidence may have a number of causes, such as insufficient focus on word forms leading to mistaken recognition of words or, perhaps, confusion between newly learned words. Since V_States has typically been used in longitudinal case studies with individuals, comparison between participants' individual confidence and accuracy rates has not been an issue, although where within subject V_States ratings vary unexpectedly from session to session, it would clearly affect the reliability of data. We will consider below how this problem may be addressed.

Regarding the second hypotheses, we have already pointed out the danger of drawing conclusions about the effect of dictionary use based simply on final V_States session scores. Since we may assume that words that are already known are those that the participants would have been less likely to look up, much of the data relating to confidence and word knowledge would be likely to relate to prior knowledge rather than reflecting the effects of guessing from context as compared to dictionary consultation.

One aspect of the general data for translation equivalents for target words that does stand out is the greater proportion of partially correct equivalents for not looked-up words for both participants. This may be due either to inaccurate or fuzzy guessing from context, or because participants had prior inaccurate understandings of the words' meanings but, because they were confident about their knowledge of the words, did not feel the need to look them up.

A focus on words that were initially rated as *I do not know* or *I'm not sure* confirms that while the undergraduate student Hiromi gave no partially correct equivalents for looked-up words, she did so for close to a quarter of state 2- and 3-rated words that were not looked up. This suggests that the contexts in which she encountered these words gave her confidence that she knew the meanings of these words, but were not in fact sufficient for her to accurately grasp the meanings. This also accounts for the large proportion, 50 per cent, of not looked-up state 3-rated items for which she gave wrong answers.

There were very few target words that were initially unknown to the graduate student Yoko that she did not subsequently look up. There is, therefore, little data available for comparison with results for looked-up words. She did, however, rate 27 of the 29 words that were initially unknown, then looked up, as probably or definitely known, and for all but one of these gave a correct translation equivalent.

Given the above, we may say that the second hypothesis is confirmed, although the data are incomplete and not altogether conclusive. In the case of the postgraduate student, we can say that her dictionary use, together with the encounter of words in context, was effective both in increasing her knowledge of the target words and in providing her with a realistic understanding of her word knowledge gained through these means. For the undergraduate student, Hiromi, for words not looked up, the higher proportion of wrong or only partially correct words which she rated as definitely known does support the hypothesis, but the large number of wrong translation equivalents for words which were looked up suggests that a number of factors may contribute to the results obtained. Further research is needed into this question.

Conclusion

The results bring us back to the issue of how to deal with overconfidence in vocabulary testing. A meaning test of all test items such as that used in this study is generally unfeasible, given the time it takes, and also somehow self-defeating, since the value of V_States is as an instrument for the self-rating of vocabulary knowledge, but there are some ways forward that are worth investigation. One way might be to ask participants to give meanings for a random sample of, for example, 10 per cent of test words. Another approach could be to focus on the set of words that were rated as unknown in earlier V_States sessions but rated as definitely known in the final session; data for this set of words could then be used to adjust overall test results to account for participants' varying confidence levels.

Pedagogical implications and suggestions for further research

The two studies reported in this chapter do not claim to address all issues related to vocabulary knowledge, confidence and testing. However, through these studies we have been able to demonstrate some ways in which confidence-related issues in vocabulary testing, such as guessing or overconfident self-rating, may be identified, quantified and addressed with some success. More generally, we believe that through these studies we have been able to show that confidence is an aspect or dimension of vocabulary knowledge that is worthy of greater attention.

With regard to testing, confidence about word knowledge is clearly an element in measures of depth of knowledge, such as VKS (Wesche and Paribakht 1996) or V_States (Meara, 2001), with the latter measure showing particular potential for tracking changes in vocabulary knowledge and confidence over time. The use of specific confidence rating methods, as employed with the VLT in the study reported here or by Iso and Aizawa (2008), demonstrates the value of adding confidence rating to tests that focus on one aspect of word knowledge.

The research reported here also indicates that confidence about word knowledge is a clear and meaningful concept for language learners. Further research with languages other than English and native speakers other than Japanese would help confirm these findings. Increasing awareness of the dimension of confidence about vocabulary knowledge and, more specifically, confidence to use that knowledge for specific purposes would also help language teachers and language learners to get beyond simplistic representations of knowing or not knowing a word towards representations that are closer to their experience: various degrees of word knowledge tempered by confidence to use the words that depends on the context and purpose of use.

Questions for discussion

- In light of the differences reported between undergraduate and postgraduate participants, what do you think has the greater influence on test-taker confidence – personality or experience?
- To what extent do the findings reported in this chapter undermine the performance of **yes/no** tests of vocabulary knowledge, and other tests of vocabulary knowledge and performance?
- Do you think confidence is a facet of vocabulary knowledge in the same way at the other elements which comprise Nation's list of knowing a word?
- If you had learners who, you felt, were under-representing their vocabulary knowledge through lack of confidence, or were misrepresenting their knowledge through overconfidence, how might you set about compensating for this to get better and more strictly comparable knowledge scores?

Conclusion: Reconstructing Vocabulary Knowledge

Tess Fitzpatrick and James Milton

12

The studies and approaches outlined in this volume are motivated by a common belief that by understanding more thoroughly the component parts of the phenomenon we refer to as 'word knowledge' we can attain a fuller understanding of the entity itself. There is a tension here, though, between understanding the parts and understanding the whole, and few of the authors here would argue that one automatically presupposes the other. It is also the case that word knowledge cannot be straightforwardly equated with lexical competence: although there is undoubtedly a strong connection here, 'lexical competence is probably not just the sum of speakers' knowledge of the items their lexicons contain' (Meara, 1996a, p. 52). And, of course, vocabulary knowledge, or competence, is in turn a component of language knowledge, or language competence, and as such its boundaries are blurry. For example, it is strongly implicated in competencies concerning phraseology and discursive cohesion, which do not sit wholly in the 'lexical knowledge' domain, but rather stray into syntactic and stylistic territory. Similarly, to return to Nation's taxonomy of dimensions, there are overlaps between knowledge of word form and knowledge of word parts, between grammatical knowledge and collocational knowledge (as exemplified by Treffers-Daller and Rogers in this volume), and so on. This is true of all divisions into academic disciplines, of course; we use labels for convenience, but in furthering depth of knowledge or application of knowledge, boundaries become fuzzy and topics or subject areas refuse to be ring-fenced.

The divisions we make, then, into dimensions or aspects or competencies or topics, are by necessity artificial and approximate, but we make them nonetheless, and with good reason. Large, dynamic, complex, multi-dimensional entities, of which language use, lexical competence and vocabulary knowledge are examples (see Larsen-Freeman and Cameron, 2008) do not lend themselves easily to micro-examination or theoretical modelling or empirical investigation. Dividing them into smaller component entities facilitates detailed examination, and Nation's word knowledge framework (1990, 2001), itself based on Richards' taxonomy of assumptions and implications (1976), fits well with and formalizes the ways in which researchers conceptualize vocabulary knowledge. It is important to note that the framework is applicable in a relatively straightforward way to language teaching and learning in practice, too (see, for example, Zimmerman's 2009 teachers' handbook). Nation's framework is certainly not the only way of modelling lexical knowledge. Other approaches focus on the interaction between, or the integration of, L1 and L2 vocabulary systems (e.g., De Groot, 1992; Kroll, 1993), on notions of breadth versus depth of vocabulary knowledge (e.g., Anderson and Freebody, 1981) or lexical size and lexical organization (e.g., Meara, 1996a), on knowledge for understanding (**receptive**) and knowledge for expression (**productive**) (see discussion in Read, 2000) and on partial as opposed to complete knowledge (e.g., Henriksen, 1999). One of the most compelling features of Nation's 'dimension' framework is that it facilitates exploration of these models too: partial knowledge can be interpreted as having mastery of some, but not all, dimensions; L1 influence on the L2 lexicon can be more easily identified by considering dimensions discretely, and researchers have argued that the notion of 'depth' of vocabulary knowledge should be reframed as knowledge of the multiple dimensions of a word (e.g., Read, 2004).

The chapters in this volume offer evidence of the potential of Nation's dimensional framework to extend and refine our understanding of word knowledge and lexical competence. The definition and examination of precise aspects of knowledge contributes to the quality of our engagement with the whole in a number of important ways. First, it facilitates interdisciplinary perspectives on our field, by enabling the researcher to identify and apply relevant information and analytic methods from other areas of research. This is difficult to do in the context of vocabulary knowledge in the round, as, with so many intradisciplinary influences and implicational connections to be considered, studies can become messy and unwieldy. Other areas of research clearly have enormous relevance to the study of vocabulary knowledge, though, and in several chapters in this volume we see them applied precisely and in a principled way to aspects of lexical knowledge. Miralpeix and Meara, for example, relate findings from experimental psychology to knowledge and processing of written word form; Treffers-Daller and Rogers draw on corpus linguistics approaches to investigate grammatical dimensions of word knowledge; and Milton, Alexiou and Mattheoudakis relate use of learning strategies to knowledge of spoken word form.

Following from this, it is also the case that a focus on a specific dimension of knowledge can clarify directions for wider applications of the methods and findings used in our own field. Examples of this in these chapters include the application of our understanding of knowledge of association to psychology-centred research into lexical retrieval and storage in language impaired individuals (Fitzpatrick and Munby); the application of findings from studies of word part knowledge to pedagogical approaches (Mäntylä and Huhta) and Pajoohesh's discussion of word **referent** knowledge in the context of the bilingual child.

A third advantage to studying specific aspects of vocabulary knowledge is that this can yield precise information about the influence of other salient variables. Perhaps the most pervasive of these in the study of L2 vocabulary knowledge, is the learners' L1. Milton, Alexiou and Mattheoudakis's chapter here reports that L1 Arabic speakers associate written and spoken representations of English words in a different way from L1 speakers of Greek. Mäntylä and Huhta suggest that the relationship between L1 and L2 morphological systems is so salient to L2 processing that a comparative analysis approach might benefit acquisition of knowledge of word parts in the L2. Fitzpatrick and Munby, in relation to associative knowledge, and Wilks in relation to knowledge of usage constraints, touch on a less frequently considered influence on qualitative aspects of vocabulary knowledge: cultural background. Brown, informed by the relevant psycholinguistics literature, considers as a salient variable the typically analytic approach of the adult language learner, and discusses the effect of this on the acquisition of **collocation** knowledge. Teaching and/or learning method can also be regarded as a salient variable in this way; several of the chapters here are concerned with learning approaches or teaching interventions, and their effect on performance in specific areas of vocabulary knowledge or use (see Brown's overview of the role of learning and teaching in the acquisition of collocational knowledge, and Milton Alexiou and Mattheoudakis's consideration of learning strategies).

There are, however, potential pitfalls in the multi-dimensional approach to vocabulary knowledge. Richards in 1976, Nation in 2001 and almost every publication in which their frameworks have been reproduced, present the dimensions of knowledge in list, or table, format. In a novice reader, this can give rise to a number of misleading assumptions – namely, that in vocabulary growth these dimensions develop in lock-step with each other; that the dimensions are equivalent in importance; that the development of the dimensions is linear in nature. The 'lock-step' assumption is implicitly, if not explicitly, challenged by scholars who claim, for example, that word form recognition has to be the initial dimension of knowledge on which other aspects of knowledge rest (see Agustín Llach and Moreno Espinosa in this volume, who propose that, in terms of numbers of items known, 'knowledge of word and form combined may be smaller than knowledge of form alone'). This claim is not universally agreed, though, with others regarding the point at which knowledge of form can be mapped to conceptual meaning as the threshold of knowledge, and Wolter, for example, controversially proposing a 'meaning last' model of vocabulary acquisition, where knowledge of meaning drags behind the other dimensions (2009). In practice the fundamental nature of the form–meaning link means that, in teaching and testing, this is usually regarded as the most important aspect of word knowledge.

The dynamic nature of the lexicon, though, and variables such as target language (L2), individual learner approaches and differing task demands, mean that the importance, or salience, of particular dimensions is dependent on specific time, task and user, and development is not always related in a linear way.

Miralpeix and Meara, in this volume, find no consistent relationship between speed of word recognition and quantitative knowledge of written words (in terms of number of words known); Pajoohesh makes the insightful suggestion that 'deep lexical knowledge … is not always immediately perceptible and can be hidden behind other language skills and knowledge'. It follows from this that we should not expect vocabulary knowledge to develop along a continuum, in a linear fashion (see Meara, 1997; Melka, 1997, for discussion of this). Agustín Llach and Moreno Espinosa support this, observing that the form–meaning link is not straightforward, but is incremental in nature; their demonstration of variation and inconsistency in learner production of target words urges us to look for developmental thresholds for each dimension, and for implicational relationships between them. Dynamic systems approaches, which have been applied to the study of language in a number of recent publications (Larsen-Freeman and Cameron, 2008; Verspoor et al., 2011) and which present an extremely useful and relevant perspective on language use, offer a means of developing this kind of exploration.

There is a clear value, then, to the discrete identification, definition and investigation of dimensions of vocabulary knowledge, and to the design of adequate tools for measuring them. Once this has been achieved, though, it is essential to return to a wider perspective, and to review the dimensions in a contextualized way. This might entail, for example, the investigation of the relationships and interactions between dimensions of knowledge in dynamic states, such as acquisition (of L1 or L2), on-line (real time) language use, and language attrition. A number of studies have attempted to address the first of these, by measuring separately the aspects of lexical knowledge demonstrated in second language acquisition. Some of these (e.g., Wesche and Paribakht, 1996; Schmitt and Zimmerman, 2002) have used an incremental scale model of acquisition, while others (Fitzpatrick, 2012; Webb, 2007) have attempted to identify patterns in the acquisition of multiple components, but these studies are tentative and do not yet offer sustainable hypotheses. Concern with the relationship between aspects of knowledge forces us to focus more on the cognitive, processing elements of these dynamic states, and this in turn facilitates the application of tools, theories and findings beyond the boundaries of L2 vocabulary knowledge – for example, to natural language processing, or to L1 attrition or aphasia.

Concern with the relationship between aspects of knowledge also introduces the larger-scale macro-theories of language acquisition and the way vocabulary develops as part of the overall language learning process. There are theories – for example, the lexical learning hypothesis – which encompass the idea that syntactic development is driven by lexical development. The hypothesis can provide accounts for the incremental nature of syntactic development as well as for the observed correlations between lexical and syntactic development and the developmental dissociations that have been observed in children's grammatical development. To cling too strongly to the aspects of vocabulary knowledge in Nation's (2001) table as separate and separable elements of knowledge may blind us to their common development and the strength of their inter-relationship. It is even possible, through frequency (Ellis 2002a, 2002b), to explain the driver behind all the aspects of knowledge in the table, although in second language learning we are far from demonstrating the way this is operationalized in any generalized sense. Current thinking suggests that details may vary according to both the first language of the learners and the language being learned (Eisenbeiss, 2007) as the occurrence of similar structures will vary in frequency from one language to another. This is probably the greatest emerging challenge for research in vocabulary knowledge: how can our growing understanding of the influence of frequency and the inter-relationship of the aspects of vocabulary knowledge be combined in a comprehensive description of the process of language acquisition?

It remains the case, therefore, that, despite arguments against the assumption of lock-step or equivalent development, studies have shown time and time again that learner performance on one dimension of word knowledge enables us to predict performance on other dimensions. Equally, vocabulary knowledge itself, especially when measured using quick, quantitative tests such as **yes/no** word recognition tests (Meara and Buxton, 1987), levels tests in their various incarnations (Nation, 1983; Schmitt *et al.*, 2001; Laufer and Nation 1999) and text-based measures such as the Lexical Frequency Profile (Laufer and Nation, 1995), is often used by researchers and by teachers as a proxy for language proficiency. This approximate relationship, though, certainly masks the complexity of the interconnections between different kinds of word knowledge; Schmitt and Meara claim that 'a better understanding of these inter-relationships could go a long way toward developing an explanatory model of vocabulary acquisition' (1997, p. 19). This volume has demonstrated the impressive amount of ground that has been covered, since Nation's model was first published, in furthering our understanding of dimensions of lexical knowledge. We propose that in moving our focus to the study of the reconstructed lexicon, and by focusing on the lexicon as a complex and dynamic entity, we can use our enhanced understanding of the component parts to investigate more deeply the whole.

Appendix 1:
The Non-Word-Based Test
of Derivation (Chapter 4)

B. Täydennä annetut sanat lisäämällä niihin sopiva **etu- tai jälkiliite**. Lihavoidut 'sanat' eivät ole oikeita englannin sanoja, vaan keksittyjä. (Fill in the words by adding an appropriate **prefix or suffix** to them. The bolded 'words' are not real English words, they are invented.)

Seuraava suomenkielinen esimerkki havainnollistaa, miten tehtävään vastataan. *(The following example in Finnish illustrates how to do this task.)*

Tehtävä *(task)*:
Hän oli hyvä **rakentamaan** taloja eli hän oli hyvä _____**rakenta**_____. *(He was good at building houses, that is, he was a good ___ build ____.)*
(= henkilö joka tekee lihavoidun sanan ilmaisemaa toimintaa / työtä (*a person who does the action described by the bolded word*))

Vastaus *(reply)*:
Hän oli hyvä **rakentamaan** taloja eli hän oli hyvä _____**rakenta ja**. *(He was good at building houses, that is, he was a good ___ build er___.)*

Huomaa, että joihinkin sanoihin voi liittää etuliitteen eikä jälkiliitettä kuten tässä esimerkissä. *(Note that you can add a prefix to some of the words rather than a suffix like in this example.)*

---

1. She could **bourble** animals very well because she was a good _____**bourble**_____.
    (= henkilö joka tekee lihavoidun sanan kuvaamaa toimintaa/työtä (*a person who does the action described by the bolded word*))
2. The first time they **prinkled** the cake was no good so they had to _____**prinkle**_____ it. (= tehdä uudestaan toiminta, jota lihavoitu sana kuvaa (*do again the action described by the bolded word*))
3. They did not want to **skey** the ticket, they wanted to _____**skey**_____ it.
    (= tehdä päinvastoin/vastakohta sille, mitä lihavoitu sana kuvaa (*do the contrary of the action described by the bolded word*))
4. It was quite easy to **pranelit** the old job but the _____**pranelit**_____ of my new work is much more difficult. (= sen asian tekeminen, jota lihavoitu sana kuvaa (*doing what the bolded word describes*))

5. This one here is not a big **gabl** but that one there, it's really a _____**gabl**_____.
    (= pienikokoinen gabl (*a small-sized gabl*))
6. Before we can finally **honch** this car you need to _____**honch**_____ it.
    (= tehdä ennen/etukäteen toiminta, jota lihavoitu sana kuvaa (*doing in advance the action described by the bolded word*))
7. I like this flower: it is very **liffear** but that flower over there is _____**liffear**_____.
    (= vastakohta lihavoidulle sanalle (*the contrary to the word described by the bolded word*))
8. I did not **monadate** the story that your friend told me yesterday but what you tell me now is much more _____**monadate**_____. (= sisältää asiaa, jota lihavoitu sana kuvaa (*contains the thing that is described by the bolded word*))

Appendix 2

List of test items in word definition task

Word definition items
Vegetables
Nose
Bicycle
Violin
Elephant
Bread
Ambulance
Duck
Earth
Equator
Sculptor
Surgeon
Fear
To perform
To write

Categories	Scale	Examples	Relevant processes
Syntax	■ Evaluates how closely a definition matched the ideal syntactic structure of standard definitions ■ A scale of 1 to 4 ■ Four was awarded for definitions matching the format of 'X is a Y + (relative clause)'	■ Score of 4:'Nose is a part of body/ something that helps you breathe and smell.' ■ Score of 3: definitions lacking *is* or *that* ■ Score of 2: an incomplete definition, as in 'a nose is something for like on your face' or 'It is a thing for smelling.' ■ Score of 1:'Nose is a body part.'	■ Control of linguistic knowledge ■ Awareness of the format of a standard definition as a school-based genre
Superordinate	■ Evaluated the type of superordinate used ■ A scale of 0 to 5	■ Score of 5:'Real superordinates' such as 'part of body/body part' ■ Score of 4:'Qualified empty superordinates' (or 'not best') e.g., 'a facial thing' ■ Score of 3:'Empty superordinates' such as 'thing/something/someone' or 'what we use for breathing/where we breathe through' ■ Score of 2: Synonyms ■ Score of 1:Translations	■ Analysis of word knowledge ■ Shift of paradigmatic to syntagmatic knowledge
Complement (relative clause)	■ Evaluates the semantic content of the relative clause in a definition based on the decontextualized meaning relations ■ A scale of 0 to 3	■ Score of 3: a properly restrictive complement 'It's (*equator*) a line that separates the north from south and it's a really hot place … goes all around the earth.' ■ Score of 2: a correct but insufficient complement as in: 'equator is --- that turns the world in half.' ■ Score of 1: an incorrect/misleading part in the complements such as:'equator is … that … and they are on the tips of the earth.' ■ Zero: definitions with no complement	■ Analysis of word knowledge of sense relations ■ Shift of paradigmatic to syntagmatic knowledge

(continued)

Appendix 2 Continued

Categories	Scale	Examples	Relevant processes
Definitional feature	■ Measures the syntagmatic knowledge in a definition ■ Includes the composition and attributions of the item ■ Score of 1 for each correct feature	■ 'a bicycle is fun to ride'/'is fast' ■ 'a nose can be triangle shape'/'pointy'/'long' etc.	■ Control of linguistic knowledge in inclusion/exclusion of syntagmatic knowledge

Glossary of Terms

Affix: A word part added, usually at the beginning or end of a word to indicate grammatical information or addition meaning.

Assimilation: The manner in which two phonemes when they occur together in normal speech will change the way one or both of them are pronounced.

CEFR: The Common European Framework of Reference for languages, providing a common set of terminology for language levels and performance.

Cloze test: Test comprising a text from which certain words have been removed.

Cognates: Words which have a common origin.

Collocation: The way words or terms co-occur more often than would be expected by chance.

Connotation: The commonly understood cultural or emotional association that a word or phrase carries.

Corpora: A collection of texts which are mined for information, such as the frequency of occurrence of words.

Declarative knowledge: The factual information stored in memory.

Elision: The omission of individual language sounds in speech.

Formulaic sequences: Fixed combinations of words that can facilitate fluency.

Frequency band: Usually groups of 1000 words taken from a list of words in a language arranged in frequency order.

Hyponymy: The relationship between a specific word and a general word, as in *dog* and *Alsatian*.

Incidental vocabulary learning: The learning of vocabulary while the focus of attention is doing something else.

Lemma: A word family comprising a base word and its most frequent and regular inflections and derivations, which do not change the part of speech.

Lexical decision tasks: A procedure used in experiments which involves measuring how quickly or accurately people classify stimuli as words or non-words.

Lexical set: A group of words with similar features.

Lexical space: A hypothetical three-dimensional construct defining a speaker's vocabulary knowledge and comprising vocabulary breadth, depth and fluency.

Morpheme: A unit of meaning.

Paradigmatic analysis: Analysing the relationship among linguistic elements that can substitute for each other in a given context.

Polysemy: The capacity for a word to carry several different meanings.

Priming: An implicit memory effect in which exposure to a stimulus influences a response to a later stimulus.

Procedural knowledge: The knowledge needed to carry out a task.

Productive/active vocabulary: The body of words that a person recognizes and understands well enough to comprehend them when read or heard.

Pseudowords: Invented words designed to look and sound like real words in a language and used in some Yes/No tests to provide a check on the integrity of learner responses.

Receptive/passive vocabulary: The body of words that a person knows well enough to produce in speech or writing when needed.

Referents: A person or thing to which a linguistic expression refers.

Register: A variety of a language used for a particular purpose or in a particular social setting.

Syntagmatic analysis: Analysing the relationship between linguistic elements that occur sequentially.

Think-aloud protocol: A method used to gather data which involves inviting the subject to say what they are thinking and wondering while carrying out a task.

Vocabulary breadth: Vocabulary breadth or size refers to the number of words a person knows.

Vocabulary depth: The quality of lexical knowledge, or how well the learner knows a word.

Word associations: Words that associate with each other through links in meaning or co-occurrence or form.

Yes/No tests: Also sometimes called checklist tests, where a learner is presented with a series of single words and is required to indicate whether these are known.

References

Adjémian, C. (1983) 'The Transferability of Lexical Properties', in S. Gass and L. Selinker (eds), *Language Transfer in Language Learning*, 1st edn (Rowley: Newbury House), 250–68.

Adolphs, S. and Schmitt, N. (2004) 'Vocabulary Coverage According to Spoken Discourse Context', in P. Bogaards and B. Laufer (eds), *Vocabulary in a Second Language* (Amsterdam: John Benjamins), 39–52.

Agustín Llach, M. P. and Terrazas Gallego, M. (2009) 'Exploring the increase of Receptive Vocabulary Knowledge in the Foreign Language: A Longitudinal Study', *International Journal of English Studies*, 9(1), 113–33.

Aitchison, J. (1987) *Words in the Mind*, 1st edn (Oxford: Blackwell).

Aitchison, J. (1994) *Words in the Mind*, 2nd edn (Oxford: Blackwell).

Aitchison, J. (2003) *Words in the Mind*, 3rd edn (Oxford: Blackwell).

Aizawa, K., Mochizuki, M. and Meara, P. (2001) 'Intuition about Word Frequency: What Does it Tell us about Vocabulary Knowledge?', *Research Reports of the Faculty of Engineering*, Tokyo Denki University, 20, 75–82.

Albrechtsen, D., Haastrup, K. and Henriksen B. (2008) *Vocabulary and Writing in a First and Second Language: Processes and Development* (Basingstoke: Palgrave Macmillan).

Alderson, J. C. (2005) *Diagnosing Foreign Language Proficiency: The Interface between Learning and Assessment* (London: Continuum).

Alderson, J. C. (2007) 'Judging the Frequency of English Words', *Applied Linguistics*, 28(3), 383–409.

Alsaif, A. and Milton, J. (2012) 'Vocabulary Input from School Textbooks as a Potential Contributor to the Small Vocabulary Uptake Gained by EFL Learners in Saudi Arabia', *Language Learning Journal*, 40(1), 21–33.

Anderson, R. C. and Freebody, P. (1981) 'Vocabulary Knowledge', in J. T. Guthrie (ed.), *Comprehension and Teaching: Research Reviews* (Newark, DE: International Reading Association), 77–117.

Anglin, J. M. (1985) 'The Child's Expressible Knowledge of Word Concepts', in K. E. Nelson (ed.), *Children's Language: Vol. 5* (Hillside, NJ: Lawrence Erlbaum), 77–127.

Arnaud, P. (1990) 'Subjective Word Frequency Estimates in L1 and L2', paper presented at the 9th World Congress of Applied Linguistics, Thessaloniki, ERIC Document ED329120.

Bahns, J. (1993) 'Lexical Collocations: A Contrastive View', *ELT Journal*, 47(1), 56–63. doi: 10.1093/elt/47.1.56.

Ballard, K. (2002) *The Frameworks of English* (Basingstoke: Palgrave Macmillan).

Barfield, A. (2009) 'Exploring Productive L2 Collocation Knowledge', in A. Fitzpatrick and A. Barfield (eds), *Lexical Processing in Second Language Learners* (Bristol: Multilingual Matters), 95–110.

Barfield, A. and Gyllstad, H. (eds) (2009) *Researching Collocations in Another Language* (New York: Palgrave Macmillan).

Barnting, I. and Schlyter, S. (2004) 'Stades et itinéraries acquisitionnels des apprenants suédophones en françaisL2', *Journal of French Language Studies*, 14(3), 281–99.

Bates, E. and Goodman, J. (1997) 'On the inseparability of grammar and the lexicon: Evidence from acquisition, aphasia and real-time processing', in G. Altmann (ed.), Special issue on the lexicon', Language and Cognitive Processes, 12(5/6), 507–86.

Bauer, L. and Nation, I. S. P. (1993) 'Word Families', *International Journal of Lexicography*, 6(3), 253–79.

Bayley, R. and Regan, V. (eds) (2004) 'The Acquisition of Sociolinguistic Competence', *Journal of Sociolinguistics*, Special Issue, 8(3), 323–38.

BBC frequency list, retrieved from http://www.kilgarriff.co.uk/BNClists/lemma.al [accessed 21 February 2012].

Beavers, J., Levin, B. and Tham, S. W. (2009) 'The Typology of Motion Expressions Revisited', *Journal of Linguistics*, 46, 331–77.

Beck, I. L., McKeown, M. G. and Omanson, R. C. (1987) 'The effects and uses of diverse vocabulary instructional techniques', in M. G. McKeown and M. E. Curtis (eds), *The Nature of Vocabulary Acquisition* (Hillsdale, NJ: Erlbaum) 147–63.

Beeckmans, R., Eyckmans, J., Jansens, V., Dufranne, M. and van de Velde, H. (2001) 'Examining the Yes/No Vocabulary Test: Some Methodological Issues in Theory and Practice', *Language Testing*, 18(3), 235–74.

Beglar, D. and Hunt, A. (1999) 'Revising and Validating the 2000 Word Level and University Word Level Vocabulary Tests', *Language Testing*, 16(2), 131–62.

Benelli, B. (1988) 'If it is a Dog, Can it be an Animal? The Role of Metalinguistic Knowledge in the Acquisition of Linguistic Superordination', *Journal of Psycholinguistic Research*, 17(3), 227–43.

Benson, M., Benson, E. and Ilson, R. F. (1986) *The BBI Combinatory Dictionary of English* (Amsterdam: John Benjamins).

Bialystok, E. (1986) 'Factors in the Growth of Linguistic Awareness', *Child Development*, 57, 498–510.

Bialystok, E. (1991) 'Metalinguistic Dimensions of Bilingual Language Proficiency', in E. Bialystok (ed.), *Language Processing in Bilingual Children* (Cambridge: Cambridge University Press), 113–40.

Bialystok, E. (2001a) *Bilingualism in Development: Language, Literacy and Cognition* (Cambridge: Cambridge University Press).

Bialystok, E. (2001b) 'Metalinguistic Aspects of Bilingual Processing', *Annual Review of Applied Linguistics*, 21, 169–81.

Bialystok, E. (2007) Acquisition of literacy in bilingual children: a framework for research. *Language Learning*, Suppl. 1, 45–77.

Bialystok, E., Craik, F. and Luk, G. (2008) 'Lexical Access in Bilinguals: Effects of Vocabulary Size and Executive Control', *Journal of Neurolinguistics*, 21, 522–38.

Bishop, H. (2004) 'The effect of typographic salience on the look up and comprehension of unknown formulaic sequences', in N. Schmitt (ed.), *Formulaic Sequences* (Amsterdam: John Benjamins Publishing Company), 227–48.

Bloomfield, L. (1933) *Language* (New York: Holt).

Boers, F. and Lindstromberg, S. (2009) *Optimizing a Lexical Approach to Instructed Second Language Acquisition*. Basingstoke: Palgrave Macmillan.

Brown, J. D. and Hudson, T. (2002) *Criterion-referenced Language Testing* (Cambridge: Cambridge University Press).

Cameron, L. (2002) 'Measuring Vocabulary Size in English as an Additional Language', *Language Teaching Research*, 6(2), 145–73.

Carlo, M., August, D., McLaughlin, B., Snow, C. E., Dressler, C., Lippman, D., Lively, T. and White, C. (2004) 'Closing the Gap: Addressing the Vocabulary Needs of English-Language Learners in Bilingual and Mainstream Classrooms', *Reading Research Quarterly*, 39(2), 188–215.

Carrasquillo, A., Kucer, S. B. and Abrams, R. (2004) *Beyond the Beginnings: Literacy Interventions for Upper Elementary English Language Learners* (Bristol: Multilingual Matters).

Carroll, J. B. (1964) 'Words, Meanings and Concepts', *Harvard Educational Review*, 34(2), 178–202.

Carroll, J. B. (1971) 'Measurement Properties of Subjective Magnitude Estimates of Word Frequency', *Journal of Verbal Learning and Verbal Behavior*, 10, 722–9.

Carstairs-McCarthy, A. (2002) *An Introduction to English Morphology* (Edinburgh: Edinburgh University Press).

Carter, R. (1998) *Vocabulary: Applied Linguistic Perspectives* (London: Routledge).

Carver, R. P. (1990) *Reading Rate: A Review of Research and Theory* (Boston: Academic Press).

CEFLING homepage, retrieved from http://www.jyu.fi/cefling [21 February 2012].

Chikamatsu, N. (1996) 'The Effects of L1 Orthography on L2 Word Recognition: A Study of American and Chinese Learners of Japanese', *Studies in Second Language Acquisition,* 18(4), 403–32.

Chomsky, N. (1959) 'A Review of B. F. Skinner's "Verbal Behavior" 1957', *Language*, 35, 26–58.

Chomsky, N. (1965) *Aspects of the Theory of Syntax* (Cambridge, MA: MIT Press).

Chomsky, N. (1986) *Knowledge of Language: Its Nature, Origin and Use* (Praeger, Westport).

Chomsky, N. (1995) *The Minimalist Program* (Cambridge, MA: MIT Press).

Chomsky, N. and Lasnik, H. (1995) 'The Theory of Principles and Parameters', in N. Chomsky (ed.), *The Minimalist Program* (Cambridge, MA: MIT Press), 13–127.

Cobb, T. (2000) 'One Size Fits All? Francophone Learners and English Vocabulary Tests', *The Canadian Modern Language Review*, 57(2), 295–324.

Cobb, T. and Horst, M. (2004) 'Is There Room for an Academic Word List in French?', in P. Bogaards and B. Laufer (eds), *Vocabulary in a Second Language* (Amsterdam: John Benjamins), 15–38.

Collins WordBanks Online (2004) HarperCollins, retrieved from http://www.collins language.com/content-solutions/wordbanks

Coltheart, M. (1978) 'Lexical Access in Simple Reading Tasks', in G. Underwood (ed.), *Strategies of Information Processing* (London: Academic Press), 151–216.

Conklin, K. and Schmitt, N. (2008) 'Formulaic Sequences: Are They Processed More Quickly than Nonformulaic Language by Native and Nonnative Speakers?', *Applied Linguistics,* 29(1), 72–89. doi: 10.1093/applin/amm022.

Cook, G. (1998) 'The uses of reality: a reply to Ronald Carter', *ELT Journal, 52*(1), 57–63. doi: 10.1093/elt/52.1.57.

Cook, V. (1999) 'Going beyond the Native Speaker in Language Teaching', *TESOL Quarterly, 33*(2), 185–209.

Corson, D. (1995) *Using English Words* (Dordrecht: Kluwer Academic).

Coulson, D. (2010) 'Q_Lex: A Quick Test of Visual Recognition for Learners of English', unpublished PhD thesis, Swansea University.

Coulson, D. (2011) 'Measuring Ability in Foreign Language Word Recognition: A Novel Test and an Alternative to Segalowitz's "CV-rt" Fluency Index', *Journal of International Studies and Regional Development*, 2, 1–22.

Council of Europe (2004) *Reference Supplement to the Preliminary Pilot Version of the Manual for Relating Language Examinations to the Common European Framework of Reference for Languages: Learning, Teaching, Assessment* (Strasbourg: Council of Europe).

Coxhead, A. (2000) 'A New Academic Wordlist', *TESOL Quarterly*, 34, 213–318.

Coxhead, A. (2008) 'Phraseology and English for academic purposes: Challenges and opportunities', in F. Meunier and S. Granger (eds), *Phraseology in Foreign Language Learning and Teaching* (Amsterdam: John Benjamins Publishing Company), 149–61.

Cronbach, L. J. (1942) 'An Analysis of Techniques for Diagnostic Vocabulary Testing', *Journal of Educational Research*, 36, 206–17.

Cruse, D. A. (1986) *Lexical Semantics* (Cambridge: Cambridge University Press).

Cummins, J. (1978) 'Bilingualism and the Development of Metalinguistic Awareness', *Journal of Cross-Cultural Psychology*, 9(2), 131–49.

Cummins, J. (2000) *Language, Power, and Pedagogy: Bilingual Children in the Crossfire* (Bristol: Multilingual Matters).

Cvikić, L. (2007) 'The Importance of Language Specific Features for Vocabulary Acquisition: An Example of Croatian', in Z. Lengyel and J. Navracsics (eds), *Second Language Lexical Processes* (Bristol: Multilingual Matters), 146–65.

Dale, E. (1965) 'Vocabulary Measurement: Techniques and Major Findings', *Elementary English*, 42, 895–901, 948.

Daller, H., Milton, J. and Treffers-Daller, J. (2007) *Modelling and Assessing Vocabulary Knowledge* (Cambridge: Cambridge University Press).

Dang, H. T., Kipper, K., Palmer, M. and Rosenzweig, J. (1998) 'Investigating Regular Sense Extensions Based on Intersective Levin Classes', proceedings COLIng-ACL. http://acl.ldc.upenn.edu/C/C98/C98-1046.pdf [accessed 20 July 2011].

David, A. (2008) 'Vocabulary Breadth in French L2 Learners', *Language Learning Journal*, 36(2), 167–80.

David, A., Myles, F., Rogers, V. and Rule, S. (2009) 'Lexical Development in Instructed L2 Development of French: Is There a Relationship with Morphosyntactic Development?', in B. Richards, H. M. Daller, D. Malvern, P. Meara, J. Milton and J. Treffers-Daller (eds), *Vocabulary Studies in First and Second Language Acquisition* (Basingstoke: Palgrave Macmillan), 147–63.

Davies, M. (2004–) *BYU-BNC: The British National Corpus*. http://corpus.byu.edu/bnc

Davies, M. (2008–) 'The Corpus of Contemporary American English (COCA): 400+ million words, 1990-present', Retrieved February 14, 2011, http://www.american-corpus.org

Davies, M. and Gardner, D. (2010) *A Frequency Dictionary of Contemporary American English* (New York: Routledge).

Davis, B. J. and M. Wertheimer (1967) 'Some Determinants of Associations to French and English Words', *Journal of Verbal Learning and Verbal Behaviour*, 6(4), 547–81.

De Groot, A. M. B. (1992) 'Bilingual Lexical Representation: A Closer Look at Conceptual Representations', in R. Frost and L. Katz (eds), *Orthography, Phonology, Morphology and Meaning* (Amsterdam: Elsevier), 389–412.

De Groot, A. and Keijzer, R. (2000) 'What is Hard to Learn is Easy to Forget: The Roles of Word Concreteness, Cognate Status, and Word Frequency in Foreign Language Learning and Forgetting', *Language Learning*, 50(1), 1–56.

De Groot, A., Borgwaldt, S., Bos, M. and van den Eijnden, E. (2002) 'Lexical Decision and Word Naming in Bilinguals: Language Effects and Task Effects', *Journal of Memory and Language*, 47, 91–124.

Den Dulk, J. J. (1985) 'Productive Vocabulary and the Word Association Test', unpublished Master's thesis, University of Utrecht.

Dewaele, J.-M. (2004a) 'The Acquisition of Sociolinguistic Competence in French L2', *Journal of French Language Studies*, 14 (3), 301–19.

Dewaele, J.-M. (2004b) 'Colloquial Vocabulary in the Speech of Native and Non-native Speakers: The Effects of Proficiency and Personality', in P. Bogaards and B. Laufer, *Vocabulary in a Second Language* (Amsterdam: John Benjamins), 127–53.

Dewaele, J.-M. and Regan, V. (2001) 'The Use of Colloquial Words in Advanced French Interlanguage', in S. Foster-Cohen and A. Nizegorodcew, *EUROSLA Yearbook 2001* (Amsterdam: John Benjamins).

DIALANG http://www.dialang.org. retrieved from http://urn.fi/URN:NBN:fi:jyu-20080 8255677 [accessed 21 February 2012].

Droop, M. and Verhoeven, L. (2003) 'Language Proficiency and Reading Ability in First- and Second-language Learners', *Reading Research Quarterly*, 38, 78–103.

Duncan, L. G., Casalis, S. and Colé, P. (2009) 'Early Meta-linguistic Awareness of Derivational Morphology: Observations from a Comparison of English and French', *Applied Pscyholinguistics*, 30, 405–40.

Durrant, P. (2009) 'Investigating the viability of a collocation list for students of English for academic purposes', *English for Specific Purposes,* 28(3), 157–69. doi: 10.1016/j. esp.2009.02.002.

Durrant, P. and Schmitt, N. (2009) 'To what extent do native and non-native writers make use of collocations?', *International Review of Applied Linguistics*, 47(2), 157–77.

Eisenbeiss, S. (2007) 'The Lexical Learning Hypothesis', *Essex Research Reports in Linguistics,* 54, 1–4.

Ellis, N. C. (2002a) 'Frequency Effects in Language Acquisition: A Review with Implications for Theories of Implicit and Explicit Language Acquisition', *Studies in Second Language Acquisition*, 24, 143–88.

Ellis, N. C. (2002b) 'Reflections on Frequency Effects in Language Acquisition: A Response to Commentaries', *Studies in Second Language Acquisition*, 24, 297–339.

Ellis, N. C. (2005) 'At the Interface: Dynamic Interactions of Explicit and Implicit Language Knowledge', *Studies in Second Language Acquisition*, 27, 305–52.

Ellis, N. and Simpson-Vlach, R. (2009) 'Formulaic language in native speakers: Triangulating psycholinguistics, corpus linguistics and education', *Corpus Linguistics and Linguistics Theory*, 5, 61–78.

Ellis, N. C., Simpson-Vlach, R. and Maynard, C. (2008) 'Formulaic Language in Native and Second Language Speakers: Psycholinguistics, Corpus Linguistics, and TESOL', *TESOL Quarterly*, 42, 375–96.

Emonds, J. (2002) *Lexicon and Grammar: The English Syntacticon* (Berlin: Mouton de Gruyter).

Entwisle, D. R., Forsyth, D. F. and Muuss, R. (1964) 'The Syntagmatic–Paradigmatic Shift in Children's Word Associations', *Journal of Verbal Learning and Verbal Behaviour*, 3, 19–29.

Ervin, S. (1961) 'Changes with Age in the Verbal Determinants of Word Association', *American Journal of Psychology*, 74, 361–72.

Eyckmans, J. (2004) 'Measuring Receptive Vocabulary Size', unpublished Doctoral dissertation (Utrecht: LOT).

Eyckmans, J. (2010) 'Innovation in Language Teacher Education: Fostering Learner Autonomy through Phrasal Awareness', paper to symposium on Language Teachers: Training for a New Paradigm, held in Udine on 7–8 September 2010. Text at http://in3.uoc.edu/opencms_in3/opencms/webs/projectes/EUNOM/EN/results/index.html [accessed 30 March 2012].

Faerch, K., Haastrup, K. and Phillipson, R. (1984) *Learner Language and Language Learning* (Bristol: Multilingual Matters).

Fairclough, N. (1989) *Language and Power* (London: Longman).

Firth, J. R. (1957 [1968]) *Papers in Linguistics 1934–1951 (1957)* (London: Oxford University Press).

Fitzpatrick, T. (2006) 'Habits and Rabbits: Word Associations and the L2 Lexicon', *EUROSLA Yearbook 2006* (Amsterdam: John Benjamins), 121–45.

Fitzpatrick, T. (2007) 'Word Association Patterns: Unpacking the Assumptions', *International Journal of Applied Linguistics*, 17(3), 319–31.

Fitzpatrick, T. (2009) 'Word Association Profiles in a First and Second Language: Puzzles and Problems', in T. Fitzpatrick and A. Barfield (eds), *Lexical Processing in Second Language Learners* (Bristol: Multilingual Matters).

Fitzpatrick, T. (2012) 'Tracking the Changes: Vocabulary Acquisition in the Study Abroad Context', *Language Learning Journal*, 40(1), 81–98.

Fitzpatrick, T. and Clenton, J. (2010) 'The challenge of Validation: Assessing the Performance of a Test of Productive Vocabulary', *Language Testing*, 27(4), 537–54.

Fodor, J. A. (1983) *The Modularity of Mind* (Cambridge, MA: MIT Press).

Forster, K. I. and Forster, J. C. (2003) 'DMDX: A Windows Display Program with Millisecond Accuracy', *Behaviour Research Methods, Instruments & Computers*, 35(1), 116–24.

Foster-Cohen, S. (1999) *An Introduction to Child Language Development* (London: Longman).

Fotos, S. (1991) 'The Cloze Test as an Integrative Measure of EFL Proficiency: A Substitute for Essays on College Entrance Examinations?', *Language Learning*, 41, 313–36.

Fountain, R. L. and Nation, I. S. P. (2000) 'A Vocabulary-based Graded Dictation Test', *RELC Journal 2000*, 31, 29–44.

García Hoz, V. (1977) *Estudios experimentales sobre el vocabulario* (Madrid: Consejo superior de investigaciones científicas).

Gass, S. M. and Selinker, L. (2008) *Second Language Acquisition: An Introductory Course*, 3rd edn (New York: Routledge).

Genesee, F. (1994) *Educating Second Language Children: The Whole Child, the Whole Curriculum, the Whole Community* (Cambridge: Cambridge University Press).

Gervais-le Garff, M.-M. (2002) 'Liberté, égalité, sororité: A New Linguistic Order in France?', *Women and Language*, 25, 1–7.

Goldinger, S. D. (1996) 'Auditory Lexical Decision', *Language and Cognitive Processes*, 11(6), 559–67.

Granger, S. (2009) 'Commentary on part I: Learner corpora: A window onto the L2 phrasicon', in A. Barfield and H. Gyllstad (eds), *Researching Collocations in Another Language: Multiple Interpretations* (Basingstoke: Palgrave Macmillan), 60–5.

Granger, S. and Paquot, M. (2008) 'Disentangling the Phraseological Web', in S. Granger and F. Meunier (eds), *Phraseology: An Interdisciplinary Perspective* (Amsterdam and Philadelphia: John Benjamins), 27–49.

Graves, M. F. (1987) 'The roles of instruction in fostering vocabulary development', in M.G. McKeown and M. E. Curtis (eds), *The Nature of Vocabulary Acquisition* (Hillsdale, NJ: Erlbaum), 165–18.

Halliday, M. A. K. (1994) *An Introduction to Functional Grammar* (London: Edward Arnold).

Halliday, M. A. K. and Hassan, R. (1976) *Cohesion in English* (London: Longman).

Harley, B. (1996) 'Introduction: Vocabulary Learning and Teaching in a Second Language', *The Canadian Modern Language Review*, 53(1), 3–12.

Harrington, M. (2006) 'The Lexical Decision Task as a Measure of Lexical Proficiency', in S. H. Foster-Cohen, M. Medved Krajnovic and J. Mihaljevic Djigunovic (eds), *EUROSLA Yearbook 2006* (Amsterdam: John Benjamins), 147–68.

Harrington, M. and Carey (2009) 'The On-line Yes/No Test a Placement Tool', *System*, 37(4), 614–26.

Hartmann, R. R. K. (1981) 'Style Values: Linguistic Approaches and Lexicographical Practice', *Applied Linguistics*, 2, 263–73.

Hatch, E. and Brown, C. (1995) *Vocabulary, Semantics and Language Education* (Cambridge: Cambridge University Press).

Hatzigeorgiu, N., Mikros, G. and Carayannis, G. (2001) 'Word Length, Word Frequencies and Zipf's Law in the Greek Language', *Journal of Quantitative Linguistics 2001*, 8(3), 175–85.

Hauk, O., Patterson, K., Woollams, A., Watling, L., Pulvermüller, F. and Rogers, T. T. (2006) '[Q:] When Would You Prefer a SOSSAGE to a SAUSSAGE? [A:] At About 100 msec. ERP Correlated of Orthographic Typicality and Lexicality in Written Word Recognition', *Journal of Cognitive Neuroscience*, 18(5), 818–32.

Hawkins, R. (2001) *Second Language Syntax: A Generative Introduction* (Oxford: Blackwell).

Hazenberg, S. and Hulstijn, J. (1996) 'Defining a Minimal Receptive Second-language Vocabulary for Non-native University Students: An Empirical Investigation', *Applied Linguistics*, 17, 145–63.

Henriksen, B. (1999) 'Three Dimensions of Vocabulary Development', *Studies in Second Language Acquisition*, 23, 303–17.

Heuvelmans, T. (2009) *TiaPlus Users Manual* (Arnhem: CITO).

Hindmarsh, R. (1980) *Cambridge English Lexicon* (Cambridge: Cambridge University Press).

Hoey, M. (2005) *Lexical Priming: A New Theory of Words and Language* (London: Routledge).

Holmes, J. and Meyerhoff, M. (2003) *The Handbook of Language and Gender* (Oxford: Blackwell).

Hornby, A. S. (1954) *A Guide to Patterns and Usage in English*, 1st edn (London: Oxford University Press).

Horst, M. and Meara, P. M. (1999) 'Test of a Model for Predicting Second Language Lexical Growth through Reading', *The Canadian Modern Language Review*, 56(2), 308–28.

Howarth, P. (1998) 'The Phraseology of Learners' Academic Writing', in A. P. Cowie (ed.), *Phraseology* (Oxford: Oxford University Press).

Hughlings Jackson, J. (1866 [1958]) 'Notes on the Physiology and the Pathology of Language', *The Medical Times and Gazette*, 1, 659–62.

Huibregtse, I., Admiraal, W. and Meara, P. M. (2002) 'Scores on a Yes/No Vocabulary Test: Correction for Guessing and Response Style', *Language Testing*, 19, 227–45.

Hulstijn, J., van Gelderen, A. and Schoonen, R. (2009) 'Automatization in Second Language Acquisition: What does the Coefficient of Variation Tell Us?', *Applied Psycholinguistics*, 30(4), 555–82.

Hunston, S. (2001) 'Colligation, Lexis, Pattern, and Text', in M. Scott and G. Thompson (eds), *Patterns of Text: In Honour of Michael Hoey* (Amsterdam: John Benjamins), 13–33.

Hunston, S. and Francis, G. (2000) *Pattern Grammar: A Corpus-driven Approach to the Lexical Grammar of English (Studies in Corpus Linguistics 4)* (Amsterdam: John Benjamins).

Inagaki, S. (2001) 'Motion Verbs with Goal PPs in the L2 Acquisition of English and Japanese', *Studies in Second Language Acquisition*, 23, 153–70.

Ishikawa, S., Uemura, T., Kaneda, M., Shimizu, S., Sugimori, N., Tono, Y., Mochizuki, M. and Murata, M. (2003) *JACET 8000: JACET List of 8000 Basic Words* (Tokyo: JACET).

Iso, T. and Aizawa, K. (2008) 'Revisiting Learners' Vocabulary Size Estimation: The Effects of Randomization and Confidence', *KATE Bulletin*, 22, 13–22.

Jackson, H. and Zé Amvela, E. (2000) *Words, Meaning and Vocabulary* (London: Continuum).

Jean, M. and Geva, E. (2009) 'The Development of Vocabulary in English as a Second Language Children and its Role in Predicting Word Recognition Ability', *Applied Psycholinguistics*, 30(1), 153–85.

Jiang, N. (2002) 'Form-meaning Mapping in Vocabulary Acquisition in a Second Language', *Studies in Second Language Acquisition*, 24(4), 617–37.

Jiang, N. and Nekrasova, T. M. (2007) 'The Processing of Formulaic Sequences by Second Language Speakers', *The Modern Language Journal,* 91(3), 433–45.

Johnson, C. J. and Anglin, J. M. (1995) 'Qualitative Development in the Content and Form of Children's Definitions', *Journal of Speech and Hearing Research*, 38, 612–29.

Kaftandjieva, F. (2004). *Standard setting. Section B of the Reference Supplement to the preliminary version of the Manual for relating language examinations to the Common European Framework of Reference for Languages: Learning, teaching, assessment* (Strasbourg: Council of Europe).

Kent, G. H. and Rosanoff, A. J. (1910) 'A Study of Association in Insanity', *American Journal of Insanity*, 67, 37–96, 317–90.

Kilgarriff, A. (1998) BNC database and word frequency lists, http://www.itri.brighton. ac.uk/~Adam.Kilgarrif [accessed February 2006].

Kiss, G. R., Armstrong, C., Milroy, R. and Piper, J. (1973) 'An Associative Thesaurus of English and its Computer Analysis', in A. J. Aitken, R. W. Bailey and N. Hamilton-Smith (eds), *The Computer and Literary Studies* (Edinburgh: Edinburgh University Press), 153–65.

Koda, K. (1996) 'L2 Word Recognition Research: A Critical Review', *The Modern Language Journal*, 80(iv), 450–60.

Konishi, T., and Minamide, K. (2001) *Taishukan's Genius English–Japanese Dictionary*, 3rd edn (Tokyo: Taishukan).

Konstantakis, N. and Alexiou, T. (2012) 'Vocabulary in Greek Young Learners of English as a Foreign Language Course Book', *Language Learning Journal*, 40(1), 35–45.

Kroll, J. F. (1993) 'Accessing Conceptual Representations for Words in a Second Language', in R. Schreuder and B. Weltens (eds), *The Bilingual Lexicon* (Amsterdam: John Benjamins), 53–81

Kruse, H., Pankhurst, J. and Sharwood Smith, M. (1987) 'A Multiple Word Association Probe in Second Language Acquisition Research', *Studies in Second Language Acquisition*, 9(2), 141–54.

Kurland, B. F. and Snow, C. E. (1997) 'Longitudinal Measurement of Growth in Definitional Skill', *Journal of Child Language*, 24, 603–25.

Lambert, W. E. (1955) 'Measurement of the Linguistic Dominance of Bilinguals', *The Journal of Abnormal and Social Psychology*, 50(2), 197–200.

Lambert, W. E., Havelka, J. and Gardner, R. C. (1959) 'Linguistic manifestations of bilingualism. *The American Journal of Psychology*, 72, 77–82.

Larson-Freeman, D. and Cameron, L. (2008) *Complex Systems and Applied Linguistics* (Oxford: Oxford University Press).

Laufer, B. (1990) 'Why are Some Words More Difficult than Others? Some Intralexical Factors that Affect the Learning of Words', *International Review of Applied Linguistics*, 28, 293–307.

Laufer, B. (1997a) 'The Lexical Plight in Second Language Reading', in J. Coady and T. Huckin (eds), *Second Language Vocabulary Acquisition* (Cambridge: Cambridge University Press), 20–34.

Laufer, B. (1997b) 'What's in a Word that Makes it Hard or Easy: Some Intralexical Factors that Affect the Learning of Words', in N. Schmitt and M. McCarthy (eds), *Vocabulary: Description, Acquisition and Pedagogy* (Cambridge: Cambridge University Press), 140–55.

Laufer, B. (1998) 'The Development of Active and Passive Vocabulary in a Second Language: Same or Different?', *Applied Linguistics*, 19, 255–71.

Laufer, B. (2010) 'Form focused instruction in second language vocabulary learning', in R. Chacón-Beltrán, C. Abello-Contesse, M. M. Torreblanca-López and M. D. López-Jiménez (eds), *Further Insights into Non-native Vocabulary Teaching and Learning* (Bristol: Multilingual Matters), pp. 15–27.

Laufer, B., Elder, C., Hill, K. and Congdon, M. (2004) 'Size and Strength: Do We Need Both to Measure Vocabulary Knowledge?', *Language Testing*, 21(2), 202–26.

Laufer, B. and Goldstein, Z (2004) 'Testing Vocabulary Knowledge: Size, Strength, and Computer Adaptiveness', *Language Learning*, 54(3), 399–436.

Laufer, B. and Nation, P. (1995) 'Vocabulary Size and Use: Lexical Richness in L2 Written Production', *Applied Linguistics*, 16, 307–22.

Laufer, B. and Nation, P. (1999) 'A Vocabulary-size Test of Controlled Productive Ability', *Language Testing*, 16, 33–51.

Laufer, B. and Nation, P. (2001) 'Passive Vocabulary Size and Speed of Meaning Recognition: Are They Related?', in S. Foster-Cohen and A. Nizegorodcew (eds), *EUROSLA Yearbook 2001* (Amsterdam: John Benjamins), 7–28.

Laufer, B. and Paribakht, T. S. (1998) 'The Relationship Between Active and Passive Vocabularies: Effects of Language Learning Context', *Language Learning*, 48(3), 365–91.

Leech, G., Deuchar, M. and Hoogenraad, R. (2006) *English Grammar for Today,* 2nd edn (Basingstoke: Palgrave Macmillan).

Leopold, W. (1939) *Speech Development of a Bilingual Child: A Linguist's Record* (Evanston, IL: Northwestern University Press).

Levin, B. (1993) *English Verb Classes and Alternations: A Preliminary Investigation* (Chicago: University of Chicago Press).

Lewis, M. (1993) *The Lexical Approach* (Hove: Language Teaching Publications).

Lewis, M. (1997) *Implementing the Lexical Approach* (Hove: Language Teaching Publications).

Lewis, M. (2000) *Teaching Collocation: Further Developments in the Lexical Approach* (Hove: Language Teaching Publications).

Litowitz, B. (1977) 'Learning to make definitions', *Journal of Child Language*, 4, 289–304.

Liu, D. (2010) 'Going Beyond Patterns: Involving Cognitive Analysis in the Learning of Collocations', *TESOL Quarterly, 44*(1), 4–30. doi: 10.5054/tq.2010.214046.

MacWhinney, B. and Bates, E. (1989) *The Crosslinguistic Study of Sentence Processing* (New York: Cambridge University Press).

Malakoff, M. (1988) 'The Effect of Language of Instruction on Reasoning in Bilingual Children', *Applied Psycholinguistics*, 9, 17–38.

Marchman, V., Martínez-Sussmann, C. and Dale, P. (2004) 'The language-specific nature of grammatical development: Evidence from bilingual language learners', *Developmental Science*, 7(2), 212–224.

Maréchal, C. (1995) '*The Bilingual Lexicon: Study of French and English Word Association Responses of Advanced Learners of French*', M. Phil. Dissertation, University of Dublin.

McBride-Chang, C., Wagner, R. K., Muse, A., Chow, B. W.-Y. and Shu, H. (2005) 'The Role of Morphological Awareness in Children's Vocabulary Acquisition in English', *Applied Psycholinguistics*, 26, 415–35.

McCrostie, J. (2005) 'A Further Investigation of Word Frequency Intuitions', *The East Asian Learner*, 2(1) 26–36.

McCrostie, J. (2007) 'Investigating the Accuracy of Teachers' Word Frequency Intuitions', *RELC Journal*, 38(1), 53–66.

McGee, I. (2006) 'Lexical Intuitions and Collocation Patterns in Corpora', unpublished PhD thesis, Cardiff University.

McGee, I. (2008) 'Word Frequency Estimates Revisited: A Response to Alderson (2007)', *Applied Linguistics*, 29 (3) 509–14

McGee, I. (2009) 'Adjective-noun collocations in elicited and corpus data: Similarities, differences, and the whys and wherefores', *Corpus Linguistics and Linguistic Theory, 5*(1), 79–103. doi: 10.1515/cllt.2009.004.

McGhee-Bidlack, B. (1991) 'The Development of Noun Definitions: A Metalinguistic Analysis', *Journal of Child Language*, 18, 417–34.

McIntosh, C., Francis, B. and Poole, R. (2002) *Oxford Collocations Dictionary* (Oxford: Oxford University Press).

Meara, P. (1983) 'Word Associations in a Foreign Language: A Report on the Birkbeck Vocabulary Project', *Nottingham Linguistic Circular*, 11(2), 29–38.

Meara, P. (1986) 'The Dígame Project', in V. Cook (ed.), *Experimental Approaches to Second Language Learning* (Oxford: Pergamon Press), 101–10.

Meara, P. (1994) 'The Complexities of Simple Vocabulary Tests', in F. G. Brinkman, J. A. van der Schee and M. C. Schouten van-Parreren (eds), *Curriculum Research: Different Discimplies and Common Goals* (Amsterdam: Vrije Universiteit), 15–28.

Meara, P. (1996a) 'The Dimensions of Lexical Competence', in G. Brown, K. Malmkjaer and J. Williams (eds), *Performance and Competence in Second Language Acquisition* (Cambridge: Cambridge University Press), 35–53.

Meara, P. (1996b) 'The Vocabulary Knowledge Framework', retrieved from Vocabulary Acquisition Research Group Virtual Library, http://www.swansea.ac.uk/cals/calsres/vlibrary/pm96d.htm [accessed December 2000].

Meara, P. (1997) 'Towards a New Approach to Modelling Vocabulary Acquisition', in N. Schmitt and M. McCarthy (eds), *Vocabulary: Description, Acquisition and Pedagogy* (Cambridge: Cambridge University Press), 109–21.

Meara, P. (2001) *V_States* (Swansea: Lognostics).

Meara, P. (2005a) 'Designing Vocabulary Tests for English, Spanish and Other Languages', in C. Butler, M. Gómez-González and S. M. Doval-Suárez (eds), *The Dynamics of Language Use* (Amsterdam: John Benjamins), 271–85.

Meara, P. (2005b) 'Lexical Frequency Profiles: A Monte Carlo Analysis', *Applied Linguistics*, 26(1), 32–47.

Meara, P. (2006) 'Emergent Properties of Multilingual Lexicons', *Applied Linguistics*, (27,4), 620–44.

Meara, P. (2009) *Connected Words: Word Associations and Second Language Vocabulary Acquisition* (Amsterdam: John Benjamins).

Meara, P. and Bell, H. (2001) 'P_Lex: A Simple and Effective Way of Describing the Lexical Characteristics of Short L2 Texts', *Prospect*, 16(3), 323–37.

Meara, P. and Buxton, B. (1987) 'An Alternative to Multiple Choice Vocabulary Tests', *Language Testing*, 4, 142–54.

Meara, P., Coltheart, M. and Masterson, J. (1985) 'Hidden Reading Problems in ESL Learners', *TESL Canada Journal*, 3(1), 69–79.

Meara, P. and Fitzpatrick, T. (2000) 'Lex30: An Improved Method of Assessing Productive Vocabulary in an L2', *System*, 28, 19–30.

Meara, P. and Jones, G. (1988) 'Vocabulary Size as a Placement Indicator', in P. Grunwell (ed.), *Applied Linguistics in Society* (London: CILT).

Meara, P. and Jones, G. (1990) 'The Eurocentres Vocabulary Size Test', 10KA (Zurich: Eurocentres), *TESL Canada Journal*, 3(1), 69–79.

Meara, P. and Milton, J. (2003) *X_Lex, The Swansea Levels Test* (Newbury: Express).

Meara, P. and Miralpeix, I. (2006) *Y_Lex: The Swansea Advanced Vocabulary Levels Test*, v2.05 (Swansea: Lognostics).

Meara, P. and Wolter, B. (2004) 'V_Links: Beyond Vocabulary Depth', in D. Albrechtsen, K. Haastrup and B. Henriksen (eds), *Angles on the English-speaking World 4*, (Copenhagen: Museum Tusculanum Press), 85–96.

Melka, F. (1997) 'Receptive vs. Productive Aspects of Vocabulary', in N. Schmitt and M. McCarthy (eds), *Vocabulary: Description, Acquisition and Pedagogy* (Cambridge: Cambridge University Press), 84–102.

Millar, N. (2011). 'The Processing of Malformed Learner Collocations', *Applied Linguistics*, 32(2), 129–48.

Miller, G. A. and Johnson-Laird, P. N. (1976) *Language and Perception* (Cambridge, MA: Harvard University Press).

Milton, J. (2006) 'Language Lite: Learning French Vocabulary in School', *Journal of French Language Studies*, 16(2), 187–205.

Milton, J. (2007) 'Lexical Profiles, Learning Styles and Construct Validity of Lexical Size Tests', in H. Daller, J. Milton and J. Treffers-Daller (eds), *Modelling and Assessing Vocabulary Knowledge* (Cambridge: Cambridge University Press), 45–58.

Milton, J. (2008) 'Vocabulary Uptake from Informal Learning Tasks', *Language Learning Journal*, 36(2), 227–38.

Milton, J. (2009) *Measuring Second Language Vocabulary Acquisition* (Bristol: Multilingual Matters).

Milton, J. (2010) 'The Development of Vocabulary Breadth Across the CEFR Levels', in I. Vedder, I. Bartning and M. Martin (eds), *Communicative Proficiency and Linguistic Development: Intersections between SLA and Language Testing Research* (Rome: Second Language Acquisition and Testing in Europe Monograph Series 1), 211–32.

Milton, J. and Alexiou, T. (2012) 'Vocabulary Input, Vocabulary Uptake and Approaches to Language Teaching', *Language Learning Journal*, 40(1), 1–5.

Milton, J. and Hopkins, N. (2005) *Aural Lex* (Swansea: Swansea University Press).

Milton, J. and Hopkins, N. (2006) 'Comparing Phonological and Orthographic Vocabulary Size: Do Vocabulary Tests Underestimate the Knowledge of Some Learners?', *The Canadian Modern Language Review*, 63(1), 127–47.

Milton, J. and Meara, P. (1998) 'Are the British Really Bad at Learning Foreign Languages?', *Language Learning Journal*, 18, 68–76.

Milton, J. and Riordan, O. (2006) 'Level and Script Effects in the Phonological and Orthographic Vocabulary Size of Arabic and Farsi Speakers', in P. Davidson, C. Coombe, D. Lloyd and D. Palfreyman (eds), *Teaching and Learning Vocabulary in Another Language* (UAE: TESOL Arabia), 122–33.

Milton, J., Wade, J. and Hopkins, N. (2010) 'Aural Word Recognition and Oral Competence in a Foreign Language', in R. Chacón-Beltrán, C. Abello-Contesse and M. Torreblanca-López (eds), *Further Insights into Non-native Vocabulary Teaching and Learning* (Bristol: Multilingual Matters), 83–97.

Miralpeix, I. (2008) 'The Influence of Age on Vocabulary Acquisition in English as a Foreign Language', unpublished PhD thesis, University of Barcelona.

Miralpeix, I. (2009) 'Measuring Vocabulary Size: New Tools for Assessment', CRAL Conference', Logroño, Spain.

Mochida, A. and Harrington, M. (2006) 'The Yes/No Test as a Measure of Receptive Vocabulary Knowledge', *Language Testing*, 23(1), 73–98.

Mochizuki, M. and Aizawa, K. (2000) 'An Affix Acquisition Order for EFL Learners: An Exploratory Study', *System*, 28, 291–04.

Moreno, S. (2010) 'Assessing L2 Embedded Vocabulary by Means of Different Computer-Implemented Analysers', unpublished PhD thesis, University of La Rioja.

Muñoz-Sandoval, A. F., Cummins, J., Alvarado, C. G. and Ruef, M. L. (1998) *The Bilingual Verbal Ability Tests* (BVAT) (Itasca, IL: Riverside Publishing, Houghton-Mifflin).

Murphy, V. A. and Pine, K. J. (2003) 'L2 Influence on L1 Linguistic Representations', in V. Cook (ed.), *Effects of the Second Language on the First*. (Bristol: Multilingual Matters), 142–67.

Nagy, W. (1997) 'On the Role of Context in First- and Second-language Vocabulary Learning', in N. Schmitt and M. McCarthy (eds) *Vocabulary: Description, Acquisition and Pedagogy* (Cambridge: Cambridge University Press), 64–83.

Nassaji, H. (2003) 'Higher-level and Lower-level Text Processing Skills in Advanced ESL Reading Comprehension', *Modern Language Journal*, 87, 261–76.

Nation, I. S. P. (2006) 'How Large a Vocabulary is Needed for Reading and Listening?', *Canadian Modern Language Review*, 63(1), 59–81.

Nation, I. S. P. (1983) 'Testing and Teaching Vocabulary', *Guidelines*, 5, 12–25.

Nation, I. S. P. (ed.) (1984) *Vocabulary Lists: Words, Affixes and Stems* (Wellington, New Zealand: English Language Institute).

Nation, I. S. P. (1990) *Teaching and Learning Vocabulary* (Rowley: Newbury House).

Nation, I. S. P. (1996) *Vocabulary Lists,* English Language Institute Occasional Publications No. 17 (Victoria: University of Wellington).

Nation, I. S. P. (2001) *Learning Vocabulary in Another Language* (Cambridge: Cambridge University Press).

Nation, I. S. P. (2004) 'A Study of the Most Frequent Word Families in the British National Corpus', in P. Bogaards and B. Laufer (eds), *Vocabulary in a Second Language* (Amsterdam: John Benjamins), 3–13.

Nation, I. S. P. (2005) 'Teaching and Learning Vocabulary', in E. Hinkel (ed.), *Handbook of Research in Second Language Teaching and Learning* (New Jersey: Routledge), 581–95.

Nation, I. S. P. (2006) 'How large a vocabulary is needed for reading and listening?', *The Canadian Modern Language Review/La revue canadienne des langues vivantes,* 63(1), 59–81.

Nation, I. S. P. (2007) 'Fundamental Issues in Modelling and Assessing Vocabulary Knowledge', in H. Daller, J. Milton and J. Treffers-Daller (eds), *Modelling and Assessing Vocabulary Knowledge* (Cambridge: Cambridge University Press), 33–43.

Nattinger, J. R. and DeCarrico, J. (1992) *Lexical Phrases and Language Teaching* (Oxford: Oxford University Press).

NBE (National Board of Education) (2004) *National Core Curriculum for Basic Education 2004* (Helsinki: NBE), retrieved from http://www.oph.fi/english/publications/2009/national_core_curricula [accessed 23 February 2012].

Nelson, D. L., McEvoy, C. L. and Schreiber, T. A. (1998) 'The University of South Florida Word Association, Rhyme, and Word Fragment Norms', retrieved from http://www.usf.edu/FreeAssociation/ [accessed 23 February 2012].

Nelson, K. (1977) 'The Syntagmatic–Paradigmatic Shift Revisited: A Review of Research and Theory', *Psychological Bulletin*, 84, 93–116.

Nesselhauf, N. (2003) 'The Use of Collocations by Advanced Learners of English and Some Implications for Teaching', *Applied Linguistics,* 24(2), 223–42. doi: 10.1093/applin/24.2.223.

Nesselhauf, N. (2004) 'Learner Corpora and their Potential for Language Teaching', in J. Sinclair (ed), *How to use Corpora in Language Teaching* (Amsterdam: John Benjamins), 125–52.

Nesselhauf, N. (2005) *Collocations in a Learner Corpus* (Amsterdam: John Benjamins).

Nissen, H. B. and Henriksen, B. (2006) 'Word Class Influence on Word Association Test Results', *International Journal of Applied Linguistics*, 16(3), 389–408.

Nyyssönen, L. (2008) 'Understanding English Word Formation: A Study Among 6th-grade Pupils in Finnish Comprehensive School', unpublished MA thesis, University of Jyväskylä, Department of Languages, retrieved from http://urn.fi/URN:NBN:fi:jyu-200808255677 [accessed 23 February 2012].

Ordonez, C. L., Carlo, M. S., Snow, C. E. and McLaughlin, B. (2002) 'Depth and Breadth of Vocabulary in Two Languages: Which Vocabulary Skills Transfer?', *Journal of Educational Psychology*, 94 (4), 719–28.

Oxford, R. L. (1990) *Language Learning Strategies* (New York: Newbury House/Harper and Row).

Pajoohesh, P. (2007a) 'The Microanalysis of Lexical Depth: The Implicit and Expressible Aspects of the Definitional Skill', unpublished Doctoral dissertation, University of Toronto.

Pajoohesh, P. (2007b) 'A Probe into Lexical Depth: What is the Direction of Transfer for L1 Literacy and L2 Development?', *Heritage Language Journal*, Special Issue on TESOL and Heritage Language Education, 5(1), 117–46.

Pajoohesh, P. (2008) 'Exploring the Lexical Depth in a Second Language: Implications for ESL Teaching', *CONTACT*, Research Symposium Special Issue, Spring, 34(2), 19–38.

Palmberg, R. (1987) 'Patterns of Vocabulary Development in Foreign Language Learners', *Studies in Second Language Acquisition*, 9, 202–21.

Palmer, H. E. (1917) *The Scientific Study and Teaching of Languages* (London: Harrap).

Palmer, H. E. (1921) *The Principles of Language Study* (London: Harrap).

Paribakht, T. M. and Wesche, M. (1993) 'Vocabulary Enhancement Activities and Reading for Meaning in Second Language Vocabulary Acquisition', in J. Coady and T. Huckin (eds), *Second Language Vocabulary Acquisition: A Rationale for Pedagogy* (Cambridge: Cambridge University Press), 174–200.

Pavičić Takač, V. (2008) *Vocabulary Learning Strategies and Foreign Language Acquisition* (Bristol: Multilingual Matters).

Pawley, A. and Syder, F. H. (1983) 'Two puzzles for linguistic theory: nativelike selection and nativelike fluency', in J. C. Richards and R. W. Schmidt (eds), *Language and Communication* (London: Longman), 191–225.

Peal, E. and Lambert, A. (1962) *Representational Processes in Early Language Acquisition* (Boston, MA: Rowley).

Pearson, B. Z., Fernandez, S. C. and Oller, D. K. (1995) 'Cross-language Synonyms in the Lexicon of Bilinguals: One Language or Two?', *Journal of Child Language*, 22, 345–67.

Pienemann, M., Johnston, M. and Brinley, G. (1988) 'Constructing and Acquisition-based Procedure for Second Language Assessment', *Studies in Second Language Acquisition*, 10(2), 217–43.

Phythian-Sense, C. and Wagner, R. K. (2007). 'What do children know when they know a word? A study in dimensions of vocabulary knowledge', Poster presented at the Annual Meeting of the Society for Research in Child Development, Boston, Massachusetts.

Politzer, R. L. (1978) 'Paradigmatic and Syntagmatic Associations of First Year French Students', in V. Hausa (ed.), *Papers in Linguistics and Child Language* (The Hague: Mouton), 203–10.

Postman, L. J. and Keppel G. (eds) (1970) *Norms of Word Association* (New York: Academic Press).

Psaltou-Joycey, A. (2010) *Language Learning Strategies in the Foreign Language Classroom* (Thessaloniki: University Studio Press).

Pugh, R. C. and Brunza, J. J. (1975) 'Effects of a Confidence Weighted Scoring System on Measures of Test Reliability and Validity', *Educational and Psychological Measurement*, 35, 73–8.

Qian, D. D. (1999) 'Assessing the Roles of Depth and Breadth of Vocabulary Knowledge in ESL Reading Comprehension', *The Canadian Modern Language Review*, 56(2), 282–308.

Randall, M. (1980) 'Word Association Behaviour in Learners of English as a Foreign Language', *Polyglot*, 2(2), B5–D1.

Read, J. (1988) 'Measuring the Vocabulary Knowledge of Second Language Learners', *RELC Journal*, 19(2), 12–25.

Read, J. (1993) 'The Development of a New Measure of L2 Vocabulary Knowledge', *Language Testing*, 10(3), 355–71.

Read, J. (1997) 'Vocabulary and Testing', in N. Schmitt and M. McCarthy (eds), *Vocabulary: Description, Acquisition and Pedagogy* (Cambridge: Cambridge University Press), 303–20.

Read, J. (2000) *Assessing Vocabulary* (Cambridge: Cambridge University Press).

Read, J. (2004) 'Plumbing the Depths: How Should the Construct of Vocabulary Knowledge be Defined?', in P. Bogaards and B. Laufer (eds), *Vocabulary in a Second Language* (Amsterdam: John Benjamins), 209–27.

Read, J. (2007a) 'Second Language Vocabulary Assessment: Current Practices and New Direction', *International Journal of English Studies*, 7(2), 105 25.

Read, J. (2007b) 'Extending the Yes/No Format as a Measure of Vocabulary Knowledge', Paper to the Annual Congress of the Applied Linguistics Association of Australia, July.

Read, J. (1998) 'Validating a Test to Measure Depth of Vocabulary Knowledge', in Kunnan, A. (ed.), *Validation in Language Assessment* (Mahwah NJ: Erlbaum), 41–60.

Read, J. and Nation, P. (2009) 'Introduction: Meara's Contribution to Research in L2 Lexical Processing', in T. Fitzgerald and A. Barfield (ed.) *Lexical Processing in Second Language Learners: Papers and Perspectives in Honour of Paul Meara* (Bristol: Multilingual Matters), 1–12.

Revier, R. L. (2009) 'Evaluating a new test of whole English collocations', in A. Barfield and H. Gyllstad (eds), *Researching Collocations in Another Language* (New York: Palgrave Macmillan).

Richards, B. J. and Malvern, D. D. (2007) 'Validity and Threats to the Validity of Vocabulary Measurement', in H. Daller, J. Milton and J. Treffers-Daller (eds), *Modelling and Assessing Vocabulary Knowledge* (Cambridge: Cambridge University Press), 79–92.

Richards, J. C. (1974) 'Word Lists: Problems and Prospects', *RELC Journal*, 5, 69–84.

Richards, J. C. (1976) 'The Role of Vocabulary Teaching', *TESOL Quarterly*, 10, 77–89.

Riegel, K. and Zivian, I. (1972) 'A Study of Inter- and Intralingual Associations in English and German', *Language Learning*, 22(1), 51–63.

Ringbom, H. (1987) *The Role of the First Language in Foreign Language Learning* (Bristol: Multilingual Matters).

Ringeling, T. (1984) 'Subjective Estimations as a Useful Alternative to Word Frequency Counts', *Interlanguage Studies Bulletin*, 8, 59–69.

Rippey, R. M. (1970) 'A Comparison of Five Different Scoring Functions for Confidence Tests', *Journal of Educational Measurement*, 7, 165–70.

Rogers, V. (2009) 'Syntactic Development in the Second Language Acquisition of French by Instructed English Learner', unpublished PhD dissertation, Newcastle University.

Rogers, V., Milton, J. and Playfoot, D. (in preparation) 'Vocabulary Acquisition: Where are We Now?', in M. Young-Scholten, C. Wright and T. Piske (eds), *Mind Matters in Second Language Acquisition* (Bristol: Multilingual Matters).

Ronald, J. (2009) 'Repeated L2 Reading with and without a Dictionary', in T. Fitzgerald and A. Barfield (eds), *Lexical Processing in Second Language Learners: Papers and Perspectives in Honour of Paul Meara* (Bristol: Multilingual Matters), 82–94.

Rothemberg, M. (1974) *Les verbes à la fois transitifs et intransitifs en français contemporain* (The Hague: Mouton).

Saussure, F. (1916) *Cours de linguistique générale*, ed. by C. Bally and A. Sechehaye, with the collaboration of A. Riedlinger (Lausanne and Paris: Payot).

Schmitt, D. and Schmitt, N. (2005) *Focus on Vocabulary: Mastering the Academic Word List* (London: Longman).

Schmitt, N. (1998) 'Quantifying Word Association Responses: What is Native-like?', *System*, 26, 389–401.

Schmitt, N. (2000) *Vocabulary in Language Teaching* (Cambridge: Cambridge University Press).

Schmitt, N. (2008) 'Instructed Second Language Learning', *Language Teaching Research*, 12(3), 329–63.

Schmitt, N. (2010) *Researching Vocabulary: A Vocabulary Research Manual* (Basingstoke: Palgrave Macmillan).

Schmitt, N. and Carter, R. (2004) 'Formulaic Sequences in Action: An Introduction', in N. Schmitt (ed.), *Formulaic Sequences* (Amsterdam: John Benjamins), 1–22.

Schmitt, N. and Dunham, B. (1999) 'Exploring Native and Non-native Intuitions of Word Frequency', *Second Language Research*, 15(4), 389–411.

Schmitt, N. and McCarthy, M. (eds) (1997) *Vocabulary: Description, Acquisition and Pedagogy* (Cambridge: Cambridge University Press).

Schmitt, N. and Meara, P. (1997) 'Researching Vocabulary Through a Word Knowledge Framework: Word Associations and Verbal Suffixes', *Studies in Second Language Acquisition*, 19, 17–36.

Schmitt, N. and Underwood, G. (2004) 'Exploring the processing of formulaic sequences through a self-paced reading task', in N. Schmitt (ed), *Formulaic Sequences* (Amsterdam: John Benjamins Publishing Company).

Schmitt, N. and Zimmermann, C. B. (2002) 'Derivative Forms: What Do Learners Know?', *TESOL Quarterly*, 36(2), 145–71.

Schmitt, N., Grandage, S. and Adolphs, S. (2004) 'Are corpus-derived reccurent clusters psycholinguistically valid?', in N. Schmitt (ed), *Formulaic Sequences* (Amsterdam: John Benjamins Publishing Company), 127–51.

Schmitt, N., Schmitt, D. and Clapham, C. (2001) 'Developing and Exploring the Behaviour of Two New Versions of the Vocabulary Levels Test', *Language Testing*, 18, 55–88.

Schur, E. (2007) 'Insights into the Structure of L1 and L2 Vocabulary Networks: Intimations of Small Worlds', in H. Daller, J. Milton and J. Treffers-Daller (eds), *Modelling and Assessing Vocabulary Knowledge* (Cambridge: Cambridge University Press), 182–203.

Segalowitz, N. (2010) *Cognitive Bases of Second Language Fluency* (New York: Routledge).

Segalowitz, N. S. and Freed, B. F. (2004) 'Context, Contact, and Cognition in Oral Fluency Acquisition: Learning Spanish in at Home and Study Abroad Contexts', *Studies in Second Language Acquisition*, 26, 173–99.

Segalowitz, N. and Hulstijn, J. (2005) 'Automaticity in Bilingualism and Second Language Learning', in J. F. Kroll and A. M. B. De Groot (eds), *Handbook of Bilingualism: Psycholinguistic Approaches* (Oxford: Oxford University Press), 371–88.

Segalowitz, N. S. and Segalowitz, S. (1993) 'Skilled Performance, Practice, and the Differentiation of Speed-up from Automatization Effects: Evidence from Second Language Recognition', *Applied Psycholinguistics*, 14, 369–85.

Sereno, S. and Rayner, K. (2003) 'Measuring Word Recognition in Reading: Eye Movements and Event-related Potentials', *Trends in Cognitive Science*, 7(11), 489–93.

Serrano, R. and Miralpeix, I. (2010) 'Analyzing the Relationship Between Vocabulary Size and Lexical Access in Second Language Learners', paper delivered to the 11th AESLA Conference (Vigo: Universidad de Vigo).

Shapiro, B. J. (1969) 'The Subjective Estimation of Relative Word Frequency', *Journal of Verbal Learning and Verbal Behavior*, 8, 248–51.

Shillaw, J. (1999) 'The Application of the Rasch Model to Yes/No Vocabulary Tests', unpublished PhD thesis, Swansea University.

Shillaw, J. (2009) 'Putting Yes/No Tests in Context', in T. Fitzgerald and A. Barfield (eds), *Lexical Processing in Second Language Learners: Papers and Perspectives in Honour of Paul Meara* (Bristol: Multilingual Matters), 13–24.

Shin, D. and Nation, P. (2008) 'Beyond single words: the most frequent collocations in spoken English', *ELT Journal, 62*(4), 339–48. doi: 10.1093/elt/ccm091.

Shizuka, T. (2004) *New Horizons in Computerized Testing of Reading* (Osaka: Kansai University Press).

Simpson-Vlach, R. and Ellis, N. C. (2010) 'An Academic Formulas List: New Methods in Phraseology Research', *Applied Linguistics, 31*(4), 487–512. doi: 10.1093/applin/amp058.

Sinclair, J. (1991) *Corpus, Concordance, Collocation* (Oxford: Oxford University Press).

Sinclair, J. (1998) 'The Lexical Item', in E. Weigand (ed.), *Contrastive Lexical Semantics* (Amsterdam: John Benjamins), 1–24.

Sinclair, J. (2004) *Trust the Text: Language Corpus and Discourse* (London: Routledge).

Singleton, D. (1999) *Exploring the Second Language Mental Lexicon* (Cambridge: Cambridge University Press).

Siyanova, A. and Schmitt, N. (2008) 'L2 Learner Production and Processing of Collocation: A Multi-study Perspective', *Canadian Modern Language Review/La Revue canadienne des langues vivantes, 64*(3), 429–458. doi: 10.3138/cmlr.64.3.429.

Siyanova-Chanturia, A., Conklin, K. and Schmitt, N. (2011) 'Adding more fuel to the fire: An eye-tracking study of idiom processing by native and non-native speakers', *Second Language Research, 27*(2), 251–72. doi: 10.1177/0267658310382068.

Skehan, P. (2003) *A Cognitive Approach to Language Learning* (Oxford: Oxford University Press).

Slobin, D. I. (2004) 'The Many Ways to Search for a Frog: Linguistic Typology and the Expression of Motion Events', in S. Strömqvist and L. Verhoeven (eds), *Relating Events in Narrative: Vol 2. Typological and Contextual Perspectives* (Mahwah, NJ: Lawrence Erlbaum Associates), 219–57.

Snellings, P., van Gelderen, A. and de Glopper, K. (2002) 'Lexical Retrieval: An Aspect of Fluent Second Language Production that can be Enhanced', *Language Learning, 52*(4), 723–54.

Snow, C. and Kim, Y. (2006) 'Large Problem Spaces: The Challenge of Vocabulary for English Language Learners', in R. K. Wagner, A. E. Muse and K. R. Tannenbaum (eds), *Vocabulary Acquisition: Implications for Reading Comprehension* (New York: Guilford Press).

Snow, C. (1990) 'The Development of Definitional Skill', *Journal of Child Language*, 17, 697–710.

Snow, C., Cancino, H., de Temple, J. and Schley, S. (1991) 'Giving Formal Definitions: A Linguistic or Metalinguistic Skill?', in E. Bialystok (ed.), *Language Processing in Bilingual Children* (Cambridge: Cambridge University Press), 90–113.

Snyder, W. (2001) 'On the Nature of Syntactic Variation: Evidence from Complex Predicates and Complex Word-formation', *Language*, 77(2), 324–42.

Söderman, T. (1993) 'Word Associations of Foreign Language Learners and Native Speakers: Different Response Types and their Relevance to Lexical Development', in B. Hammerberg (ed.), *Problems, Process and Product in Language Learning* (Åbo, Finland: Åbo Academic), 157–69.

Sökmen, A. (1993) 'Word Association Results: A Window to the Lexicons of ESL Students', *JALT Journal*, 15(2), 135–50.

Son, M. (2007) 'Directionality and Resultativity: The Cross-linguistic Correlation Revisited', in M. Bašic, M. Pantcheva, M. Son and P. Svenonius (eds), Special issue on Space, Motion and Result, *Tromsø Working Papers on Language and Linguistics*, 34(2), 126–64, CASTL, Tromsø, http://www.ub.uit.no/baser/nordlyd/ [accessed 20 July 2011].

Staehr, L. S. (2008) 'Vocabulary Size and the Skills of Listening, Reading and Writing', *Language Learning Journal*, 36(2), 139–52.

Stanovich, K. E. (1986) 'Matthew Effects in Reading: Some Consequences of Individual Differences in the Acquisition of Literacy', *Reading Research Quarterly*, 21, 360–407.

Suárez, A. and Meara, P. (1989) 'The Effects of Irregular Orthography on the Processing of Words in a Foreign Language', *Reading in a Foreign Language*, 6(1), 349–56.

Takala, S. (1984) *Evaluation of Students' Knowledge of English Vocabulary in the Finnish Comprehensive School* (Jyväskylä: University of Jyväskylä Reports from the Institute for Educational Research).

Talmy, L. (1985) 'Lexicalization Patterns: Semantic Structure in Lexical Forms', in T. Shopen (ed.), *Grammatical Categories and the Lexicon. Volume III of Language Typology and Syntactic Description* (Cambridge: Cambridge University Press), 57–149.

Talmy, L. (2000) *Toward a Cognitive Semantics, Vol I Toward a Cognitive Semantics: Concept Structuring Systems* (Cambridge MA: MIT Press).

Thornbury, S. (2002) *How to Teach Vocabulary* (Harlow: Longman).

Tonzar, C., Lotto, L. and Job, R. (2009) 'L2 Vocabulary Acquisition in Children: Effects of Learning Method and Cognate Status', *Language Learning*, 59(3), 623–46.

Treffers-Daller, J. and Tidball, F. (under review) 'Can L2 Learners Learn New Ways to Conceptualise Events? Evidence from Motion Event Construal among English-speaking Learners of French', to appear in N. Mueller, P. Gujarro-Fuentes and K. Schmitz (eds), *The Acquisition of French in its Different Constellations* (Bristol: Multilingual Matters).

Tschichold, C. (2012) 'French Vocabulary in Encore Tricolore: Do Pupils have a Chance?', *Language Learning Journal*, 40(1), 7–19.

Tversky, A. and Kahneman, D. (1973) 'Availability: A Heuristic for Judging Frequency and Probability', *Cognitive Psychology*, 5, 207–32.

Underwood, G., Schmitt, N. and Galpin, A. (2004) 'The eyes have it: An eye-movement study into the processing of formulaic sequences', in N. Schmitt (ed.), *Formulaic Sequences* (Amsterdam: John Benjamins Publishing Company), 153–72.

Van Compernolle, R. A. (2009) 'What do Women Want? Linguistic Equality and the Feminization of Job Titles in Contemporary France', *Gender and Language*, 3(1), 33–52.

Van Compernolle, R. (2010) 'Towards a Sociolinguistically Responsive Pedagogy: Teaching 2nd Person Address Forms in French', *The Canadian Modern Language Review*, 66(3), 445–63.

Van Compernolle, R. and Williams, L. (2009) 'Learner Versus Non-learner Patters of Stylistic Variation in Synchronous Computer-mediated French: Yes/No Questions and Nous Versus On', *Studies in Second Language Acquisition*, 31(3), 471–500.

Van Ek, J. and Trim, J. (1990) *Waystage 1990* (Strasbourg: Council of Europe).

Van Gelderen, A., Schoonen, R., de Glopper, K., Hulstijn, J., Simis, A., Snellings, P. and Stevenson, M. (2004) 'Linguistic Knowledge, Processing Speed, and Metacognitive Knowledge in First- and Second-language Reading Comprehension: A Componential Analysis', *Journal of Educational Psychology*, 96(1), 19–30.

VanPatten, B., Williams, J. and Rott, S. (2004) 'Form-meaning connections in second language acquisition', in B. VanPatten, J. Williams, S. Rott and M. Overstreet (eds), *Form-Meaning Connections in Second Language Acquisition* (Mahwah: Erlbaum Press), 1–26.

Verhallen, M. and Schoonen, R. (1993) 'Lexical Knowledge of Monolingual and Bilingual Children', *Applied Linguistics*, 14, 344–63.

Verhallen, M. and Schoonen, R. (1998a) 'Lexical Knowledge in L1 and L2 of Third and Fifth Graders', *Applied Linguistics*, 19(4), 452–70.

Verhallen, M. and Schoonen, R. (1998b) 'The Word Association Task: Testing Depth of Vocabulary', paper presented at the Annual Meeting of the AERA, San Diego, July.

Verhelst, N. and Glas, C. (1995) 'The Generalized One Parameter Model: OPLM', in G. Fischer and I. Molenaar (eds), *Rasch Models: Their Foundations, Recent Developments and Applications* (New York: Springer), 215–38.

Verhoeven, L. and Carlisle, J. F. (2006) 'Introduction to the Special Issue: Morphology in Word Identification and Word Spelling', *Reading and Writing*, 19(7), 643–50.

Verspoor, M., de Bot, K. and Lowie, W. (eds) (2011) *A Dynamic Approach to Second Language Development: Methods and Techniques* (Amsterdam: John Benjamins).

Virkkunen, A. (1992) *Affixation as Part of an English Reading Proficiency Test at the University of Helsinki*, Reports from the Language Centre for Finnish Universities, 43, (Jyväskylä: University of Jyväskylä).

Vygotsky, L. S. (1962) *Thought and Language* (Cambridge, MA: MIT Press).

Vygotsky, L. S. (1986) *Thought and Language*, ed. and trans. by A. Kozulin (Cambridge, MA: MIT Press).

Walker, C. P. (2011) 'A Corpus-Based Study of the Linguistic Features and Processes Which Influence the Way Collocations Are Formed: Some Implications for the Learning of Collocations', *TESOL Quarterly*, 45(2), 291–312. doi: 10.5054/tq.2011.247710.

Wang, M. and Koda, K. (2005) 'Commonalities and Differences in Word Identification Skills Among Learners of English as a Second Language', *Language Learning*, 55(1), 71–98.

Ward, J and Chuenjundaeng, J. (2009) 'Suffix Knowledge: Acquisition and Applications', *System*, 37(3), September, 461–9.

Wardaugh, R. (1986) *An Introduction to Sociolinguistics* (Oxford: Blackwell).

Watson, R. (1985) 'Toward a theory of definition', *Journal of Child Language*, 12, 181–97.

Watson, R. and Olson, D. R. (1987) 'From Meaning to Definition: A Literate Bias on the Structure of Word Meaning', in R. Horowitz and S. J. Samuels (eds), *Comprehending Oral and Written Language* (London: Academic Press), 329–53.

Webb, S. (2007) 'The Effects of Repetition on Second Language Vocabulary Learning', *Applied Linguistics*, 28 (1), 46–65.

Webb, S. (2008) 'Receptive and Productive Vocabulary Sizes of L2 Learners', *Studies in Second Language Acquisition*, 30, 79–95.

Wesche, M. and Paribakht, T. A. (1996) 'Assessing Second Language Vocabulary Knowledge: Depth Versus Breadth', *The Canadian Modern Language Review*, 53, 13–40.

West, M. (1953) *A General Service List of English Words* (London: Longman).

Wible, D. (2008) 'Multiword expressions and the digital turn', in F. Meunier and S. Granger (eds), *Phraseology in Foreign Language Learning and Teaching* (Amsterdam: John Benjamins Publishing Company), 163–81.

Widdowson, H. (2000) 'On the limitations of linguistics applied', *Applied Linguistics*, 21(1), 3–25. doi: 10.1093/applin/21.1.3.

Wilkins, D. A. (1972) *Linguistics in Language Teaching* (London: Arnold).

Wilks, C. (2009) 'Tangled Webs ... Complications in the Exploration of L2 Lexical Networks', in T. Fitzpatrick and A. Barfield (eds), *Lexical Processing in Second Language Learners* (Bristol: Multilingual Matters), 25–37.

Wilks, C. and Brick, N. (1997) 'Langue non-sexiste et politique éditoriale', *Modern and Contemporary France*, 5(3), 297–308.

Wilks, C., Meara, P. and Wolter, B. (2005) 'A Further Note on Simulating Word Association Behaviour in a Second Language', *Second Language Research*, 21(4), 359–72.

Wilks, C. and Meara, P. (2007) 'Graph Theory and Word Association Networks', in H. Daller, J. Milton and J. Treffers-Daller (eds), *Modelling and Assessing Vocabulary Knowledge* (Cambridge; Cambridge University Press), 167–81.

Wolter, B. (2001) 'Comparing the L1 and the L2 Mental Lexicon', *Studies in Second Language Acquisition*, 23, 41–69.

Wolter, B. (2002) 'Assessing Proficiency Through Word Associations: Is There Still Hope?', *System*, 30(3), 315–29.

Wolter, B. (2005) 'V_Links: A New Approach to Assessing Depth of Word Knowledge', unpublished PhD dissertation, University of Swansea.

Wolter, B. (2006) 'Lexical Network Structures and L2 Vocabulary Acquisition: The Role of L1 Lexical/Conceptual Knowledge', *Applied Linguistics*, 27(4), 741–7.

Wolter, B. (2009) 'Meaning-last Vocabulary Acquisition and Collocational Productivity', in T. Fitzpatrick and A. Barfield (eds), *Lexical Processing in Second Language Learners* (Bristol: Multilingual Matters), 128–40.

Wolter, B. and Gyllstad, H. (2011) 'Collocational links in the L2 mental lexicon and the influence of L1 intralexical knowledge', *Applied Linguistics*, 32(4), 430–49.

Wray, A. (2002) *Formulaic Language and the Lexicon* (Cambridge: Cambridge University Press).

Wray, A. (2009) 'Conclusion: Navigating L2 collocation research,' in A. Barfield and H. Gyllstad (eds), *Researching Collocations in Another Language: Multiple Interpretations* (Basingstoke: Palgrave Macmillan), 232–44.

Yamashita, J. and Jiang, N. (2010) 'L1 influence on the acquisition of L2 collocations: Japanese ESL users and EFL learners acquiring English collocations', *TESOL Quarterly*, 44(4), 647–68.

Yap, M. J. and Balota, D. A. (2007) 'Additive and Interactive Effects on Response Time Distributions in Visual Word Recognition', *Journal of Experimental Psychology: Learning, Memory and Cognition*, 33(2), 274–96.

Yule, G. (2006) *The Study of Language,* 3rd edn (Cambridge: Cambridge University Press).

Zimmerman, C. B. (2009). *Word Knowledge: A Vocabulary Teacher' Handbook* (Oxford: Oxford University Press).

Zoccolotti, P., De Luca, M., Di Filippo, G., Jurdica, A. and Martelli, M. (2009) 'Reading Development in an Orthographically Regular Language: Effects of Length, Frequency, Lexicality and Global Processing Ability', *Reading and Writing*, 22(9), 1053–79.

Index

A-Lex   17, 20, 21, 23–7, 29, 33
academic vocabulary   81, 157–9
Academic Word List   *see* AWL
active vocabulary knowledge   3
advanced learners   19, 22, 37, 38, 48,
    120, 129, 131, 138, 139, 145, 148
affix   **3, 30, 45–52, 55, 56, 58, 59, 96**
Arabic   10, 18, 20, 21, 175
Aristotle   1–3
assimilation   14
aatrition   90, 176
Aural Lex   *see* A-Lex
automaticity   36–41, 89
AWL   41, 61, 62, 164

beginners   19, 56–8, 67, 102, 120
bilingualism   35, 37, 62, 72–5, 78–9,
    81–3, 86–91, 117, 166, 174
breadth of word knowledge   *see* lexical
    breadth
British National Corpus (BNC)   15, 38,
    55, 100, 101, 110, 111, 112, 115, 127,
    129, 130, 132, 135

CEFR   **23, 49, 55, 56, 57**
clang responses   95, 96
cloze test   **61, 98, 100, 102–4**
cognates   **31, 33, 38, 42, 68–70, 72, 88**
collocation   **3, 4, 5, 7, 8, 11, 12, 72, 94–6,**
    107, 123–39, 140, 152, 154, 173, 175
concordance lists   111
content words   83
coordinate   78, 96
corpora   **15, 16, 36, 46, 67, 71, 72,**
    108–10, 125, 127, 129, 135, 147, 150,
    151, 157, 161, 162
coverage   15, 16
Cronbach, L. J.   3, 52

declarative knowledge   **7, 145, 152**
decoding   20

density   118, 119
depth of word knowledge   *see* lexical
    depth
derivation   4, 6, 45–9, 51–9, 65, 124,
    132, 178
dictionaries   48, 65, 66, 102, 113, 125,
    134, 135, 141, 156, 162, 164, 166,
    167, 170
dimensions of knowledge   6–11, 29, 32,
    43, 60, 64, 65, 78, 81, 93, 96, 104,
    140, 141, 143, 145, 151–3, 154, 155,
    171, 172, 173–6

elementary learners   19, 56–8, 67, 102,
    120
elision   14
encoding   129
equivalence   11, 14, 18–20, 22, 38, 48,
    49, 65, 67–8, 101, 107, 110, 113, 115,
    126, 129, 136, 163, 165, 166, 127,
    169–71, 175
explicit instruction   45, 48, 58, 69, 68,
    91, 139, 142, 145, 146, 150
extensive reading   28

false words   *see* **pseudowords**
first language acquisition   14, 77, 93,
    94, 95, 121
fluency   7, 9, 28, 32, 34, 43, 128
formulaic sequences   **46, 52, 66, 89,**
    104, 123, 125, 127, 128, 129, 151,
    153, 165, 169
French   33, 35, 74, 88, 89, 106, 107,
    110–21, 143–5
frequency   15–19, 22, 23, 31, 32,
    33, 36, 41, 46–9, 52, 55, 58, 61–6,
    69, 72, 81, 96, 100, 102, 110, 111,
    115, 124, 125, 129, 130–3, 135–9,
    141–3, 146, 152, 153, 159–61,
    177
frequency intuition   147–52

General Service Wordlist (GSL)   62
generative grammar   108, 118
grammar   48, 98, 100, 108, 109, 117, 118, 126, 138, 154
Greek   18, 20–4, 26, 27, 29, 175
guessing   14, 17, 23, 32, 62, 155, 156, 159, 161, 162, 164, 166, 170, 171

Hellenic Nation Corpus   23
high frequency   65, 100, 115, 130, 132, 135, 136, 138, 146, 153
hyponomy   78, 101

implicit vocabulary learning   145
incidental vocabulary learning   141, 153
inflection   4, 6, 30, 46–8, 57, 65, 69, 117
intermediate learners   37, 58, 102, 120, 132, 135, 136, 157, 164
item analysis   97

JACET 8000 list   38
Japanese   10, 14, 31, 47, 101, 102, 126, 127, 129, 132, 135, 136, 149, 159, 156, 157, 163, 164, 165, 172

L1 influence   31, 69, 126, 145, 174
labelling   73, 74, 76, 88
learning strategies   24–9, 47, 106, 174, 175
lemma   17, 23, 110, 137
Lex30   18, 28, 131
LexCombi   131, 137, 138
lexical access   32, 34, 37–44
lexical breadth   3, 6, 7–12, 32, 47, 93, 121, 174
lexical decision tasks   31–4, 43
lexical depth   6–11, 22, 37, 47, 60, 75, 76, 80–2, 91, 93, 140, 154, 171, 173, 174
Lexical Frequency Profile (Laufer and Nation)   177
lexical frequency profiles   18, 31, 33, 63
lexical retrieval   34, 35, 90, 99, 104, 149, 174
lexical set   96, 149
lexical space   7, 9, 10
lexicogrammar   108, 109
levels test (VLT)   7, 41, 61, 62, 64, 65–7, 72, 157, 161, 162, 171

listening and vocabulary knowledge   2, 36
loan words   69, 101

mental lexicon   18, 21, 28, 42, 43, 92, 93, 96, 149, 151, 153, 155
MI (mutual information) scores   125, 129, 130, 132, 135–9
mnemonic strategies   23
modelling vocabulary knowledge   3, 6, 8, 11, 17, 29, 31, 43, 75, 77–80, 83, 87, 92, 94, 109, 128, 141, 149, 151, 159, 164, 173–7
morpheme   45–7, 47, 58
morphology   31, 45, 47, 50, 58, 117

native speakers   4, 14, 18, 20, 34, 35, 42, 47, 48, 82, 87, 89, 94, 95, 97–9, 102–4, 115, 117, 124, 127–36, 138–9, 144, 145–53, 172

order of acquisition   49, 122
orthography   2, 31, 42, 124, 136

Palmer H. E.   2, 3
paradigmatic analysis   76, 77, 78, 80, 81, 84, 89, 91, 94–6
passive vocabulary knowledge   3, 7, 17
phonology   23, 46
polysemy   3, 183
priming   31, 114
procedural knowledge   7, 152
processing theory   77
productive vocabulary knowledge   2, 3, 5–8, 14, 18, 28, 29, 30, 43, 45, 48, 58, 61, 62, 64, 66, 67, 69, 71, 83, 121, 131, 141, 142, 154, 163, 174
pseudowords   17, 23, 32, 33, 50

Q-Lex   35, 43

reading and vocabulary knowledge   2, 22, 26–31, 34, 36, 37, 40, 72, 79, 81, 82, 100, 127, 129, 157
receptive vocabulary knowledge   2, 3, 5, 6, 8, 13, 17, 28, 30, 32, 33, 36–41, 45, 48, 58, 61, 62, 66, 71, 76, 120, 121, 141, 142, 154, 174
referents   73–6, 78
register   141, 143–6, 149, 152, 153, 154

Saussure, F. 2
semantic organization 75–7, 86, 89
semantics 78
speaking and vocabulary knowledge 2,
 19, 29
spelling 15, 30, 31, 42, 50, 65, 69, 71
strategies 22–9, 47, 50, 106, 174, 175
superordinate 77, 78, 80, 81, 83, 84,
 86, 88–91, 101
synonymy 8, 72, 75, 76, 94, 96, 146,
 148, 149
syntagmatic analysis 77, 78, 80, 81, 85,
 89–91, 94–6

teaching vocabulary 48, 58, 68, 69, 71,
 72, 91, 121, 125–8, 139, 146, 151,
 153, 154, 174, 175
technical vocabulary 81
think-aloud 48, 58, 59

universal grammar 108, 118
University Word List (UWL) 61, 62,
 65

vocabulary breadth/depth 8, 121, 140
Vocabulary Knowledge Scale (VKS) 8,
 9, 75, 154, 163, 171

Vocabulary Levels Test (VLT) 7, 41,
 61, 65–72, 82, 129, 157, 161, 162,
 171, 177
vocabulary size 7, 14, 17, 20, 22–9,
 32–44, 47, 48, 58, 61, 62, 65, 66, 67,
 72, 89, 91, 93, 117, 121, 131, 149,
 150, 156, 157, 174

word associations 4, 5, 7, 8, 11, 12, 18,
 47, 60, 63, 76, 83, 88, 82–105, 123,
 130, 154, 174
word families 65, 67, 132, 135
word knowledge framework 7, 8, 12,
 96, 123, 140, 141, 143, 152, 154, 155,
 173–5
word recognition 7, 12, 16–20, 31–8,
 40–4, 61, 176, 177
writing and vocabulary knowledge 2, 10,
 15, 16, 19, 20, 27, 28, 29, 31, 34, 55,
 56, 57, 59, 61, 69, 72, 79, 81, 127, 130

X-Lex 7, 17, 20, 21, 23–7, 29, 33,
 37–40, 120

Y-Lex 37, 38, 39, 40
Yes/No tests 17, 32, 33, 36–9, 63, 156,
 172